At the Centre

Jeremy Guscott
At the Centre

with Stephen Jones

PAVILION

To my wife, Jayne, my two daughters, Imogen and Holly, and also to the relatives and friends on both sides who have had to put up with my sarcastic and cynical nature.

First published in Great Britain in 1995 by
PAVILION BOOKS LIMITED
26 Upper Ground, London SE1 9PD

Picture credits: Allsport: nos 5, 16, 28a; Mike Brett: 6, 11, 13, 19, 22; Central Television/*Body Heat*: 31; Colorsport: 7, 8, 9, 10, 12, 14, 15, 17, 18, 20, 21, 23, 24, 25, 27, 28b, 28c; Andrew Cornaga/Fotosport NZ: 26; Jeremy Guscott: 1, 2, 3, 4; Real World Associates Ltd: 29; David Woolford: 30

Designed by Cole design unit

A CIP catalogue record for this book is available from the British Library.

ISBN 1 85793 084 3

Phototypeset in Stempel Garamond with Univers
by Intype, London

Printed and bound in Great Britain by Butler & Tanner Ltd,
Frome & London

2 4 6 8 10 9 7 5 3 1

This book may be ordered by post direct from the publisher.
Please contact the Marketing Department.
But try your bookshop first.

Contents

Prologue: Thanks for all the Lasagne		1
1	Wild West Drifter	3
2	The Trick of Redemption	15
3	Spartan Days on the Rec	29
4	The Greatest Journey	38
5	Everything Comes to Him Who Sleeps	56
6	The Hammer of Brisbane	70
7	Dying Dreams of the Grandest Slam	88
8	Red Rose Speedway	100
9	Blinded by the Laws	122
10	Catching the Plane, Missing the Boat	143
11	All Roads Lead to Tormarton	167
12	The Best-Dressed Millionaire?	174
13	A Journey Below the Waist	185
14	High Veld via Hartlepool	195

15 Ambushed by All Blacks 208
Epilogue: A Question of Balance 229
Index 241

Prologue: Thanks for all the Lasagne

For most of my life as a global superstar of the sporting stage, I seem to have been a part-willing, part-cynical partner in a search – a search for me. No matter how they all phrase it, all the men and women from the rugby press and the glossy magazines and the television, the underlying question is basically the same. Who the hell are you?

It seems from some people's responses that I have put up an enormous wall between the outside world and myself – appropriately, for a man holding a City & Guilds in bricklaying. It has been put to me, across the interview table in front of the rolling tape machines, that as well as having outstanding rugby talents (their words), I am arrogant, aloof, quick to put people down. Richard Hill, my colleague at Bath, tells the story of how, when approached at some disco by a lady who asked me to dance, I replied: 'Why? It isn't Halloween yet, is it?' If I said that, I don't remember it.

I am also, as the interviewers gently suggest to me, rich from all my modelling assignments and ancillary earnings off the back of the game. Even in my rugby career, I am not a team man, just someone who lives to make individual breaks and make fun of the donkey forwards (the second bit is definitely true).

And when these interviews appear, when the writers make their judgements, it is usually impossible to recognize myself, sometimes even impossible to believe they actually listened to anything I said. I can understand some of the confusion. I will admit that, like most of the population, I have not been terribly keen to lay bare the innermost me just for the price of a lasagne and a glass of Perrier charged to a newspaper account. I like to keep the rugby media guessing. We have these little games. They know it and I know it.

I also love rugby, and am in debt to the game, as I am to my colleagues, friends and club, and to my family. I did not relish being famous in the 1993–94 season simply because I was not playing, but was stuck on the sidelines holding my groin. It was much more fun being back in the team for the World Cup.

And now the game is over. Now, at last, and for the first time, this is the whole thing – all the juice on Jeremy. The caps, the tours, the poses, the groin, the lot. This is the real me. I think.

1 Wild West Drifter

Early years and the red card of authority

My mother was called to the school and I knew before the fateful interview with the headmistress, as I was called down the dark corridor towards her room on a sunny day, that it was all over between Ralph Allen Comprehensive School and myself. We walked down the long school corridor, past the dining hall, where, in response to misdemeanours, I had frequently had to stand outside the glass doors on my own, till everyone else finished. Only then could I go in for my lunch, alone. We turned around the corner and approached the door.

In the inner sanctum of the headmistress's office, we took our seats. Miss Hayter was a kind of sub-Thatcher figure, mousy hair, medium build and half-glasses. She was actually a fair woman, but when it came to this incident she had obviously decided to accept the version of events she had been given.

This final incident – and last straw – occurred during a soccer match. Ralph Allen's Fifth Year team went to play Broadlands School in Radstock. The referee was their PE teacher and we all felt, not to put too fine a point on it, that he was a cheating bastard. We never got any free kicks, never got one of the 50/50 decisions. It began to prey on our minds. Our goalkeeper came straight to the point. 'Ref, you are a fucking cheat,' he said. The referee abandoned the whole thing. He said that he had had enough, it was all over.

If I had insulted the referee or called him a cheat or abused him in any way, then I could honestly not remember doing so. I certainly complained about his decisions, but I did not believe that I was the worst offender. The message from the head was that I had a lot to do with the situation which had brought shame on the school: to wit, the abandonment of a match because of our abuse of the referee, a member of staff of the school we were playing against. The version held that I had been attacking the referee throughout, had been giving him a lot of stick.

She said that they could not tolerate me any more. They no longer wanted me in the school. I was expelled. There was no right of appeal. The first impression I had was one of shock and anxiety. I had no idea what I would do. I walked back down the corridor to face the music with Dad in a kind of daze.

I was born at the Royal United Hospital in Bath on 7 July 1965, and my brother, Gary, followed two and a half years later. My mother, Susan, was from the West Country, although her father had been born in India. And my father, Henry – known to everyone as Slim – had come to this country from Jamaica a few years before he and my mother met. They had met in Bath in circumstances that have become legendary in our family. As my mother recalls:

'Henry used to live down the hill from me in Bath. I had seen him around, but one day I was cycling down a hill with my head down, not really looking where I was going. He saw me coming and decided to play the fool, standing in my way and assuming that I would swerve out of his way. But I saw him too late, grazed him as I went by and fell off the bike. He came over and asked me if I was all right. I could not repeat my answer. Then, he had the cheek to ask me to go for a drink with him the next night. I refused.'

My father had a very happy, but hardworking childhood in a large family, including some stepbrothers and stepsisters. My parents have been back to Jamaica several times, and it is an ambition of mine to spend more time over there if ever I can afford to.

My great-grandfather on my mother's side formed the first-ever settlement in San Carlos, scene of one of the major incidents in the Falklands War. My mother's father was born in Madras, India: the family had moved there a generation before to work for the Dutch East India Company. He returned home before the Great War, joined the London Scottish Regiment and was shot on the Somme. He was invalided out to hospital in Versailles but was soon back at the front line. One of the family stories is that he once jumped into a shell hole for cover during fierce fighting, found there a German soldier seated with gun pointing at him, and then realized that the German was already dead.

But easily the most remarkable story is that of a man we knew as Ron; his full name was Ronald Sinclair, a cousin of my grandmother, and was to become close to my mother in his later years. I knew him a little and Mum used to visit him in Plymouth, where he lived in a retirement home. He eventually died in 1988 at the age of 99. His obituary appeared in *The Times*. My mother relished her visits to see him. He lived with Taddy, who was his second wife. When Taddy died, in 1984, he invited Valya, a Russian who had been his first wife, to share his rooms in Plymouth rent-free.

My mother said in an interview in 1994: 'He was one of the most fascinating men I had ever met. I used to go down to Plymouth and sit listening to him for hours. He was a brilliant linguist, painter and photographer.' She has a number of his photographs and other memorabilia.

However, even our family and *The Times* was completely fooled about the real identity of Ronald Sinclair. His life story was more colourful and marvellous than that of any sportsman, and his real name was Reginald Teague-Jones. Visitors to the home in Plymouth and the nurses there could never understand why Taddy, when she spoke to him, always used the name Reggie, not Ron. The real story was revealed to my mother only just over a year before he died, and, until recently, I was unaware of the full details of an incredible tale.

Reginald Teague-Jones was a captain in British Intelligence during the Great War. He had been brought up in St Petersburg, educated at London University and joined the army in India at 21. He quickly passed on to Intelligence duties. According to books on his life, he was to become one of the best secret agents the country ever had.

During the War Teague-Jones was sent, disguised as a Persian-Armenian trader, to the Russian town of Baku, on the Caspian Sea. The town was held by Bolsheviks, led by Stefan Shaumian, a close friend and associate of Lenin himself. The situation was complicated because although the British were no friends of the Bolsheviks, favouring the Tsarists in the Russian civil war, it was in their interests to shore up the town in the face of the advancing Turks. It was also in their interests to have intelligence from Baku, a complicated hive of activity and different factions. Some of the coups Reginald brought off in and around Baku were staggering. Because of his vast ability as a linguist he was able to pass himself off in various guises.

Baku eventually fell to the Turks, but 26 of the Bolsheviks, including the leadership of Baku and Shaumian, a group to become known as the Baku Commissars, managed to sail away aboard a ship called the *Turkman*. At some time on the voyage to what they thought was a friendly destination, the ship changed course and arrived instead at Krasnovodsk, a Tsarist stronghold, where the Commissars were imprisoned. They were then taken by train to the countryside to be shot. The Baku Commissars became some of the most significant martyrs in Soviet history, and have been portrayed almost ever since as glorious heroes of the Bolshevik cause to generations of Russian schoolchildren. In Baku today there are monuments to them.

The villain in the eyes of the Russians has always been Captain Reginald Teague-Jones, the British Intelligence officer. The Russians have always accused British Intelligence of ordering the change of course to the *Turkman*, thereby delivering the Commissars to their enemies, and have always stated that Teague-Jones himself persuaded the Tsarist and Cossack authorities to murder the Baku Commissars. Some Russian depictions of the scene even show British Intelligence men actually taking part in the shooting, one deliberately bearing a likeness to Teague-Jones.

The British government always flatly denied that Teague-Jones was involved. He was certainly around Krasnovodsk briefly while the Commissars were imprisoned, reporting back on their fate. He was apparently over 200 miles away at the time of the shooting, and afterwards submitted documentary evidence which the British government passed on to the Russians in the 1920s. They refused to accept it. Teague-Jones, even though he was a hardened Intelligence man, was now in a serious position. The Bolsheviks had already demonstrated by their actions, including the murder of Trotsky, that they could fulfil vendettas by tracing and killing their quarry, and anti-Teague-Jones feeling in Russia was vast.

At the age of 29, Teague-Jones changed his name by deed poll to Ronald Sinclair. His two sisters also had to assume new identities, in case the Bolsheviks traced him through the family name. He dropped out of sight for almost 70 years and was only rediscovered, as it were, on his death. *The Times* reporter Peter Hopkirk recognized, when he read the obituary in *The Times* of Sinclair, that the dead man was Teague-Jones, and the next day another obituary appeared pointing out his true identity.

In fact, Sinclair stayed in the Intelligence service, and was in MI5 for many years, living an exciting life under his alias. He was still under the alias when Mum got to know him and became fascinated by his stories. It was only later that he revealed everything to Mum and the rest of our family, even though Taddy was a little paranoid about any visitors.

Teague-Jones's book, *The Spy Who Disappeared*, was published posthumously. Shortly afterwards, Peter Hopkirk's book *On Secret Service East of Constantinople* appeared, and illustrates the strong likelihood that Teague-Jones, and indeed the British, had probably been framed by people with various political axes to grind. Hopkirk, who had always admired Teague-Jones and his story, and had spent years trying to discover what had happened to Teague-Jones, concludes that Teague-Jones was not responsible at all. Interestingly, Peter is a keen follower of my rugby career, and it was only during his researches that he connected Teague-Jones to the Guscott family.

Dad's trade was carpentry. He gave that up soon after arriving in this country, and worked in a rubber factory at Melksham, Wiltshire. Later he took voluntary redundancy and did some odd jobbing in maintenance and carpentry. For a while, he sold clothes; then he became a porter at Bath's Royal United Hospital, where he still works today. Mum had been a secretary; then she moved on to work for Bell Fruit, collecting the money from their machines in the pubs and clubs. Long after she had Gary, she went back to college to do a teacher training course for teaching remedials. She now teaches at Speedwell School, along with the former Bath back-row forward and former chairman of selectors, Simon Jones.

The first place we lived in was a top-floor flat in Lansdown Road, where things were relatively hard and where my mother had to labour up no fewer than five flights of stairs carrying heavy shopping and babies. She still shudders when she remembers those days. 'When Jeremy was about six months old I sat down and asked myself why on earth we lived so high up.'

We moved on to Ringswell Gardens, just across the road from Larkhall, the suburb of Bath where I lived until recently. My first memory of the place is of me screaming and bawling and shouting from the garden up to my mother, whom I could see in the bathroom above, because I had had an accident in my trousers.

When I was six, we left Ringswell and settled in Batheaston, at 2, School Lane. We stayed there until my late teens, when the family moved on to St Saviour's Terrace, where Mum and Dad still live. But by the time of the move to St Saviour's, I was already established as one of the West Country's leading uncontrollable rebels, was thrown out of home by Dad and was heading deep into the heart of nowhere.

From the age of four I attended St Saviour's Infants School. At six I went on to Batheaston Junior School, where I stayed until the age of 11. My parents wanted me to go on to Beechen Cliff School, which Jon Hall, later to become the Bath captain, already attended. However, in Batheaston, we were just outside the city limits so had to take our chances with satellite schools. I was turned down for Beechen Cliff, and went instead to the Ralph Allen Comprehensive School. It was not the start of a happy relationship between school and pupil. It was all to end in tears.

They had apparently never come across a child like me. They said that I was disruptive and uncontrollable. I thought I was no more naughty than any other child, but they did not see it that way. It was the start of continual trouble and it seemed that the attitude of the teachers there was that I should be kept apart from the others as much as possible in case I spoilt them all. One bad apple . . . They would wait until I made a mistake, send me out for the rest of the lesson and then, apparently, all get along happily without me.

I never felt that I fitted in. Academically, I got on quite well and was in the upper stream. But most of my friends were in the middle and lower streams, and I felt that I had moved up to the ranks of the swotty. That made everything even worse because I felt alienation. Outside class I went back to my friends, the toughies, the smokers – boys like Gary Johnson, Keith Rudland, Simon Carlin and Philip Gray, most of whom lived on the Elmshurst Estate. I had more of an affinity with them, even though I did not live on the estate myself.

It was not that I disliked every member of staff there. John Johnston, a PE teacher, was always very encouraging. I had a lot of respect for him throughout my years at Ralph Allen. More than any other teacher, he could relate to me. He saw that I had some talent in almost all the sports I took part in. I remember that, after one of my altercations with authority, I was told that I could bring along a member of staff as a 'prisoner's friend' when the case was heard. I took along a Mr Rush and this obviously rather upset John at the time. A few years later, John asked me why I had chosen Rush instead of him. I couldn't remember.

I had already shown ability at judo, soccer and cricket. I started judo when I was about nine, at the Church Hall at Batheaston. Bas Lloyd was the teacher. To me, he was an old hippie even though he may only have been 35. He didn't use the full-scale bollocking technique. That always used to bring my dislike of figures in authority bubbling to the surface. It would be: 'Don't do that, Jerry.' That was enough to stop me doing it – if it came from a man I respected. I got better, and by the age of 12 I was going three times a week, although by this time the head of judo was Peter Thatcher, who was authoritarian and would snap at people. That did not work so well with me.

Nevertheless, I persevered. I won lots of tournaments around the West Country, even though I was suspended from Peter's class for insubordination. I was the West of England champion in my weight category, and went on to Crystal Palace for the National Championships, but of my three group bouts I won just one and lost the other two. My judo career fell short of the heights.

So did my soccer career. I played at school, and for Batheaston's boys' team as well. At 13, when I had already been playing mini-rugby for six years, I went for a trial to Parkway Boys, a soccer club which pulled in youngsters from the Bath and Bristol areas and which was, unofficially, a nursery for the Bristol professional teams, City and Rovers. I was not to be the forerunner of Gazza, however. In the trial they gave me one half of the action and they didn't call back.

In an interview my mother recalled an obsession with sport. 'When Jeremy was a small boy he used to drive the neighbours mad by kicking a ball around. He was always bouncing a ball in his hand, wherever you saw him. He used to kick a football against a wooden garage belonging to one of our neighbours and still, when I see her these days, she tells me that her claim to fame is that she used to tell Jeremy off.

'He used to tell me even from an early age that he would play for England one day and I had a feeling long before he ever became well known with Bath that he would keep his promise. Part of the problem at school was that he was so good and he found it difficult to tolerate others in the team making mistakes. He used to give them hell. He used to be an arrogant little so-and-so, partly, perhaps, as a defence mechanism for being black. But he had that hammered out of him when he went to Bath rugby club.'

But my escape through sport was still a long way in the future as the situation at Ralph Allen began to come to a head. The whole problem worsened in the Fifth Form, when I was suspended from school several times and rebellion against authority grew. They would have preferred to keep me back in detention, but I lived too far away and would have had to walk home; and there was no way that Mum or Dad would have come to get me.

On one occasion, we went to play a soccer match at another school, and came back afterwards to Ralph Allen on the coach. The staff member on board, who taught humanities, was reckoned to be soft on discipline, so we put him to the test. Everyone started smoking. He told us to put the cigarettes out. He remonstrated, we persisted. He confiscated the cigarettes and we were all reported to the headmistress. We were suspended.

I reported back to Dad. I told him I was suspended. 'But it wasn't me,' I said. 'I didn't do anything. It was that lot from the Elmshurst Estate.' Dad went up to the school to complain about this disgraceful victimization of his son. He was assured that I had indeed been involved. When he came back, he said that I had let him down.

On another occasion, a metalwork and technical drawing teacher called Barney Parr took strong exception to something I had done. Parr was a straight-talker. He never seemed to enjoy teaching at all. He shouted at me. I shouted back. I felt he was on my case too often, so I flipped and swore at him. I lashed out, verbally. I was taken to the deputy headmaster, a man with a frightening face and acne scars called Berry. 'Laddie,' he said, 'I knew it would be you.'

He announced that he wanted to cane me but that it was against school policy. Incidentally, the use of the strap was not against Dad's policy, and I can remember several occasions when he gave me the strap, with Gary sympathetically hovering outside the room to see if I was all right.

Berry had one weapon. Suspension. I was taken on to Miss Hayter, the headmistress. Mum and Dad were called to pick me up. I was given a two-week ban without remission, and relations with school – and between me and Dad – nosedived even further.

Then came the match of shame and the abuse of the referee at Broadlands School. Mr Rush, the member of staff on duty, drove us back in a minibus. We were laughing and joking about the whole incident, and arrived back at school in time to depart for home on the coaches. Next day, there was the come-uppance. But it was not the goalkeeper who was dragged in, or the team in general. I was carpeted entirely on my own. No one else got into trouble. As I say, I may have questioned some of the decisions, but if I did swear at their master or call him a cheat then I certainly did not remember doing so. It did me no good. Very recently, I attended a year reunion for Ralph Allen pupils. Mr Parr and myself still did not hit it off, although it was good to see all my old schoolfriends again.

After expulsion I had to find somewhere to go. I enrolled at Bath Technical College. I had been turfed out of Ralph Allen a few months before 'O' levels, and it was felt that I should not take them at the original date because I would be too disturbed. So I went to college to sit them at the re-sit stage. The freedom of college life simply added to the problems. You did not actually have to attend classes, nothing was compulsory. There was too much leeway. I spent most of my time dossing around, playing the video machines and the pool table in the common room. Eventually, I got seven CSEs and my original intention was to stay on for more qualifications.

When I was 17, education and I just drifted apart. I left college more or less by default. My tutor kept calling me in. 'You are not appearing in lessons, you are just never there,' he would point out. I would agree to attend in future. I would come in and sit at the front for about a week, then disappear again. I faded out of college, never to return.

Obviously, my father found this almost impossible to accept. At this distance, I can understand and feel sorry for what I put him through. He never had the opportunities that I had, whatever I thought at the time, and I was wasting my chances of a good education.

Relations between us pretty well broke down. I was driven into Mum's camp because Dad had to wield the big stick. He used to do a lot of shift work, so I didn't always see a lot of him anyway. Gary and I used to have our own key when we were at junior school. We would let ourselves back into the house after school, watch cartoons on the television and do our own thing. Mum would come in, and later Dad, but I never felt I could talk to him. He did not actually want to work all those hours; it was something he had to do to make ends meet.

When he came home he would be wanting his dinner, would sit down and watch the TV and then, exhausted, disappear to bed. Life revolved around Mum. She would make our breakfast, ship us off to school then go and do her work. In fact, I had always talked things over with my mother from the earliest days. I discussed with her my first experience of racism, something which, to the disappointment of some of the profile writers looking for a story in more recent years, never affected me too badly.

At Batheaston, I got into a gang which played football at the playing fields there. One day, I beat a couple of the other boys with the ball, only to run into an altercation with Keith Rudland. There was a nose-to-nose confrontation. I was tripped up, my nose rubbed in the mud. I got up and ran off and they were shouting: 'Fuck off, you black bastard' as I ran home with my face full of mud. In Batheaston, it was the first time I had been called a Nigger or a Black Sambo. But I never ran home in floods of tears and asked Mum why I was black. I never thought it was any worse than calling the overweight guy 'Fatso' or the guy with spectacles 'Four-eyes'. There used to be the odd comment from the opposition in clubs in Wales in later years. But racism was just one of many subjects I would talk over with Mum.

When it came to discipline, however, Mum would leave it to

Dad. He dealt with things, whether verbally or with the strap, in the way he thought fit. He was strict, and was always the master of his own house – even today, what Dad says in his house is law. He would not relish letting even the police in because it is, simply, his house. I don't think what he did was wrong, and it would certainly have helped me a lot more if there had been strict discipline like that at school.

When I was 17 there came the big break. Dad said that I was wasting my life, I was treating his home like a hotel, I did not care for anyone but myself. 'The way you are living your life shows a lack of respect for everyone and everything. I don't want you living in my house any more.' There was no ultimatum or discussion. I was out.

I found a home from home with the Allen family. Judy Allen lived with her three teenage daughters, Tracey, Geta and Wendy, in Hill View Road, about a mile up the road from my parents' house. Judy and her husband were separated; she became like a second mother to me, and the girls became like sisters. I shared a room with Tracey for about a year.

The family were later to move to the South London area and I still visit them occasionally, especially after squad sessions in London. I still feel very grateful and very friendly towards them all. Wendy is now in the RAF, and Judy lives in Orpington, but Tracey and Geta have returned to Bath.

I had already returned to Bath to play rugby after some time at Walcot Old Boys. I had a strong group of friends, including Peter Blackett, Tony (Chalkie) Wardle, Gary Frankcom and Steve Knight.

At the time I was on the dole; doing odd jobs here and there to pay rent to Judy. There might also be enough left over for a few extras, to go down to the pub with Peter Blackett, my friend from the Bath Colts. I was still too young to realize that life was in danger of passing me by. I certainly did not feel like begging Dad to take me back. I didn't enjoy his company and he didn't enjoy mine. I could have said: 'Let me come back. I promise I'll get a job.' But that would have meant swallowing too much pride. And in any case, we had no communication at all. I can hardly remember seeing him in the year or so I lived elsewhere. I kept in touch through Mum, but no fences were mended.

'It was a very difficult time,' my mother recalled last year. 'Slim used to be at his wits' end with it all. Jeremy was naughty but never malicious. If I had gone and sat with him all day at school he would have been fine, but they let him get away with murder there. We wanted him to go to Beechen Cliff, because they kept children there under their thumbs, which is just the approach that Jeremy wanted.'

Naturally, this was all very upsetting for Mum. I used to call in when I knew that Dad would be out working. She never wanted me to go, but she realized that Dad was the lawman in the home. I did eventually start making overtures to return, but it took a year before Mum and I plucked up courage to ask Dad for the reprieve.

2
The Trick of Redemption
Emerging from the limbo with a kick in the leg

I was aware of the rumblings at the Bath club. I knew that some of the players thought of me as an arrogant little shit who cared for nothing. I was too mouthy. I would get on people's nerves with descriptions of my playing brilliance. I used to take them through how I side-stepped the openside, ran through with only the full-back to beat (piece of piss), ran under the posts, thank you very much. There was nothing really overt in the reaction of the others, but you would have to be totally insensitive not to pick up the general tone.

Early one season, I arrived at the Rec for training. We found there that training had been switched to Lambridge, Bath's other ground next to the A4 on the road out of town. It was raining hard. David Trick arrived at the same time. Trick was, and is, extremely popular, a very nice man, slow to anger and slow to condemn. I got into his Golf GTi for the short trip to Lambridge with the knowledge that here was the ideal man from whom to find out if other people really did dislike me – however arrogant I was, I did not want to be disliked. He was honest, and experienced enough to give me a proper view, but not so near to the inner circle that I would be out of order even asking him.

I broached the subject as soon as we started off from the Rec. I asked Tricky what the boys thought of me – did they think I was arrogant? 'Yes, they do,' he said. 'And they are right. You are, aren't you?' Coming from Tricky this was all a salutary experience. He kept it up all the way to Lambridge, and even if I did not exactly emerge from the car a new man, perhaps I was on the way. All because training had been switched.

The journey from the Rec to Lambridge has now become one of the most famous episodes in my life. It has been trotted out in scores of profiles of me as the day when I received redemption, became a changed man. And all down to Tricky. Perhaps that is overstating the case, perhaps not. But at least it all made me stop to think. And David and I have remained close friends.

Eventually, we plucked up courage to ask Dad to have me back. Mum talked to Dad. I reappeared and mumbled that I would change, would promise to be as normal as possible, or at least, would try to be whatever was normal in his eyes. One day, I packed my haversack and left the Allens with grateful thanks, and moved back home to St Saviour's Terrace.

I was not quite given the best suite in the house. They were doing up the place, so when I arrived, I was put in the top room that was not yet decorated. There was one bed, no bookshelves, and dust all over. Still, it was home. The atmosphere was frosty, but better. I was still an arrogant handful whether at home or outside, and I had no real job, but we had to sort out some kind of working relationship.

It was at this time that rugby took a hand. I was at Bath RFC, gaining the kind of sporting education that stands you in good stead for other things. As my mother says, some of the arrogance was hammered out of me by the people at Bath – but that was much later.

It was time to sign off the dole. In an extremely rare, almost unique burst of ambition in my school days I had contemplated becoming a PE teacher. That ambition soon faded, but I had to find something. For the first time, I saw what rugby contacts could do as my life and contacts began to be centred around rugby and around the Recreation Ground, the home of Bath RFC, where I had played since mini-rugby years.

I had recently moved up from the Colts to the Spartans, the third XV; George Norman was a Spartan, and I now started working for him. He had permission to fell dead trees up at the Bath Golf Club. We chopped down the trees, sawed them up, moved them by tractor and took them away in George's pick-up to sell for firewood.

After I had been driving round for some time in the pick-up it struck me that one day I ought to take a driving test and try to get a licence.

Before that, I had stacked shelves for Keymarkets. It was not as dreary as it might sound, because the people were colourful. In particular Steve Davies, the fruit and veg manager, and Carlton Dixon, the warehouse manager, were good company.

Even then, I was possessed of no great ambition and no sense of panic that I was going next to nowhere. I still tried to arrange it so that I had the summer months off, on the dole. I would go and watch the cricket, or hang around on the weir on the River Avon outside the Recreation Ground; I was swimming, wasting time. I was floating in mental limbo.

I was, by most accounts, insufferable when playing rugby in those days. Some of the players who were around at the time, or who were just about to join, were interviewed recently in a magazine article about me. 'He was impetuous,' said Gareth Chilcott. 'He came across as conceited in his early days,' said Richard Hill. 'You have got to have some arrogance,' said David Trick. 'But he had too much. I told him that he was a great player, but a prat to himself.'

That was why I was secretly grateful for that lucky switch of training and the talking-to from Tricky.

While I was still cutting down trees there came another major step on the road to recovery. I spent a Saturday evening at Nero's night club, Bath, with Peter Blackett. I was 19. There are two versions of what happened at some stage of that evening. My version is that I felt a kick on the back of my leg, which I ignored. Then I was kicked again and turned round. There were two attractive girls, one black and one white with dark hair. Their names, although I did not know it at the time, were respectively Sharon Williams and Jayne Aland. I looked straight at Jayne and asked her why, if she wanted to talk to me, she did not just introduce herself. She claimed immediately that she did not kick me and that it was her friend. After that top-level discussion the conversation drifted on, then faded. Later in the evening, Jayne started to leave. She gradually got nearer the door. I realized it was now or never. I chased her, asked for her phone number and that was that.

Jayne's story is that she was trying to pair me off with her friend, and that also, when she asked me to dance, I made a feeble excuse that I had hurt my foot playing rugby. 'I told Jeremy that he didn't even look like a rugby player,' Jayne recalled later. She assumed that all rugby players must be massive.

Whatever the actual details, I established that she lived in Holt, that she was going out with another boyfriend at the time, that she was at college and that she was working at a factory at Trowbridge at night to earn some extra cash.

From then on we used to spend hours on the phone, talking. She used to call me in her break and, as it was a payphone, I would call her back. I could imagine her workmates queueing up to use the phone and waiting impatiently. For three months, when Jayne was still officially going out with her boyfriend, we saw each other regularly, although there was nothing sexual in the relationship. Then came a kind of ultimatum from me, because I could hardly go on like that and neither could Jayne. It was him or me, and her answer was that it was me.

It was a brave choice, especially after our somewhat disastrous first date. I arranged to go out with her one evening and told her that I would collect her at Bath Station. I was still logging at the time and managed to commandeer a Datsun pick-up in a horrible dirty yellow. Inside, it was filthy. I was parked outside the station when Jayne arrived. She walked out on to the forecourt, dramatically attractive in her best clothes, and looked expectantly up and down for me, completely ignoring the shambolic pick-up. I pressed the horn to draw her attention. Suddenly, she realized. I saw her wilt, almost sink as the full impact hit her.

Jayne remembers the encounter all too well. 'As it was the first time we had ever arranged to go out, I was all dolled up, trying to make an impression. He said that he would pick me up because he had borrowed the work vehicle. When I got over the shock of this old pick-up truck, Jeremy got out of the truck wearing dirty waterproof trousers and an old cagoule over the top. I got into the van. Inside, it was covered with old newspapers, old Coke cans and crisp packets. My first thought was that I would very much like to get back on the train and go home again. At least Jeremy went home to change first before we went out for the evening.'

We went to the Marlborough Tavern, had a drink and a chat. We took it from there. We eventually went on holiday together, reckoning that if we got on all right then we could safely move in together. Jayne got a job in Bath, we went on holiday without major disasters, came back and we rented a little flat on the ground floor of one of the tall terraces in the city. It was not exactly a cosy love nest. In fact, it was freezing. We had one gas heater around which we would form a huddle every winter evening. We used to run from the bedroom into the bathroom; we used to drag the heater around after us like a faithful little pet. Sometimes, the loo froze totally and you had to pee on it to de-freeze it. We slept in tracksuits, bobble hats and scarves. We used to leave the clothes dryer on to keep warm. Now that is what I call a cold flat. But for the first Christmas we spent there, we bravely invited round half the world – we invited both our families and Peter Blackett and had a great laugh.

By this time I had moved up the employment ladder with a vengeance. I had begun to work as a bus driver with Badgerline. You had to sit a test to get your PSV licence and then took these little mini-buses on various routes around Bath. Unfortunately, the Gloucester crowd got to hear of it with disastrous consequences. One afternoon when I was playing for Bath at Kingsholm, the crowd in The Shed, the popular side of the stadium, began to shout: 'Badgerline, Badgerline, Badgerline . . .' I left the buses and went back to labouring work.

I worked for Ernest Ireland, the builder, and met a man called Roger Hill, who was a bricklayer subcontracted to Irelands for a job at Bath University. I acted as the bricklayer's mate. Roger would let me lay some bricks where they would never be seen – down manholes and so on. He had a calm outlook on life, never seeming to be worn down with worries or hang-ups. If any problems arose, he would decide to sort them out tomorrow. I admired that laid-back lifestyle, and decided to become a bricklayer myself. I went to Fishponds, near Bristol, for a six-month course, and eventually acquired my City & Guilds in bricklaying. There were times when some of the lecturers almost caused me to repeat my old rebellion against authority, but eventually I did manage to get along with them.

The final test for the certificate was to build a miniature version of the front of a house. The bricks were tested for level and strength, and the facial work had to be spotless. I passed. My wall was quite good. It was very satisfying. And that was not all. I was with Jayne,

I had undergone the David Trick course on being a human being, I was making occasional appearances for Bath's first XV, I was establishing a warmer relationship with my father, if not with our flat. Things were looking up a little.

I also received another education with a trip to Wollongong, New South Wales. John Morrison, the Bath lock who had joined from Loughborough and whose sister, Samantha, was later to marry Andy Robinson, the Bath flanker, had spent a season with the Waratahs, a relatively small club which played in the league structure in New South Wales. I was invited there, through the Bath club, to play a season in succession to Morrison. I felt very torn, because Jayne and I had all but decided that we could afford to buy a small flat in Bath and escape from our igloo. Meanwhile, Morrison told me what a great time he had had, what an opportunity it was. Tough choice.

I decided to go. I had to give up my job, and as we could not afford the flat if I was not working, we had to give that up as well. Had I not gone to Australia, and had we gone ahead and bought a place, we could have made a killing on the property market, which was booming. However, we worked out instead that Jayne would move in with my parents while I was away. I left in April 1987, for six months. I had a wonderful time.

I stayed in a flat with a character called Ronnie Wessels, who was a player and an official of the Waratahs. He was balding on top, had a wavy moustache. We trained twice a week, and attacked the juice with enthusiasm on occasions. It was good fun, the pressure was low. The team did not go well. In the previous year, John Morrison had won all the line-out ball for them, and they also had Peter Williams, later to become the England fly-half, playing for them. By the time I arrived they had nosedived a little and we were not successful that season. There was not much I could do in the centre with the lack of ball, but I made sure that when the ball did come I made as much use of it as I could. I lapped up the experience on and off the field.

The actual club was based in the back room of a bowling club, where all the pictures of past teams were hung. The bar was shared with the bowling club. On one day per week there used to be a giant meat raffle. Everyone would buy raffle tickets and there would be a big draw, with sacks of meat going to the winners. I often wondered how many of the participants realized where the money went. It went to me. It was my pocket money for the trip, and came out at about 150 Australian dollars per week. I have never checked how that affected my amateur status, but I do not expect Twickenham to set a major enquiry in motion at this stage.

Or the police. But the truth is that I had my first drugs experience in Australia. I was invited around to the house of the captain of the club one evening. I knew that some of the club members smoked dope, and sure enough, as the night wore on, they produced a bag of the stuff and proceeded to skin up some large joints.

'I'm driving,' I said.

'Have one for later,' they replied.

I had a couple (of drinks), went back to the flat where I stayed and decided it was time to write a letter to Jayne. I decided to try the joint too. When I was half-way through it, I began to feel light-headed. As I wrote, I was touched by dazzling flights of writing brilliance, and the eloquent prose simply flowed. It was a letter of heartfelt love and pain.

I put out the joint, laid down the letter to post in the morning, still feeling impressed. As I put my head back on the pillow, it seemed as if a smile was creeping all around my face. When I shut my eyes, stars were blasting out through my head. It was an incredible experience.

On waking in the morning, I picked up the letter and read it through. It was complete and utter drivel.

For the last two months at Wollongong, Jayne came out and joined me, which was great. I had written scores of letters, made dollars and dollars worth of phone calls. During those two months, we decided that we were going to get married. The proposal was not especially romantic. We were in bed. 'What do you think about getting married?' I said.

We spent two years with my mother and father in St Saviour's Terrace. We had two rooms in their house but we had started saving seriously. I was back at bricklaying for a subsidiary of John Mowlem and, since my return from Wollongong, rugby had begun taking over in a big way. I became a regular with Bath, and at the start of the 1988–89 season I was the first choice centre, alongside Simon Halliday.

At the end of that season we bought a terraced house in Larkhall, not too far on foot from my parents' home. We could have got something bigger in somewhere like Bristol, but we decided that we would rather stay in Bath. Mum and Dad helped us with the mortgage and, as the place needed a lot of work on it, we rolled up our sleeves to begin a summer of hard toil. Then I was chosen for the Lions tour, so I rolled my sleeves back down again, went to Australia and left it all to Jayne. Luckily, our friends rallied round. My father did a great deal of work, and loads of people helped in different ways.

And Jayne and I were married, at St Saviour's Church, in Larkhall, at the end of the next season. The local papers made a lot of the fact that I could not choose between Pete Blackett and Chalkie Wardle for best man, so I chose them both. England were away on tour at the time, so some of the lads were unable to attend the wedding, but Simon Halliday was there and it was a wonderful day. Some of the Bath minis formed a guard of honour in their kit as we emerged from the church.

Once again, the papers pulled out all the stops. 'News of the nuptials will no doubt cause a few tears to be shed among female rugby supporters, for whom Jeremy has become something of a heart-throb,' said one account. 'But a family friend tells me that the burly centre, aged 25, has had eyes only for Jayne since meeting her several years ago . . .' How do these people get their jobs? We held the reception at the Rudloe Park Hotel, as well as an evening reception in a marquee in the familiar surroundings of the Recreation Ground. We went to Florida for a fortnight on honeymoon.

When it comes to the big events in our life, Jayne is usually the driving force. Perhaps because my mind is on other things, I tend not to see what is approaching – like a hedgehog on the motorway. Then suddenly it all becomes clear! In 1990, for example, when we had been engaged for some time, Jayne was a little tired of the lack of a final decision on the wedding itself. While I was still humming and hawing, she suddenly had church and vicar booked, and the reception into the bargain. Looks like we're getting married, I thought.

Now, in 1991, Jayne started talking about having children. She also started saying that she didn't want to take the pill any more. Looks like we're having a baby, I thought. Our first child was duly conceived, if memory and maths serve me correctly, on the night of the 1991 World Cup final. Later, she bought a home pregnancy kit. She woke me after a major night out. She held up the kit.

'Can you see a black dot there?' she asked. I could see hundreds of black dots. I was just coming out of a coma. Looks like Jayne's pregnant, I thought. We told Mum and Dad. Dad was in a trance of joy, cuddling Jayne and patting her on the back.

But if I was blasé then, I stopped being blasé quickly. On 4 August 1992, we had a daughter; we called her Imogen. Her arrival was the most profound thing which ever happened to me or is ever likely to happen to me. Even though billions of people have the same experience, I still found it unique and brilliant. Through the pregnancy – leaving aside the temporary threat of a miscarriage, which thankfully did not occur – I watched the change in Jayne with fascination. I watched my share of the bed shrink down to six inches.

One day, when I came home from work, she told me that she had been having contractions. With my usual helpfulness and thoughtfulness when it comes to the housework, I suggested that she should make my dinner. We had scampi and chips. We went to Bath Hospital and after a 23–hour labour, ending up with me trying to be at both ends, to encourage Jayne but also to see our baby actually being born, Imogen arrived.

She made all the local papers, pictured with a dad bursting with pride. I explained the one dodgy moment. 'Her umbilical cord became wrapped around her neck. I was scared silly, but the staff were cool and calm and took care of it.'

I was totally besotted by her then and I have remained besotted ever since. I still cannot believe that she is ours. I have so much love and affection to give and to share. The birth brought us all closer together as a family, and made me less selfish. Everything I have done since the birth has been motivated by the desire to make everything better for the family. I have become quite callous and single-minded in devoting everything to Jayne and our daughters.

Even rugby, mentally, takes a back seat. I suppose it brings part of the story full circle.

The arrival of Holly, our second daughter, had a different story attached. In 1994 I co-presented *Body Heat*, the ITV programme. It was a great opportunity and I was asked to do the second series as well, which was to be filmed in the middle of 1995. Some of the filming was to take place in Atlanta, Georgia, at around the time when the baby was due. It was a dilemma, but we decided that the role was such an outstanding opportunity, especially with the possibility of a third series later, that I would go ahead.

For a time, there were visa problems with the Atlanta trip and it seemed as if filming might be switched to Britain, so that I could nip down to be with Jayne when the time came. However, the problems were sorted out just before the due date and I set off for America. One day, Jayne started having contractions. We left the hotel to go out filming, white-water rafting and mountain biking in Tennessee and so the production manager took along a Motorola telephone for Jayne to ring with any news. However, the signal was weak up in the mountains, Motorola could not help in Britain because it was a bank holiday and Jayne could not get through.

When I got back to the hotel in the evening there was a message to ring Jayne. She sounded so matter-of-fact when I rang that I assumed at first that nothing had happened. But it had. Holly was born on Easter Sunday, Jayne sounded great and had abandoned her campaign for the name Romany. She had stayed at home with Helen, the midwife, until the last moment. She went into hospital at 5, gave birth at 7, and was back at home at 9.

It was strange being so far away, but at least as Holly was a few days late, it meant that she would be only two days old when I returned. I am envious of the midwife, who was there at the birth in my absence, but at least we now have a second treasure.

It is almost impossible to describe the appeal of living in a certain place if that is the only place where you have ever lived. But I do realize how lucky Bathonians are. It is a city, but it is very small. It is quite difficult to do anything without everyone else knowing. That suits me because I am essentially nosy. I like to know what is happening around me. I don't like large open spaces and I don't like large cities. Bath, when the old stone is cleaned, looks stunning. It reminds you of old paintings. In a sense, you could be in a time warp, a time warp of atmosphere as well as architecture.

I am told that I could have made a financial killing by uprooting myself and moving to London to join a club like Harlequins. I am obviously not suggesting that they would have paid me, but they do have access to some major and highly-paid jobs. Briefly, for a month or two some years ago, I did contemplate moving. But it was never on the cards. It seems you would have to harvest money then wait for the weekend to spend it all. Now, I could not even begin to consider the idea. Nor could I face the idea of living in a place like Richmond, relatively near to the centre of London on the tube, but still a long way out. I have a running joke with Colin Herridge, the former secretary of Harlequins who is now the media adviser for the England team, about my impending arrival at the Quins. But with great respect to the Quins, if you have experienced the atmosphere of the city of Bath then you don't want to change, and if you have experienced the atmosphere of Bath Rugby Club, you don't want to swap that either. I have stayed with the city and the club through thick and thin, and at the time of writing I cannot see anything changing that, apart from a massive league offer.

Even Larkhall, up on the hill from the A4 on the way into Bath from the London side, is a nice community within a community. We had our own celebrations and party to turn on the Christmas lights, when the streets were blocked off to traffic. We had Ron the Butcher, Roger the Newsagent and Tony the Greengrocer. Ron asked for signed autographs for a Scottish delivery man of his who likes rugby. We moved on to a bigger house across the city in March 1995.

The only real hassle I have from being a well-known face these days is from odd drunks in Bath, especially when they dredge things up they have read, or they think they have read, about me – especially the hoary old chestnut about me having lots of money, walking round in a big coat and driving a massive car. That is hardly my style, which in fact has not changed very much. I still ring Peter and Chalkie and suggest a day out now and again. If I'm not playing, I might suggest some lunch in Bath, a walk down to the Rec to see the game and a drink afterwards. Sometimes we might make a night of it by going on to the Pig & Fiddle, and maybe ending up at Joe Bananas or the Island Club.

The hassle factor has increased as I have become better known. I have cut down the excursions a good deal because if I lost my temper and lashed out and the other guy was taken to hospital, I would be the one who lost out. Usually, I finish my drink, jump in a cab and go home. It is part of the price that you pay. So are the letters I receive. I try to reply to them all, especially those from children asking for autographs and pictures. I am always fascinated by the more pointed ones from female admirers, although Jayne tends not to exhibit the same fascination.

After the tour of Australia in 1989 and with the glories of that tour still in my veins, I had worked out that I did not want to be a bricklayer at 45. Dave Robson, who was then coaching at Bath, arranged a meeting with John Day, then the Deputy Chairman of British Gas South Western. I then had a follow-up interview with John Day and Bill Edwards, the PR manager. They said that there was a position in their PR department for me if I wanted it. I duly joined British Gas on 2 January 1990, as a PR assistant.

For that read office boy. I filled in invoices, took telephone messages, helped the press officer. I couldn't have been more like an office boy if I had been appointed office boy. Meanwhile I could have time off for any rugby-related activities – training, tours, tests, interviews, photographic shoots, golf days. It was as loose as that. I averaged two days a week in the office. I never sat down and thought, 'Wait a minute. This isn't working.' I thought it was brilliant.

But gradually, I became more attracted to the company, and more involved. I spent time with the internal communications manager, I spent a year in the PR department and some time with the PR and sales manager, was put on secondment to sales and spent time with the technical sales reps. Not all the time was particularly well spent, but some if it definitely was, and I learned more and more about the company. I eventually met my current boss, Trevor Cooper, and made known my wish for something a little more specific. Eventually, I became a representative for the housing department, dealing directly with the developers. My job title became marketing co-ordinator (housing promotions), and I was given a long job description. This included the promotion of British Gas show homes, personal appearances, and a special responsibility for Gaswarm, a promotion and incentive scheme that we ran as a benefit for developers opting to use gas exclusively.

When I started, Christine Foster, a colleague, said: 'How long are you here for? Three months? Six months? When does your sponsorship run out?' I think many people thought I would be up and away very rapidly. However, in July 1995 I was well into my sixth year with British Gas. It took me time to be accepted and perhaps there are still people who find it difficult to accept me completely as I am allowed time off for rugby and, within limits, for other activities. But acceptance has gradually come. I think my colleagues recognize that I am trying to be as successful with my business life as I have been in sport.

I perhaps don't see myself working for British Gas for my whole life. But I do have strengths in the job. My biggest asset appears to be my mouth. I enjoy talking to people, influencing their choice. I get a kick from feedback I receive after making a speech or a presentation, or from the sales manager's reaction to some work I have done. It's certainly a lot better than driving the dirty yellow pick-up truck with the logs.

When my father threw me out of his house in my late teens, I was on the surface shattered and it was not a feeling I enjoyed at all. Where am I going to go? What am I going to do? Those were just two of the questions I was asking. But it did not shake me to the roots. I had what could be called a premonition. I knew even then that the only way it would all come crashing down was if I had an injury which finished my sporting career at a very young age.

Otherwise, I knew that I would get by with my rugby talents. I always sensed that the route would be open. Whether, in order to take that route, I would have to move to London or Manchester or even into rugby league, or whether I would stay in Bath, was another question. But I always knew the answer.

After the grim days of the non-relationship, Dad and I began to thaw. Jayne only came on the scene a couple of years after I had returned home, but she remembers both the original problem and the change. 'It was generally accepted,' she says, 'that Sue was the one you had the laughs with and Slim was the one you were a bit reserved with. But things changed dramatically over the years. Slim and Jeremy both have relaxed with each other. They have fun together. They are more like friends.' I would go along with that.

3
Spartan days on the Rec
Gathering strength

Stuart Barnes and I played so many times alongside one another that we had an excellent understanding. But we did not always live in complete harmony, especially when I wanted the ball to run with, and he wanted to kick it. When he was in a more conservative mode, lining up and waiting for the forwards to win the ball, I used to say: 'Go on. Kick it like you always do.' Or if we were near their posts: 'Drop a goal like you always do.' Stuart used to get angry. 'Jeremy can be a right bastard,' he once told a newspaper.

But I changed policy at Twickenham in 1992, in the cup final. We were level with Harlequins at 12–12, it was the last second of extra time in an amazing match at the end of a hard season, and because of everything we stood for at Bath, to lose to Harlequins, or even to have to share the Cup – our Cup – with them would have been unbearable.

We won a line-out about 35 metres out. It was bound to be the last move of the match. 'Pass it on. I'll try a drop goal,' I said to Barnes. 'No, I'm going to try one myself,' said Barnes. For once, he got no argument from me.

Nigel Redman won the line-out. Richard Hill passed to Barnes. Pictures of the instant he struck the ball show me beside him with hands on knees, completely knackered. Time seemed suspended as the ball approached the posts and all 30 players, 62,000 in the crowd and a huge live TV audience held their breath. It went over. For me it was the best thing that ever happened in rugby, until a similar incident in the quarter-final of the 1995 World Cup. I celebrated as I have never celebrated before or since, gesticulat-

ing towards Harlequins and almost jumping on Stuart's back. It was another cup final triumph. And it was another part of what Jack Rowell, who finally left the post as coach in 1994 to become England's team manger, calls 'The greatest journey any club has ever had'. This is the story of that journey, and of an institution that has meant more to me than anything in my sporting career – and which, however, is nothing like what it seems on the surface.

At the annual Christmas party of the Bath mini-rugby section, Gareth Chilcott was always Father Christmas. I remember how ridiculously easy it was to tell it was him. These were the mid-1970s. At the time when I joined the section Bath were still watched by a few hundred people and there was no inkling at all of what lay ahead for the club.

Or for me – no inkling of how I would eventually become the first player to play for Bath's first XV who had begun in the mini section. Or of how influential Chilcott would prove in my sporting career. The only certainty was that there, under the red cloak, was Chilcott. Bath were a friendly club, but just another club. We were still the good guys who lost.

My parents had been down to Bath with John Taylor, my mother's brother, who was a keen supporter. They had a good time, felt welcome and heard through the grapevine that there was a mini-rugby section. On the first day I ever went, practically the first time I ever took to a rugby pitch, it was a foul day and I remember the mud being reddish and thick. I took a tumble, was covered in the thick, red stuff. As my father told a newspaper in later years: 'I could see Jeremy's lip quivering as he picked himself up. But he carried on playing, and never looked back after that.'

But the Bath years are not an unbroken line. Bath did not run youth teams between 11 and 16, so for those formative years we all moved up to Walcot Old Boys. A sort of 'Bath in exile', Walcot used to rent Lambridge, Bath's second ground.

The Walcot days were great days. Every year we seemed to have a tiny team, far smaller than the opposition. We seemed to be various bits of riff-raff thrown together to play against well-organized rugby teams. But we played with tremendous heart, we loved the concept of playing for each other. I sometimes managed a jinking kind of try from my normal position as fly-half, and when we won, it was a fantastic feeling. We enjoyed the team spirit in adversity, a factor which saw both Walcot and Bath teams through in my later career. Tony Wardle, who with Peter Blackett was to be joint best man at my wedding, was in the team. We used to go up to the ground together to play, on Sundays, and revelled in it.

Andy Michael, a coach at Walcot, was one of my early influences. He was a taskmaster who would never tolerate larking about if there was serious work to be done, but he put himself out for us. When the time came to return to Bath, when I was invited to train with them at the age of 16, it was a wrench to leave. The club have always kept in touch, sending me messages of congratulations at various points in my subsequent careeer, and I owe them a debt of gratitude.

As a newly installed member of Bath Colts, it would be wrong to say that I dreamed of future glories. I realized in a sort of arrogant way that I could play rugby well. I was confident on the ball. I also had two chips on each shoulder, but if I offended other people (and I did), then my circle of friends seemed to put up with me.

And it was that feeling of comradeship, the game followed by a night out with the other colts, which was basically the summit of ambition. We would travel away in a nice, posh coach, play big clubs on big grounds, like Leicester, Coventry, Cardiff and Llanelli. There was often a ritual debagging of a new player on the return coach trip. His trousers and underpants would be thrown off the bus, and Deep Heat administered to the appropriate places – appropriate unless you were the victim. I was so engrossed in the life that, even though we unquestionably played against some colts in other teams who were to become extremely famous, I never noticed one of them. Even now, I never study the opposition team sheet and worry about them. If they run past me it simply registers that they may be a bit quick.

Geoff Pillinger and Tom Martland were the coaches of the colts team. Tom was a former first-team coach. John Morrison, Peter Blackett and Gary Frankcom, all to figure strongly with Bath later, were in the team. But it was still the short-term view which appealed: play the game, have the social fun afterwards.

The next step up on leaving colts rugby at 18 was to join the

Spartans, Bath's third XV. It may not sound glamorous. Perhaps today, emerging talents might turn up their nose at playing for a third XV, and many clubs simply don't have a third string. But again, this was another chapter which I can look back on with delight.

By the time I arrived in the Spartans, Bath had started their run. On a Colts tour of St Ives, in 1984, we took time off on a Sunday to watch *Rugby Special*. The day before, Bath had beaten Bristol 10–9, to win what was then the John Player Cup, after Bristol's fly-half, Stuart Barnes, had missed a penalty in the last seconds that would have given Bristol the cup. We watched the rerun as Roger Spurrell, the captain, walked up the steps to claim the trophy. It was the first trophy of national significance that we had won.

Obviously, things at Bath were gradually improving, and Jack Rowell, the coach, was finally achieving some success after lean years. But there was still no real sense that the club was on the threshold of a dream.

For me, the first XV were, for the moment, out of reach, too serious. The second XV were full of the bitter and twisted, who thought they should be in the first XV or who had just been dropped. That left the Spartans. They used to play the first teams of local clubs and the third teams of the major clubs – Coventry, Bristol and so on. I was still at fly-half. Indeed, at this time I never dreamed that I would ever move to another position. We had a brilliant team, and we were captained by the great Robbie Lye, who played over 500 matches for the first team. A tremendous competitor and player, Robbie was wonderful company for the younger players. His philosophy was that we should run everything from any part of the pitch. Great days. Robbie Lye is still a very close friend. During my absences on long tours, he and his wife, Teresa, keep in contact with Jayne, ring her every Sunday to ask her around or to see if everything is all right. Friends like that in rugby tend to be friends for life.

Black Two was one of our favourite moves. We would call it at a scrum near our own goal-line, and, best of all, with a blind side of about 15 yards. Our No. 8 would pick up and take out their scrum-half on the blind side. Our scrum-half would take out their blind-side wing. That left the left wing to set off down the touch-line and the wing would usually be away to score. We scored so many tries with that movement. We used to beat teams by 40 and 50 points every week – and celebrate appropriately after the game.

And the most amazing thing was that Robbie, the experienced veteran who used to guide a team of youngsters, was always the biggest casualty. The Spartans' drink was rum coolers – rum, orange juice and lemonade with lots of ice. We would mix it all up in an ice bucket and you would get 10 seconds each with a straw. It gave you a buzz. It gave Robbie more than that. He would be legless by 6.30, his wife would come to collect him and Robbie would be gone.

With growing maturity as I developed on and off the field of play, I consciously tried to become less of an annoyance to people and was helped, as we have seen, by what has apparently been immortalized by all profile writers as 'The Journey', the trip from the Rec to Lambridge described earlier, during which David Trick favoured me with some home truths about my behaviour and demeanour. Bath, meanwhile, were becoming an annoyance to everyone standing in their way. I started looking to leave the Spartans, one of my favourite teams, behind.

The first team would train on their own. Looking over to them as they went about their business, I was always impressed by two in particular. Spurrell, the captain, was an incredible figure, whose commitment bordered on the dangerous. It was something I have seen in very few other players. I would certainly class him with Peter Winterbottom. As a captain, Spurrell would never ask anyone to do things he wouldn't do himself.

Spurrell once led a Bath tour party to Boston, where we played in an international tournament. Before one of the matches a sizeable American came up for what he thought would be a spot of psyching out. He looked at Chilcott. 'I kick ass, man,' he said, and walked away.

Chilcott looked at Spurrell. Spurrell looked at Chilcott. The American was carried off the field in the first few minutes. At the end of the final itself, we were losing but we had a chance to take the title with a long penalty. Spurrell called me up, and gave me the Spurrell look. 'You are going to take it and you are going to get it,' he said. If I had missed it, I wouldn't be here today. I kicked it and Bath won.

In the backs, I used to watch John Palmer, in the centre. If anyone in my time at Bath has cause to moan, it was Palmer – that he did not win 40 caps for England. He would mesmerize people with the ball. He would hold it out as he approached, show it to them, then take the ball back under his arm and go on. He wasn't the quickest centre, but he was a footballer, he had all the ball skills. A remarkable player.

If I was to join him, it seemed in the mid-1980s that I was in a queue of three for the fly-half position. John Horton, the great club servant who had been England's fly-half in their Grand Slam season in 1980, was expected to retire at the end of the 1984–85 season. The talk of the city was that the three pretenders were myself, Charles Gabbitas, who had joined the club from Plymouth Albion, and Alun Watkins, who had played for Newport. I was seen as the long shot because I was still the Spartans' fly-half. Robbie put in a word for me in the *Bath Evening Chronicle*. 'Jeremy's always got so much time to do things,' he said. 'If he continues to develop he is going to make one hell of a player.'

My attitudes changed substantially for the 1984–85 season. I trained throughout the summer at Bath Sports Centre. I would go out and do sprints before the five-a-side soccer. I realized that, not being very big, I would have to make up for it with speed.

In early January 1985, Bath were away to Waterloo. I was on standby for the big time because there was a doubt whether Palmer could escape from a commitment at his school in time to travel on the Friday. I arrived in bad humour. My inclination was to stay in Bath and go on the piss with my friends, not travel to the far north with people I knew only to nod to. But Palmer failed to arrive, and I was on the coach, the Bath first XV coach. I was not to play at fly-half. I was to play in the foreign land of the centre, alongside a player who was just beginning to make a mark at the club, Simon Halliday, a well-spoken public schoolboy and Oxford blue.

Next morning, at the team meeting, Jack Rowell took control and I was impressed by his forcefulness. But I was so nervous that I had not the faintest idea what he said. It slowly dawned that what every Bath Colt wanted was going to happen to me. I was terrified of making mistakes. All I wanted to do was play well, get home and go back and tell my mates about it.

Bath won, 23–13. I even got two headlines in the papers, dutifully clipped out by my mother for the scrapbooks. 'Guscott shines in Bath win,' and, in the *Sunday Telegraph*, 'Guscott Gusto.' I kicked four penalties and put Barry Trevaskis in for one of his two tries. The *Bath Evening Chronicle* said that I had 'a splendid game'. Unfortunately, they only had on file one stock photograph of me, with a full-scale Afro-style haircut. It appeared again and again until they sent someone to take another.

I did not realize until it actually happened what making the first XV meant in the eyes of the average Bathonian in the city. But people started to look at you in a different way – friends, neighbours, strangers. There was more respect and also, in the time-honoured tradition of British people, there was jealousy. It seems that almost a majority of British people hate success. American sports followers have far more respect for it.

I played a few more games as the season progressed, gradually feeling less of an outsider. The *Daily Telegraph* records that I scored 'a lovely solo try' when Bath beat Ebbw Vale; the *Western Mail* went further. According to them, I 'ripped the defence to shreds'.

And at the end of the season, after Bath had fought their way through to the John Player Cup final again, against London Welsh, I was chosen as replacement for Twickenham itself. I was 19. I was measured up for the blazer. I got the special kitbag. Pete and Chalkie took it badly. 'You lucky bastard,' they said. We stayed in a fine hotel overnight, as part of the build-up. It was a taste of the real big-time.

There was a nasty moment during the match. I had to come on. Barry Trevaskis left at half-time and I played the second half, on the wing and out to lunch. The wing is the worst position in rugby. For an English wing, it is even worse than that, because you never get the ball. After the match, which we won 24–15, I could remember hardly anything.

I did remember one moment. John Palmer jinked and we went away. Chris Martin, the Bath full-back, took it and he had time to pass to me, but didn't. I am sure I would have scored because there was only one man left to beat. Still, I was up on the platform with the lads as Roger Spurrell lifted the cup again. I had a winners' tankard. I still had the massive Afro.

We then moved under the stand for the television interviews.

Nigel Starmer-Smith moved among the team, asking for reactions. Palmer gave his views, then Starmer-Smith reached me. 'What was it like out there?' he asked brightly. I was still out to lunch. 'The Blood done it,' I said. It was an expression black kids use, but it must have been completely lost on every TV viewer. I laughed, the team laughed, and old Starmer looked a bit blank. It was a wonder that the BBC ever had me back.

Next day, we rode round the city of Bath on an open-topped bus. This tradition was not quite so well established then, and you felt like a complete pillock. A few hundred people came to the Rec to see us off, and then we watched, sipping champagne on the top deck, as they all went running like hell around the city to make it seem that 100,000 people had turned out.

It seems surprising now to look back and remember that it was to be almost another three years before I became a full-time Bath regular. In a later age I would unquestionably have been snapped up by another club with a major package deal. But people were more loyal, were prepared to wait for their chance. And the grapevine was not so extensive – fewer people would have known about me.

And Palmer and Halliday were such an outstanding partnership. In 1986, Palmer assumed the captaincy, and Halliday began his England career. Palmer's short Test career had begun when England toured South Africa in 1984. To be shut out of the first XV was not frustrating when you realized how well they were playing. There was no sense of injustice when I was competing against two legends.

What I did accept was that centre was to be my position. When I did play for the first team, I would follow John Horton with his left and right dart. If you had any pace you could come up on his shoulder and cut straight through, so there were more attacking opportunities. On the other hand, I now had to make a career out of tackling, whereas fly-halves at that time were not really expected to get their hands dirty with that kind of thing.

The 1985–86 season provided several more walk-on parts as I waited in the wings. Palmer was duly back at Twickenham at the end of the season, waving from the rostrum to mark Bath's third successive cup final win, over Wasps, 25–17.

I was trusted for several of the bigger matches, notably when Palmer stood down for a match against Gloucester. We won 22–9, and the *Daily Express* recorded that one of 'three breathtaking first half tries' was scored by 'Jeremy Gosport'! I made *The Times* late in October 1985 when Peter West tried to predict the next black player to play for England. He named three possibles – Ralph Knibbs, Eddie Saunders of Coventry and myself. The other two never made it.

And at last I approached the inner circle at Bath. It was easy. To become one of the inner few you played cards. On the coach, others mellowed out or watched the videos. The inner circle played cards – Horton, Chilcott, Palmer, sometimes Jon Hall, the flanker, the local boy who was already an incredible force. Halliday sometimes joined in too. It was always a red-letter day when Halliday graced the game with his presence.

There was something else remarkable about 1985–86. We had a new fly-half. At the start of the 1985–86 season, Stuart Barnes had joined. He came from Bristol, our deadly rivals. Before that, he had left Newport for Bristol and had also left Wales, where he went to school and had made the Welsh squad, for England.

I could not accept him. Barnes wrote in 1994: 'Jerry hated me at the start. He was the worst. He couldn't accept that anyone from outside Bath's world could come in.' Nor could many Bath followers, who were devoted to John Horton. It was all handled badly by the club. Horton, who had done so much for Bath, had to leave for Bristol almost in a hurry, to accommodate Barnes. I can remember talking about Barnes to Pete Blackett, and asking: 'What is he doing here?'

Barnes just got on with the job. Before we knew it, he was in the card circle. Then he was organizing the backs. Before we knew it, he had wormed his way in and become one of us, part of the long march.

4
The Greatest Journey
Jack Rowell and the years of domination

Everyone at Bath had known that something was stirring, especially when John Palmer led the team to the 1985 cup final win over London Welsh. But I don't think that anyone really appreciated the possibilities and what was going to happen in the decade ahead, the total dominance we exerted not only over the league and cup competitions, but in providing Bath players for England squads at all levels. Many commentators believe that no club will ever approach the achievements again. I feel certain they are right.

By the end of the 1994–95 season, the club had become part of rugby history and sporting and West Country folklore. We had won the cup nine times in twelve years; we had won the league five times in the seven years since the league system operated, and for four times in succession. We had won the double three times, and 1987–88 was the last season in which we won neither trophy. I have played in three more finals in addition to appearing as replacement in the 1984 final, but missed the 1994 battle with Leicester because of injury. For everyone involved at the club, it has been an unforgettable ride.

The club has meant everything to me. It has been a huge part of my life, and indeed, until four years ago, when I was married, everything in my life revolved around the club. My friends all played. There was the match on Saturday, there was Sunday in the pub discussing the game; on Monday, everyone at work or around the city wanted to talk about it, too. Monday and Wednesday nights were training nights, then there was the excitement of being selected for the weekend; and then the whole cycle began again. If I was in the first XV – I became a regular in 1987–88 and the unquestioned first choice by the start of 1988–89 – I would spend Friday evenings quietly at home (and if I was in the second XV, I would have six to eight pints of Guinness).

How have Bath done it? How have Bath managed to keep it up for so long, to send back all the pretenders to our crown empty-handed? Even with a depleted team, and expected to lose, we won the Cup yet again in 1995. It is partly an accident of birth, obviously, that so many talented players were born in roughly the right place and the right time and have come through together. We are lucky that so many of us live near to the ground. We have always been outstandingly dedicated trainers. We start training at 7. If you are not there by 7, you may as well not come at all. As Gareth Chilcott always says: 'Even on the training pitch, you never wanted to be the player who let Bath down.'

There is also the incredible succession of strong characters, down the years: Roger Spurrell helped to begin it all; Gareth Chilcott is simply an overpowering character, a great influence; there was John Palmer, Richard Hill, Stuart Barnes, John Horton and Jon Hall. Off the pitch, there has been, obviously, Jack Rowell, who retired after 17 years as Bath coach only when the post of England team manager became available. Tom Hudson, who had a relatively short stay at the club, chiefly as fitness adviser, also left a lasting impression. He laid the foundations of a training regime of harsh proportions.

He was a taskmaster. He used to ask me, say, to fetch some balls during a training session. I would refuse. 'I don't fetch balls,' I would say.

'Right,' Tom would retort. 'Go and have a shower.' This would happen three or four times per season. We look back on it together now and almost wet ourselves with laughter.

But there is far more to it. People expect us to have the most incredible team spirit and togetherness. They would not be disappointed, but they would be shocked by the way in which that team spirit actually shows itself. Any outsider looking in, anyone coming close to the centre of the club, would assume in a very short space of time that we all hate each other, that we truly and deeply do not like each other at all.

The back-chat or, to give it its street term, the piss-taking, even the bickering, operates to a degree that few people would believe. It is the combination of huge egos in the club, the huge characters throughout the dressing-room. In a way, it is the battle between the players off the field to see who can give the shit, how long we can keep it on someone. It is as if we are doing it to see how much people take before cracking. It seems to be the way we get along.

I have escaped quite lightly. I have never been seriously targeted, partly because my tactics have always been very good. They started on me in the early days. 'Hey, you flash bastard, you scored all the tries again.' I learned that the easiest way was to nod, say nothing and smile. They would soon get bored and try it on someone else.

Some of the lads have not been so successful. Nigel Redman gets it all the time. He is the most clumsy, awkward, accident-prone player in the club. Before one of the semi-finals, he took the field with eight stitches in the top of his head after some dressing-room accident. On another occasion, when the chant of the warm-up had begun in the dressing-room, Redman, running on the spot like the others, accidentally stepped into a bucket and collapsed on to the floor with a mighty clatter.

Tony Swift can also attract the wrong sort of interest. It is over 20 years since he came down from the Fylde in the north, but he is still attacked as a northern softie, a pie-eater. He has his defence a bit better organized these days. He stores up embarrassing moments he has witnessed when other people are drunk, retorts with some of his own ammunition when the attack comes on. He has successfully moved to the periphery, glides around the edge to escape. He announced his retirement after the 1995 Cup Final, scoring a typically brilliant try. He was a great player; totally underrated.

Even the heart of the team is more cliquey than people would expect. Redman and Jon Callard are close; so were Hill, Chilcott and Graham Dawe – Hill and Chilcott have now retired to coach. I am not in any particular grouping. Perhaps it is no wonder, because I have been one of the ringleaders when it comes to winding up people past the point of no return. When I have had a drink I may go overboard in telling people about their weaknesses. Many things are too precious to the moment to recreate, but I do remember a grade one disagreement or two.

One came on the night of the annual club dinner in 1991. We had repaired to the Oldfield club's bar after the dinner and everyone was in belligerent mood. I tore into Paul Simpson, our back-row man. I was about to tour with England to Australia in our pre-World Cup tour. My last dart was to say: 'Look, it isn't my fault if you are not good enough to go. I'm going.' Simpson connected with a decent punch, and thankfully, some friends dragged us apart. His 17 stone and my 13 stone might have been a mismatch.

On the Bath New Year training camp in Lanzarote, a few seasons ago, I started on Tony Swift. Apparently, I told him he was crap, that he shouldn't be in the side, that he should retire – we say the same things to him every season. Swifty was soaking it all up very well, so I turned on Richard Hill, then my closest friend in the team. We used to room together when we were away, and Hilly used to drive me to the Recreation Ground on match days. We were always close. Hill eventually reacted. 'Well,' I said. 'Come on then.'

That round gradually died down, Hill went back to the room we were sharing. When we got back to the room, Hilly had prepared some food for me. I can remember standing up against the wall, slagging off Hill with abandon. I heard later that I was denying his right to call himself a British Lion. He had played for the Lions in the International Board celebration game, but never on a proper Lions tour. Hilly stood up slowly, walked across and whacked me. I slid, legless, to the floor.

In the morning, I woke on the settee with an aching jaw. Swift was still there. He filled me in with the full story of what had happened. Jon Webb had just joined the club from Bristol. He really made himself useful as a doctor. Apparently, when the argument reached its height he hid underneath the bed. Hilly and I lost some of the old closeness after that.

Most of the team, from Spurrell onwards, have had a few bouts. Even the backs. Phil de Glanville was chatting to Jack Rowell late at night after England played Ireland in 1994. Barnes was at the end of his tether, still stuck on the bench behind Rob Andrew. Barnes and de Glanville started with a playfully heavy whack each; Barnes, in no mood for jesting anyway as he was still out of the England side, lost it completely and came in with a head-butt. Barnes and I had a major disagreement at my stag night. Even at the dinner to celebrate Jack Rowell's departure after the double-winning season of 1993–94 there was a good deal of ill feeling as the testing comments from Jack struck home. Jack would often begin a team meeting by looking at one of the team he felt was underachieving and asking: 'What on earth are you doing here?' De Glanville is now one of the ringleaders of the whole thing.

It is not, quite, as malevolent as it might sound. It is a collision of egos, a way of relieving the pressure by letting off steam. Tension is created by operating at such a high level.

And as Chilcott says, the continuing success comes from the desperate wish not to be the one who lets Bath down, in training or on the field. People find it remarkable that we are never mentally satisfied. Other clubs might settle mentally for one cup or league title, but we rejuvenate ourselves for every season.

The new captain comes in. We sit down and discuss our goals. They are always the same – to win the cup and the league. That creates a pressure because it means that unless we win the double we look upon the season as being a failure. We treat the trophies as our own, as personal treasures, family heirlooms.

This probably sounds arrogant, but if you are a Bath player you feel yourself in the ascendancy. No one can ever question what we have done; the more I have been through it, even though it has not all been plain sailing, the more it comes home to me. I tell myself: 'You are a lucky bastard to have been part of all that.' I know that we have some matches won before they even start. You can see it in the eyes of the opposition players.

Of course, I was a senior player as we reached a decade and more of triumph. Yet I have never really considered myself a contender to lead the team. In fact, I would hate it. There are too many egos, too many difficult explanations to give to people who have been left out. That situation altered slightly when Barnes retired before the start of the 1994–95 season, because Barnes would always be the tactical controller, relegating the captain into second place. If I finished playing for England and carried on for Bath, I might just consider it, because the captain should be someone who is there all the time, not someone dashing up to London every week for the England squad sessions. But don't hold your breath for me to take over.

Even among all the egos and the strong characters, some egos and characters stand out. The England manager's job was the only post in rugby which Jack Rowell could have gone to after Bath. It was the only bigger thing. It was a massive wrench for him to leave, as anyone who heard his emotional speech at the Rec after we had won the 1993–94 league title (with a drastically limited contribution from me) will testify.

So now Jack is the top man and took England into the World Cup.

He is an extremely complicated man. His lifestyle is complicated too. He had to juggle the commitments at Bath with life as a high-flying businessman, and so his time management must have been brilliant. It was announced only in September 1994 that he would step down from the board of Dalgety and that he would have far more time to devote to his England rugby tasks. It was also announced by Jack that he had dispensed with the services of Dick Best, and that he would take on the coaching duties himself – so he needed the extra free time.

When I first came into the Bath team, Jack tried to do a bit with the threequarters. He gave me a fair bit of advice, some of it very useful. He would be encouraging. Well done, keep it going, you're doing very well; but watch out for this, work on that. That dwindled down to nothing over the years, largely because Jack switched his interest to forward play. He would concentrate on the ruck, the maul, the scrummage and the line-out. All the time, he would be drawing advice and help from Gareth Chilcott.

His particular love was the back row. He would dwell on the back row for half the season. Whenever he mentioned the back row in any context, he would kiss the tips of his fingers in celebration of this key part of his philosophy. In team meetings, whenever he mentioned the back row himself, every player in the room would kiss the tips of their fingers. We also used to rib him about his habit of being seen with the Loughborough College boys – Andy

Robinson, David Egerton and John Morrison. They used to walk around the training field together.

People often ask me if Jack Rowell is a great coach. He might not be the best technically; he might not be able to tell the prop how to alter the position of his feet in the scrum, or how the second row might be able to jump into the space better. But he knows what works, he knows what a team should do in given situations. He is outstanding in creating a game plan. He is also outstanding at drawing in knowledge and experience from a wide variety of areas.

When a major match approaches you can see the tension and the energy growing in him. He has even had to leave important matches because he simply can't stand to watch. He did tend to say the same things week after week. We would meet, for the home games at least, in the Dukes Hotel. The routine rarely varied.

'Barnesie, what are cup games all about?' he would ask Stuart before every cup game.

'Winning.'

'Coochie, what are the opposition like?'

Coochie (Chilcott) also said the same thing, every match, every season. 'They are big, strong and robust.' I swore that if Coochie said that one more time I would fall down laughing in the team meeting. We met so many teams that were, apparently, big, strong and robust that it is a wonder we ever won a match.

Jack is also extremely cunning. He would always bring a list with him to the team meeting, noting the points he wanted to cover. Sometimes, he would religiously go through the list. Other times, he would ignore it, become sidetracked and emotional. He knew the characters of his players. He would look into the eyes of certain players. 'This is your stage, this is what you do best, do it again today as you have always done.'

Then he would look at someone like Andy Reed and tear in. 'You started this season playing for the Spartans. Then you went on a Lions tour. Why aren't you playing like a British Lion?' I have also seen Jack, minutes before a final, so emotional that I thought he was going to cry.

He has never given me a major telling-off; or at least, he may have done so without me noticing. People ask me what Jack, or any coach, has done for me. The truthful answer is that I don't know.

Stuart Barnes once assessed the relationship between Jack and myself. He said that I pretended not to like Jack but that, really, I did like him.

It may surprise people who have read the publicity about Jack and his harsh ways, to learn that he does not like confrontation. He will sometimes start it between some players for his own ends, then walk away whistling as it all comes to a boil. He is not good when it comes to dropping players. When I was dropped from the team, he tried to defuse the situation completely. When I walked up to him he immediately blurted out that I would be back for the next match.

Jack is an amazing man. He did not create the Bath legend – there were many others involved – but he is a huge part of the Bath legend, and his personality makes him the ideal coach for our strange environment. When he finally switches off and relaxes, he becomes as big a liability as any of the players.

In the final analysis, his rugby philosophy is very similar to mine, if not quite so adventurous – as was proved in the 1995 World Cup. His instinct is to get the team to function well in the forwards to win our ball, and only then, after getting the best out of the forwards, to be flamboyant. At Bath, he created a platform for world-class players to play their game. He gave a public farewell speech on the podium at the Rec after we were awarded the Courage trophy for winning the league in 1993–94. That was when he described the Bath march as the 'greatest journey any club have ever undertaken'.

Jon Hall is one of the world-class players who flourished under Jack's regime. In fact he is more than that. When people ask me who is the best player I have ever played with, they always seem to expect me to name a back. Wrong. Hall is unquestionably the best player. The older I have become, the better I am able to appreciate talent and ability and exceptional players. When fit and injury-free, Hall could do everything, and he was still a fantastic player when he retired after the 1994–95 season, a major decision and a major blow.

Like any top-class sportsman, Hall had all the skills of the game at his command without even thinking about them. He had a fantastic natural ability, and even in his young days in the Bath team, he was always a step ahead of the others in play, and years ahead of his time. He may have been a flanker, he may have weighed 17 stone, but he was an athlete too. Before his run of serious knee injuries slowed him down, he used to train with the backs, and in the sprints he was never the slowest.

He was a truly great forward. He has looked after generations of Bath line-out jumpers, standing behind everyone from Ronnie Hakin to Andy Reed. He has the knack of seizing the ball if the main jumpers don't get it; he is like an ox at close quarters. He has his eye on everything and he is a tactician too.

And yet the best tribute comes from the opposition. They all say the same thing: that Hall is a horrible person to play against – always there, always with his hands on the ball, always stopping them winning it. I remember arriving at Northampton to play a league match a few seasons ago. Hall had been left behind because he was not quite fully recovered from injury. Tim Rodber, of Northampton, was delighted. He told us that if he was picking a team he would chose Hall at 70% fit ahead of other players who were fully fit.

His injuries were a tragedy. He has won only 21 caps when he could have had 50, and only one since 1990, when they called him back to play in the Calcutta Cup at Murrayfield in 1994 and he prevented a certain Scottish try by catching Gary Armstrong near the England line. There were times when he seemed to disappear off the face of the England squad. He may have had a disagreement behind the scenes, too, especially in his wilder early years. Yet I still thank goodness I never had to play against him.

And another of the players who thrived on the Bath platform was Simon Halliday. I have already put on record my debt to him as a mentor from the time I came into the team, and my admiration for him as a player. It was not necessarily the centre partnership that was the key to the success of our back play in the seasons after we teamed up in earnest in 1988. It was more the combination of all the backs.

Technically, it usually worked like this. Stuart Barnes would take out the opposition open side by running straight; that would give Halliday around six to ten yards to work in before the back-row tackles. He might also be faced with a fly-half who didn't fancy tackling someone as powerful and hard as Halliday.

Halliday would run towards the inside centre then break out towards his outside shoulder. This would take the attention of their outside centre too, who would suddenly start to wonder if Halliday was going to get through. Hallers would eventually run towards the space between the two centres. Even if he was heavily tackled he would usually manage to get the ball away; then it would be on to me and, as I have said before, it was usually so easy from there that either I or Audley Lumsden, the full-back, used to score without the need to pass to the wings.

At the start of our partnership, the biggest advantage was that I was unknown. No one knew who I was till the word got round after a season or two. Barnes was well known; Halliday was a Test player; Tony Swift was ex-England. The rest of us were spring chickens. Halliday did the work and I played off him.

He remains the best centre I played with and the perfect mentor. The roles always stayed roughly the same over the years as we played through league and cup triumphs, even though, contrary to what people always assume, we played left and right centre instead of inside and outside. Rowell used to speak of Halliday as the colossus behind the triumphs.

It was sad that the parting was marked with something of a falling out. Halliday played the 1990–91 season like a man possessed. He was so strong, he nagged people on throughout the season, he was almost like a wild man. He tried to involve himself in everything. I sensed from all this that he might be moving on, that he was trying to go out in the best possible style. There were always rumours behind the scenes that he would leave for London – purely because Susanne, his wife, was always expected to go back to London to join her father's medical practice.

Initially, Hallers denied, notably to Barnes and one or two others, that he was leaving. When he made the announcement that he was indeed to move to London, it came as a shock and some people felt badly let down. There was friction between Barnes and Halliday and between Halliday and Swift. I never shared the feeling. I could fully understand his departure, and wished him nothing but good luck.

By the 1992 cup final, of course, Halliday was a Harlequin. After the epic battle, he came into our dressing-room, and said that if he had to lose, then he was glad that he had lost to Bath. I had no problem with that, but even as he departed there were sharp retorts from some of the team. Happily, old friendships have been gradually mended, notably between Barnes and Halliday, and I could never take anything away from Halliday's contribution to the club.

People assumed that I would feel exposed after his departure, that all our tactics and my game would be thrown off course. But I knew Bath better than that. I knew instinctively from what I had seen of Phil de Glanville, our young centre from Durham University, that he was going to slot in. In any case, I never think that far ahead or try to anticipate something which might happen.

When de Glanville arrived I was as selfish as ever, unlike Halliday. When I had arrived, he had asked me how I wanted to play – left and right or inside and outside. It was typical of Halliday to be so considerate. I never gave de Glanville the choice. I told him that I was still going to play left, implying that he should just get on with it. But after a few games settling in, we carried on the progress without a hitch. That is one of the great Bath achievements. It has happened so many times. A star player moves on or retires, and even our own supporters doubt that we will ever be the same. Then, the position is filled so quickly that no one mentions it again.

Gareth Chilcott is the soul of our club, even after his retirement from the playing side in the 1993–94 season. By then he had become the elder statesman, the television rugby pundit, the man recognized even by people who knew nothing about rugby. It was a long way from his early days, when apparently he was too violent for his own good and was at one time in grave danger of being banned for life.

I owe almost everything to Cooch. Of the ancillary things I've learned in rugby – how to listen to people, which people are worth listening to, how to understand people and be accepted by people, how to act as an international player – most were learned from Cooch, or from observing how he acted. He is always himself, never mind if he is talking to the Queen or to a group of five-year-old children.

He has to be at the centre of everything that happens, on or off the field. He can be a liability with some of his pranks and strong-arm stunts. You have to listen to his long stories (whether you want to or not). He is in almost every one of his stories. They usually start with him making a fool of himself, but there is always a happy or flattering ending for him!

There are those who question the Chilcott legend, but I have always found him to be exactly the bloke he appears to be, whether taking the rough with the smooth on the field or taking part in charity events. He was also a very, very underrated player. People used to write him off as a toby-jug prop, and so on. But he was amazingly skilful. When we played five-a-side soccer he showed deft little touches that Gascoigne would have been proud of. His handling skills were as good as anyone in our threequarter line, his basic speed was passable, and he had a technique in forward play second to none. I never saw him in trouble in the scrums.

I always felt almost sorry for opposing front rows coming to Bath to take him on. To take on Graham Dawe on his own is enough, but Dawe with Coochie alongside him . . . I was proud to play with Gareth Chilcott. I have nothing but nice things to say about him. He typified, as he admitted many times, what rugby could do for people. He is a great friend and a fantastic personality, and he is a man who is always going to be liked by people who really know him. He is now trading on his name and his aura – and rightly so.

Thankfully, the likes of Chilcott and Richard Hill have stayed in the club after leaving the playing side. It can sometimes cause problems if players immediately go into coaching. Some of the players have difficulty coping with Cooch cracking the whip when they recall his excellence at cutting corners himself on the training field! Hill used to be the ringleader for pissing it up and sticking in the famous Bath knife. Now, he rides at the front of the coach and knows that the real power rides at the back. But for them both to keep up their contribution when they might be expected to step away for a few seasons is admirable, especially Hilly's commitment to the development of the young players.

By 1986–87 Barnes was in his second season, I often played next to him when the Halliday-Palmer partnership was broken for some reason and, after initial reluctance, we began to establish a rapport on the field. We began to thrash top teams from England and Wales by wide margins. There have been so many epic battles down the years, and I don't think it is blowing the Bath trumpet too much to say that Bath have won a vast percentage of the tight games.

There have been very few bad memories. One came in 1987–88 when we had been playing superbly but managed to lose 4–3 to Moseley in the cup. The truth is that we had played well in beating Leicester at Welford Road in the previous round and were overconfident against Moseley. That ended our chances of winning the cup for the fifth time in succession. It was the first year of Courage Leagues, but we were sloppy in some matches and finished in the pack.

But at that time, local newspapers began to speculate seriously about my chances of playing for England at some future date. 'Will Jeremy Guscott become the next Bath player to earn representative honours?' asked John Stevens in an article in the *Bath Evening Chronicle*.

By the start of the 1988–89 season, when my career took off so quickly that I had difficulty keeping up, Stuart Barnes was captain and our dominance simply increased. Practically the only moment which gave us pause for thought that season, on our way to a double of cup and league, came before the match against Nottingham at home which we needed to win to make sure of our first league title, with two matches still remaining. Barnes noticed beforehand that the trophy itself had arrived but that it had already been engraved with our name! Luckily, we weren't superstitious, and won anyway. And a few weeks after that, they stopped talking about me being an England possible; chiefly because I became an England player, in Bucharest against Romania.

We were also league champions in 1990–91, finishing three points clear of Wasps; in 1991–92, when we finished level on points with Orrell but took the title on points difference (we were docked a point for failing to register a player, and that angered the team enough to ensure our trophy); in 1992–93, when we beat Saracens in the last game and bungee-jumped in triumph; and in 1993–94, when we hammered Leicester in the key game.

Among all the peaks, two in particular stand out in my memory. The first was when we smashed Gloucester 48–6 on a hot day at Twickenham in the 1990 cup final. To crush our deadly rivals was obviously an incredible result. We scored eight tries, some of them from long range.

In fact, I am quite critical of that performance. There wasn't quite the continuity of performance that the score suggests, and a good deal of the scoring came from Gloucester mistakes. But it was a true reflection of where the two clubs stood at the time, and it shook the Gloucester club to their foundations. If anything, we became even stronger in the seasons ahead.

The other was the final of 1992 against Harlequins. Geoff Cooke, then the England manager, said that it was a game played near to international standard. That surprised me, because personally I did not rate it so highly, although many of the press agreed with Cooke. But as an occasion it was fantastic. There was a world record crowd of 60,500, and some of the papers wrote that not even an international match could have held as much drama.

I hid it well at the time, but I probably should never even have played. I had a damaged ankle. Will Carling was in the Harlequins team and I was anxious taking the field for the game; if Will had got past me I would not have been able to turn properly to catch him, and yet I could hardly put up my hand and complain about a bad ankle. I was never going to score the try that lit up the place, but at least, when Will did try to cut past me, I just managed to catch him by the bootstraps, so no one really noticed that I was off the pace.

We were a little off the pace in other areas. Paul Ackford was making a one-off appearance, because Harlequins had two forwards sent off against Gloucester in a league match the week before the final. If he was out of condition, however, he didn't play like it. He cleaned up the line-out.

We were down 12–3 at half-time, with a try by Peter Winterbottom, but we drew level with only eight minutes remaining when Phil de Glanville scored and Jon Webb kicked the conversion. It was already a long afternoon at the end of the longest season in English rugby history, but we had to play on into extra time.

Partly because everyone was too tired to make the decisive plays, the scores were still level with seconds remaining. Then, amazingly, Nigel Redman won a line-out in front of Paul Ackford's nose. Barnes had already told me he was going to try a drop goal. It went over, we all celebrated the kick and the final whistle, which went immediately. As I said earlier, it was one of the sweetest feelings I have ever experienced. For Harlequins, robbed of at least a share of the trophy, I felt nothing.

No doubt, the players on the field in the 1993–94 season – largely a write-off for me – felt the same when Bath thrashed Leicester, who regarded themselves as a major threat to us, first on the Rec to settle the league title and then again, soon afterwards, at Twickenham to seal the double.

It was all different from the start of the 1994–95 season. Rowell had departed, and so had Barnes, Hill and Chilcott. For the first match of the season, against the Barbarians, Barnes was perched up in a TV studio at the Rec in his new job as a presenter for BSkyB's rugby coverage. Mike Catt was in his place at fly-half, and in place of Rowell was Brian Ashton, a man highly respected by myself and all the players from his years as coach to Bath's backs. But was it so different? We were still the team to beat, just as we had been for the previous 11 seasons.

There was no double in 1994–95. Leicester managed to sneak a draw at the Rec in the league and they beat us at Welford Road in the return. They took the League on the last Saturday of the programme. I missed the trip to Leicester and that was symptomatic of the season. We had so many people going off to take part in different squads: England, England A and England Emerging Players, plus Scotland and Ireland, that there were many comings and goings. I played some games but was unavailable for others, and tried to play a rota in some positions. It all meant that we became disrupted and lost our focus. The strength of the Bath club has always been in picking our best side and letting people fight for positions. That is what will happen next year when, I am sure, there will be no rotas. We will all be focused again. I have absolutely no doubt that we are still the best team in Britain when we are focused on the job.

We demonstrated our focus in the Cup run and yet another Cup Final triumph. We have still never lost a Cup Final. I was by this time one of the senior players in the side, but the Cup run was still a thrill for me; it is the thought that it is a one-off, that if you get it wrong on the day you are dead. We played superbly in the second half to beat Harlequins in the semi-final, and went through to Twickenham to play Wasps, who had been making noises all season about what a good side they were, how brilliant their all-out attacking policy was. We had something of a strange-looking team, with our Scottish contingent ruled out, and Graham Dawe on the bench.

The team became stranger as the game approached. Jon Hall had announced that he would retire after the Cup Final, but he was injured in the league match against Sale the week before the Cup Final, a match we somehow contrived to lose. He did his best to make the big day but it was obvious in training that he would not be able to. Phil de Glanville took over and Hall had to watch from the stands.

It was a great day. We won 36–16, and kept the Bath run going. It was brilliant. There was a major distraction on the day because the Carling Affair broke only a few hours before the kick-off but that was something to worry about after the match. We soaked up a good deal of pressure from Wasps but they didn't have anything like our ability to make and take chances. As Dean Ryan, their captain, said afterwards, they were given a lesson in rugby. I made a break after a short pass from Richard Butland to set up one of our four tries for Jon Callard.

It was Tony Swift's last game and he celebrated in the best possible style. He was 35, marking Nick Greenstock on the wing. He once got the ball, shimmied past Greenstock and other Wasps as he has been doing for season after season, and scored by the posts. Only the selectors know why Swifty was not used to much better value by England.

At the end, Hall led us up to take the trophy. There had been no plans worked out with Phil de Glanville. It was just understood that when the time came, he would be the man to lead us. He hoisted the trophy and set off another major weekend celebrating. The atmosphere among the team was outstanding, there was a great reception at the club when we returned, and the euphoria continued through the usual open-top bus ride next day, and beyond. And throughout the Cup campaign, all the savage Bath piss-taking simply flowed on as usual. Nothing changes. It must have been a huge disappointment to Hall to leave on such a down note, defeat against Sale and missing the Cup Final. But having been the heart and soul of the club for so long, I am sure that watching us win was some compensation.

It was also a great moment for Brian Ashton, the coach who had the task of taking over from Jack Rowell. At the start, surrounded by strong characters inside the team and with Gareth Chilcott and Richard Hill coaching off the field, he found it a little difficult. It seems in 1995–96 that Ashton, a superb coach, will revert to taking charge of the backs since he has school commitments which will prevent him from attending some of the matches. It was announced just after the Cup Final that Hall will take over the role of team manager.

We are also forming the Bath Players Initiative. Hall, Swift, Nigel Redman, Jon Callard and myself were discussing the prospects of forming our own company, and in conjunction with Malcolm Pearce, the businessman who does so much to help the players in the club, BPI was set up. Just as the England players' Playervision took on the Parallel Media Group, our affairs will be under the umbrella of Carnegie. They have effectively subcontracted the work out to Peter Downey, who successfully negotiated the sponsorship for the Teachers Stand at the Rec. The idea is to look after the development and future of Bath players, especially the younger players. Carnegie will market the packages we have drawn up to companies, the players will take part in a range of activities and the proceeds at the end of the season will be divided between the squad. Furthermore, if some of the younger players, such as Gareth Adams or Kevin Yates, are called up to attend some sort of function it will be helpful to them to go along with someone like Ben Clarke or myself, who are used to that kind of public appearance.

Players have always joined Bath because we are winners, and most players who establish themselves with us win some sort of international recognition. But that may not always be enough, given the variety of inducements now on offer throughout the club game. Players' welfare is important, and we hope with the full backing of the club the scheme will assure Bath's progress.

Perhaps I still do not take as full a part as I might as senior player, but it is difficult with my increasing commitments. Last season, I hardly stayed over after a game once. There was either an England squad session in London, or I had to be back at home to help out Jayne and the family, or there was a business commitment. I still enjoy the rugby sides as much as ever at Bath, but the social focus has changed quite considerably from the old days. On the field, I am as committed to the cause as anyone else but I am also occasionally away doing other things. Some people seem to have difficulty coming to terms with that. Perhaps I have become more selfish but, on the other hand, I don't believe I owe the club anything after all the years I have played there. And I still have a thrill from the successes.

Being at Bath has not always been a brilliant experience. We have had too many silly arguments with the committee. There are still no special facilities for wives and girlfriends to have an area of their own in the clubhouse. Facilities at Lambridge, our training ground, have not been upgraded since I started at the club. Also, an organization as successful as Bath should never lose money and yet, sometimes, we do. We need a paid administrator to sort out the club, but at the moment, all the club does is talk about it, not act on it.

Still, the club partly funded an outstanding trip to Barbados in the summer of 1994, in which almost the whole first-team squad and their families had a great ten days, and in which hardly any of the traditional micky-taking occurred. Before Barbados, all we had to show for all our triumphs was a weekend in the Cotswolds.

It isn't easy, as I have said, to sum up achievements and experiences while you are still playing. There is no time to reflect and to work out whether or not you are indeed having the time of your life. It is also difficult to judge a club when it is the only club you have known, and you therefore have nothing to compare it with. But I do know enough to realize that what Jack Rowell calls 'the greatest journey' has been an unforgettable experience. I also know that, together, we all made the homely club I joined as a seven-year-old into the greatest the rugby world has seen.

5
Everything Comes to Him Who Sleeps
My brilliant season, 1988–89, from Pontypool to Perth

It was just like John Morrison to phone on a Monday morning, when I was still asleep. I was still living with my parents, but because they had had enough of the volume of phone calls, I had my own phone line in my bedroom. It was May 1989 and I was still suffering from the celebrations of Bath's cup final victory over Leicester that weekend.

Morrison, then Bath's lock, had a repertoire of accents and practical jokes. This time, he was giving it his best South Walian. He claimed to be Clive Rowlands, the manager-elect of the British Lions party which was to tour Australia in a few months' time. The voice purporting to be Rowlands explained that as Will Carling had withdrawn from the party originally selected owing to a shin injury, I had been chosen to take his place. Morrison had obviously been working on the accent. He offered, in a perfect Rowlands-like rasp, many congratulations. He even started to go through the arrangements for the tour.

I never said a word, waiting patiently for Morrison to run out of his accent and his repertoire and to start laughing. Morrison kept it up for such a long time that I was beginning to get bored. Then, realization began to dawn. Maybe it wasn't John Morrison after all.

Bath's preparations for the start of the 1988–89 season were the fiercest in the history of the club. In the previous season, we had failed to win either the cup or the league, an unheard of state of affairs. The incentive to put things right, under the new captaincy of Stuart Barnes, was powerful.

Even though I had become a regular player in the previous season, this was the first time I had begun a season as Bath's first choice. John Palmer had duties on Saturdays as a schoolmaster and was slowly scaling down his appearances, so Simon Halliday and myself were the starters in the centre. Our preparation had included a tour of the Far East and a tournament in Leiden, Holland, which we had won by beating Toulon, the illustrious French team, in the final. It was the most violent game I had ever played in. It was carnage, with kicking and punching throughout the game. Not to put it mildly, Toulon tried to kick the shit out of us. Even Jon Hall said it was a bad one, and he has played in a few.

Our first domestic match, on a sunny day in early September, was at Pontypool. They had dominated the Welsh scene, losing only two matches in the whole of the previous season, and even though their key player, David Bishop, had left for rugby league, they were still powerful on paper, and Mark Ring, the famous Welsh centre, was still there.

Welsh teams had never been a mental problem for Bath. We never crossed the Severn Bridge in the same fearful state of mind as other teams. Previously, when I had played for Bath in Wales, I had been worried about taking the mother and father of a kicking on the ground. They are canny enough there to know who the dangerous opposition players are. But people like Gareth Chilcott and Roger Spurrell tended to look after me. The Welsh clubs have their traditions, but our record there is excellent. We have always let Welsh teams worry about us.

On that day at Pontypool, with the weather warm and the ground firm, they were right to be worried. We took them apart by 50–9. I had been given a good run by the local press in the West Country, but this match marked my arrival in the national spotlight, if the newspapers are to be believed.

My mother still has the cuttings. 'No one wreaked greater havoc in the Welsh midfield than Jeremy Guscott,' said *The Guardian*. 'Glorious Guscott,' was the heading in *The People*. 'Glittering Guscott,' said the *Sunday Mirror*. 'It was Guscott who took centre stage,' said *The Times*. The *Sunday Times* tried to make a long-term prediction. 'Bath were simply magnificent. This was the first match of the post-David Bishop era (at Pontypool). However, it also may well have proved the first match of the Guscott era. It was he, more than anyone, who undermined Pontypool's morale because he simply cut their midfield to pieces.'

Meanwhile, the *Sunday Express* took a different line. 'A Champagne style display by Dublin centre Jeremy Guscott . . .' I'm still working that one out.

I can remember some of the tries, especially making a break uphill towards the Pontypool clubhouse end, and putting Audley Lumsden over. I can also remember one incident when Andy Robinson was in possession. He lined up Chris Huish, Pontypool's flanker, and tried to drive straight through him. You could almost hear Robbo thinking: 'I'm going to walk all over you.' There was an evil look on his face. But Huish was like a little battleship. He stuck his shoulder into Robbo, lifted him up off his feet and bowled him backwards.

By this time we had a luxury coach, with coffee machine, toilet and video. On the way back to Bath no one wanted to watch our tries. We kept on running and rerunning the bit when Robbo gets bowled back, time and again, to the accompaniment of loud cheering. It has always been a hard life in the Bath team . . .

That was the start of an incredible season. My rugby career changed totally. Nothing would ever be the same again. At this stage it was enough to be in the Bath team, but what was to happen to me during the season was beyond my wildest dreams.

It was a joy to play in Bath's back division. Barnes at the time did not attempt as many breaks as he did in later years. Yet he would always take out the flanker. Halliday was so strong in the inside centre position that he would often take out two men. The opposing fly-half would hardly ever be good enough to stop him. Halliday's gift was to thrust through the outside arm of the fly-half and the inside arm of the centre – and the defence was drawn.

He would find me accelerating on his shoulder. I might score myself or, if not, Audley Lumsden, who had a brilliant season, would come up outside me to score. In that season, we had wings like Tony Swift, Barry Trevaskis, David Trick and Peter Blackett, but we were so good that, often, they were just left spare outside.

It was a season in which I was free and clear. Opposition defences hadn't seen me. I and my style were new to them. These

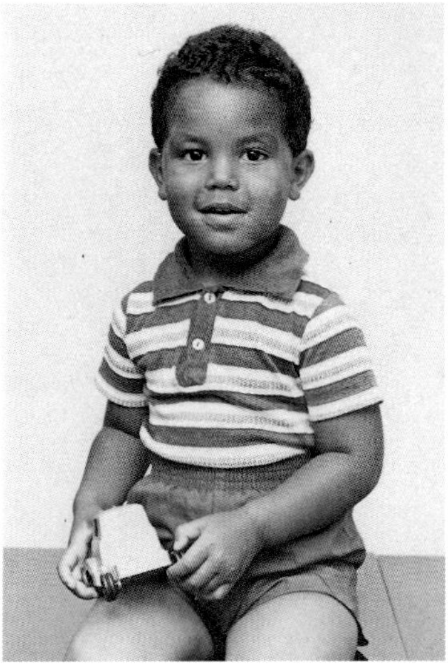

Right: Wearing unsponsored shirt at the age of three. (1)

Far right: With Mother and Gary in the garden of our home in Bath. (2)

A grim expression for the camera as the remainder of the class at Beechen Cliff School smirk at the annual photograph. (3)

Jayne and Jeremy, wedding day. (4)

The old home town. Searching for a cure at the Roman Baths. (5)

Waving the Cup after
appearing as replacement
in the 1987 Cup Final
win against Wasps. (6)

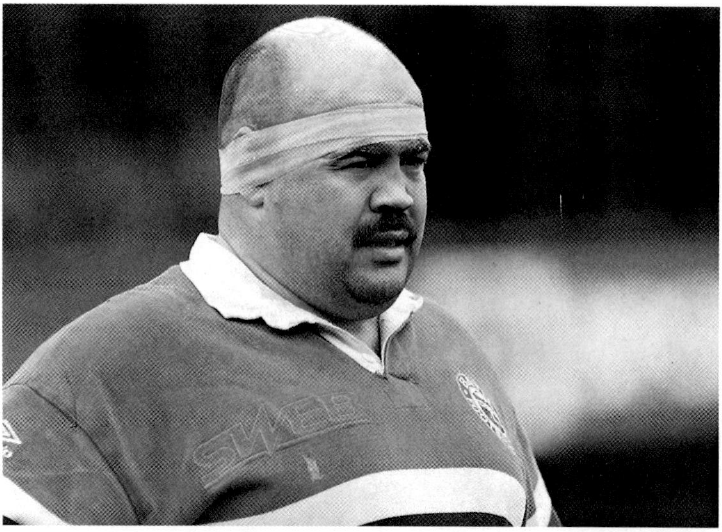

Two hearts of Bath. Top: 'Coochie' – the incomparable Gareth Chilcott. Above: Simon Halliday, the colossus, wins the Cup Final in 1977 with a vital try. (7, 8)

Two days of Bath thunder. Above: Maintaining the flow with Adedayo Adebayo and Stuart Barnes as Gloucester are incinerated in the 1990 Cup Final. Right: Unadulterated, unconfined joy. Stuart Barnes has dropped the goal, in the last second of extra time, and Bath have beaten Harlequins in the 1992 Cup Final. Barnes is mobbed by happy bystanders. (9, 10)

One of the peaks of the glorious season – playing for England in Bucharest, when the day brought a cap and three tries. (11)

Robert Jones joins me for some serious celebrating after my try to settle the Second Test in Brisbane, 1989. (12)

Will Carling about to impart some non-mystical leadership to the England team, pre-anthem at Twickenham. (13)

Progress checked by John Kirwan in the opening match of the 1991 World Cup at Twickenham, a tournament that was to begin and end in disappointment. (14)

The World Cup final. The ball kept on coming as our tactics faltered – it usually arrived in tandem with Australian defenders. (15)

Stuart Barnes is at fly-half, we have the ball in space. On the way past Scotland's noisy Scott Hastings to set up a try for Rory Underwood, Twickenham, 1993. (16)

were innocent times. In the subsequent seasons, defences were ready, and this affected my own try-scoring rate for a time. For now, we were unstoppable. I scored 28 tries in first-class games that season.

I also started to learn about media coverage, and to realize how shallow it all was. The scorers were always the players who were mentioned in reports. Even if I actually played badly, as long as I scored two tries I would get all the write-ups anyway.

Only two weeks after that Pontypool game, Geoff Cooke, the England manager, came down to Bath specifically to watch me play. 'Guscott has an enormous amount of potential,' he was kind enough to say. 'He is certainly on our list.' Jack Rowell always backed up his players. 'He is a sensation,' he told the *Daily Mail*.

It was very kind of everyone. But it was time to be realistic. For a start, I hate disappointments, so I tend to shy away from people talking about what is in the future for me in case it never happens. And it was only my first full season.

There was also a more practical reason: Will Carling was established in the England centre and he was appointed as England's captain that very autumn, an appointment that was to continue until the 1991 World Cup. Simon Halliday was established alongside him. That was that. The choices were made. It was a question of simply playing on, not stopping to dream the impossible. So when people ask me when I began to think of playing for England, the answer is: only after I heard that I had been picked.

And rugby league clubs began to circle. There was widespread coverage of a story that I had been approached by Hull Kingston Rovers. It was only after the stories appeared that they actually approached me, offering £150,000. On the day after I received Hull KR's offer, I was telephoned by Joe Pickavance, from St Helens. I never even considered the offers. I had not actually achieved anything in my rugby union career. These offers were something to tell the lads about, but not something to waste time over.

When the Courage Leagues began, we maintained our form and confidence, beating Harlequins, Gloucester, Moseley, Orrell, Liverpool-St Helens and Rosslyn Park, usually with a bagful of tries by the backs. At half-time at Rosslyn Park, after a half in which we had not played well, Richard Lee, our prop, offered the sort of tactical insight for which props are famous. 'Their darkies are quicker than our darkies,' he said.

My first representative selections came along. I was chosen for the South & South-West Division for a warm-up match against Leinster. It was hardly the start of a love affair. I have always felt that the Divisional Championship is a place where reputations can only be lost. You always feel like an individual in a scratch team, there is always the atmosphere of a trial match. If I were to be totally honest and had the confidence, I would have told the England selectors that I was not available for the divisionals. There is no reason for the Divisional Championship to take place. I would be far more in favour if they found a different format, perhaps tried to develop along the lines of the Super-10 in the Southern Hemisphere, with some of the minor European nations competing as national teams together with some of the major district and provincial teams from elsewhere. Geoff Cooke always used to say that they wanted to see players from outside the cosy club world. Fair enough, but surely it would be better to put the whole thing on a pedestal, not two grades below club stuff.

But that is with the perspective of the experienced player. To play for the South-West against Leinster on the Rec was at least a rung on the ladder. My cuttings show that, at the time, this was the limit of my ambitions. 'My personal ambition this season is to stay in the South-West side,' I told the *Evening Post* only a few months later; it looked rather a modest goal.

Shortly afterwards came the big break. The Australians were touring and I was chosen for England 'B' to play them early in their tour. I set off for Sale, where the match was to take place, in the knowledge that, if the door to the England team was shut, at least I could establish myself as one of the first in the queue. The roll continued.

The England 'B' coaches were Alan Davies and Dave Robinson, who had both been involved with the senior squad on their tour of Australia in the previous summer. Robinson, apparently, was something of a fiery customer, or so I had been told. John Buckton, from Saracens, was my co-centre, Mark Bailey was the captain and wing, and the chief interest centred around a Welshmen, Dewi Morris, who had switched allegiance to England and who had caused a stir at scrum-half in the early-season matches.

Crammed into the tiny changing-rooms at Sale, some of the lads were visibly psyching themselves up, strapping and greasing themselves. I never bother with all that angry stuff, but as I was the new boy I thought I'd better join in, so I put on my best psyched-up face and tried to look as fierce as possible.

Bailey said a few words as we sat around the tiny room. Then, he stood aside. 'It's Robbo time,' he said. It was like the announcement of Hammer Time, when MC Hammer comes on to do his act at a concert. But did I detect a note of doubt in Bailey's voice?

There was no time to wonder. Suddenly, Dave Robinson came charging into the space in the room like a raging bull at the corrida. He started barking and shouting and spittle was coming from the sides of his mouth like the Roy Hattersley puppet in *Spitting Image*. His moustache was bristling like a live thing.

He went ranting on in a full Queen and Country speech. He was going round the team one by one. 'Do you want it? Are you ready?' It was the sort of speech which had gone out of use in the Bath third XV about five years previously, together with the practice of banging your head against the wall of the dressing-room. But as the new boy, I assumed that this was all very necessary, that this was what the big-time was all about.

Robinson approached me and punched me on the bicep. It was difficult to work out whether to laugh or cry, but my first inclination was to hit him back. Eventually, we stood up to take the field, with Robbo still ranting. He stood by the dressing-room door for the final roar. He gave Andy Mullins, the prop who was near the front, a full-blooded smack across the face. By the time I reached him I was almost crawling along the ground, SAS style. We escaped to the security of the pitch. It didn't matter any more what the Australians had to offer. It couldn't be worse than Robbo.

Or perhaps it could. We lost 37–9, with David Campese scoring a hat-trick for Australia. My most vivid memory of the match is watching Dean Ryan, our No. 8, driving at Campese, of Campese suddenly ripping the ball from Ryan's hands and disappearing up the touch-line to score. For us in the midfield, it was a quiet game.

There was another representative experience later in the season.

Andy Mullins and I were called up to attend the England-Scotland international with the full England squad. It was meant to inject us with the sense of the occasion. 'It is a new idea,' said Geoff Cooke. 'It will help the younger players to see what it is all about.'

It was half a good idea. Of course I was honoured, but there was also the anxiety of feeling like a vital part of the body going spare at a wedding. We met on a Wednesday evening, checked into the Petersham, the traditional England team hotel above the river near the top of Richmond Hill.

Mullins and I took part in all the training, and I stood out to oppose the England backs, Carling and Halliday included, when they went through their moves. They roomed me with Gareth Chilcott, presumably to make me feel more comfortable under the wing of this experienced forward. He certainly taught me a lot about diet. Coochie stuffs himself stupid at breakfast, enough to make you queasy just watching him. He gravely talked me through the dangers of international rugby through the weekend, tried to give me tips. I was more worried about the dangers to Coochie's heart at breakfast.

I sat in at all the team meetings. But there was still time to kill, and I spent most of it staring out of the windows of the hotel, bored to tears. Even when I travelled in the team bus to Twickenham, there was still the feeling of not quite being part of it all. I was taking in the scene as the bus drove in. There were the Range Rovers and hampers and people waving in support – and other people waving with the famous five-finger shuffle sign, which was not very supportive. While I was taking in the scene, the old pros on the bus were discussing the girls at the Guinness caravan.

I was given a seat in the stand and settled down to enjoy the match. Whenever play moved down to one of the corners all the crowd stood up. So I stood up too. A voice behind me bawled: 'For God's sake, sit down.' It happened a few times.

I turned round and spoke to the couple behind me, who had been the ones complaining. 'I'm sorry, but if they all stand up in front of me I have to stand up too. Otherwise, I'll miss the match. I can do nothing but apologize.'

The woman nodded towards her husband and asked me: 'Do you know who you are talking to?' I didn't. Apparently, the complainant was Vic Roberts, a former England flanker on the Barbarians committee. Then I heard her whisper: 'Isn't that Jeremy Guscott?' She leaned over. 'Are you Jeremy Guscott?' Now that we had all worked out who we all were, we exchanged some pleasantries and the incident was closed. However, this too contributed to the feeling that I was in the way all weekend.

England won the match 22–12. We all filed back on to the team coach afterwards – at least, I tried to. Carmen McDonald, an RFU employee, refused to let me on because she didn't have my name on her list. Eventually they did let me on. The bus set off for Central London and the dinner at the Hilton Hotel. I was not invited. They kicked me off the bus at a roundabout in Richmond. I walked back to the hotel to pick up my car and drove home alone. It would be an exaggeration to say that I had spent the weekend in awe of the whole thing.

But the sheer enjoyment factor was still running through the season. We scored six tries and 35 points against Cardiff and could easily have scored 50; we scored 40 points against Llanelli, and I scored four of the tries, still revelling in the freedom of being the new kid.

We had the Division 1 title safely wrapped up as early as the ninth match of a 12-match programme, having blown away the rest. We secured the trophy by beating Nottingham at the Recreation Ground. It was a poor game, one of the few bad performances of the Bath season. The score was 22–16, and we were behind with less than ten minutes to go.

But we won. It was only the second year that leagues had been operating, and Bath were still known as the cup team. Perhaps that was why the feeling was not one of any fantastic delight; or perhaps it was because of the standards we had set that season. But we did a lap of honour with the trophy itself, which, after the trophy-less season before, was more like what our supporters expected.

There were also two more games for England 'B'. One was at Leicester against the French. Welford Road is one of my favourite grounds, but we played France 'B' there on a cold and wet Friday evening, the pitch was dreadful and France won 35–16. Philippe Berot and Philippe Saint-André saw loads of the ball. We saw loads of them. The best part of the whole experience was playing snooker at Willie Thorne's snooker club, near the ground. Willie himself was there.

And for a time, my modelling career hung in the balance. I took a blow in the face in that match which almost dislodged my nose. When I plucked up the courage to look in the mirror I found that it had travelled half-way across my face. I went to the Ear, Nose and Throat department of the Royal United Hospital in Bath the next day. They had a look. 'It's all right,' they said, cheerfully. 'You can have an operation once you've finished playing.'

'Look,' I said. 'There's no way I'm walking around like this till I retire.' All my future modelling contracts were at stake. Someone grabbed my nose, whacked it painfully back into place, and it came back fairly straight. Saved.

It could have gone again after the 'B' match against Italy in Piacenza. We won easily, 44–0. I put through a little grubber kick for Tony Underwood to score, and Phil de Glanville won a 'B' cap as a replacement for Leicester's Barry Evans. Afterwards, on the loose in Italy and with the likes of Mick Skinner in our team, we looked forward to a good night. Food was launched around the room at the post-match dinner, and a large piece of flying main course hit Alan Sharp, the Bristol prop. This was at a time before Sharp decided to be Scottish and to play for Scotland.

Sharp was not amused that his white shirt was spoiled. He suggested to Gary Pearce, who had nothing whatsoever to do with the incident, that they settle matters outside. Skinner, the real culprit, offered to stand in for Pearce and pushed between them. For a time, a fair-sized scrap seemed on the cards, but peace gradually broke out and the evening recommenced.

I seemed to be making good progress for England 'B'. My form with Bath was still excellent. People still kept harping on about my imminent England career. But Carling and Halliday were still there. Nothing to get excited about, I tried to tell myself.

Yet the sense of a season building to a climax for Bath was continued through the cup. In the previous season we had gone out to Moseley in the quarter-finals, a ridiculous result. This time, we were focused. We beat Oxford 82–9 and Hereford 48–0 in our first two rounds; then we played Bristol on the Rec in one of the most amazing matches. It had been raining all week, and on the morning of the match we thought the match should be postponed. Bristol disagreed, and even though the surface was a lake, we played on. Soon, the mud became shin deep. It was just the lottery Bristol wanted, and they tore into us.

Jon Webb, later to see the light and join Bath, scored a try for Bristol and I scored one for Bath. This was in the early stages, before the mud obliterated any chance whatsoever of a proper match. But we were still behind with three minutes left, and our cup dreams seemed about to disappear dramatically. Then Bristol lost control of the ball at a scrum near their own line. Richard Hill grabbed it and forced his way over. Poor old Bristol. I was heartbroken for them.

We also scraped through a very, very hard semi-final match at Gloucester, winning 6–3. We were at Twickenham. So were Leicester. The build-up was massive. It was to be my first final in the starting line-up, although I had come on as replacement four years earlier against London Welsh and also against Wasps two years after that.

We went through the whole rigmarole of being measured up for the special blazer and slacks. As usual, my old friends Peter Blackett and Tony Wardle were jealous of the finery. 'You lucky bastards,' they said. There was also the opportunity, as we stayed overnight at the Runnymede Hotel, to obtain a bathrobe.

The final was the match which at last established the cup competition as a major event. It was a complete sell-out, with 59,300 present – then a world record for a club match. The atmosphere was incredible. And it was also the last game before retirement for Dusty Hare, so there was no shortage of press hype.

We had an old full-back of our own. Audley Lumsden had suffered a serious neck injury in a match at Plymouth Albion, and John Palmer returned to the fold to stand in. It was a great occasion and, as usual for the cup, it seemed as if the town of Bath had almost been evacuated for the day. It was also the match which established the cup final as a major Bath day out. Some of our supporters now book for the final months ahead, and they still go along even if we don't make it ourselves.

We won 10–6, to complete the first ever league and cup double in English rugby. We were behind in the final quarter, but a back-row drive led by Jon Hall set up a chance and Barnes scored wide on the left. Barnesie led us up for the cup itself, and the season, which had begun so brilliantly at Pontypool back in September, was crowned in the best possible way.

After the formalities, we embarked on the return journey to Bath and to our clubhouse, where our followers were waiting to welcome us. As we were passing through Richmond on the way to the M4, another time-honoured Bath cup ritual was enacted as Jack Rowell, with a rare flash of the credit card, disappeared into an off licence to buy celebratory drinks for the homeward journey. He bought crates, heavily leaning towards rum coolers. It was a massive celebration. It was probably his company credit card. If I had known what was to happen later in the weekend, perhaps I would not have indulged so heavily. On the other hand . . .

One of Jack's best traditions was to throw a champagne breakfast on the Sunday after cup finals. He saw it as a tradition he inaugurated and which he was proud to continue. The reality was that after Bath had beaten Bristol, in 1984, in our first final, Roger Spurrell and Paul Simpson had been on an all-nighter and early on the Sunday morning, having nowhere else to drink, they arrived at Jack's house. Sue Rowell let them in, Jack was forced to break out the drinks, and the tradition was on. The tradition was extended a bit more recently when the wine threatened to run out and we discovered the real stuff hidden in Jack's cellar. His protests were overruled.

Early on the Sunday morning after the Leicester game, when I was still dazed and trying to work myself up for Jack's bash, the telephone rang. It was Don Rutherford of the Rugby Football Union. England were there to play Romania in Bucharest two weeks after the final. Already, there had come news that Will Carling was struggling. He had shin splints and was said to be doubtful.

Rutherford now told me that Will was out, I was in, and congratulations. I put down the phone, even more dazed. So the locked door had swung open. I was going to play for England. I was celebrating a league and cup double to crown my first full season as a Bath senior, and now I was going to win a cap! I told Jayne and my parents, and when I reached Jack's party I was able to spread the news further. Jack and the Bath lads were delighted.

But those early morning calls kept coming. Monday morning brought a massive hangover and the John Morrison/Clive Rowlands call, waking me from another pit. I kept totally silent through most of the call, waiting for Morrison to reveal himself and the joke. Rowlands must have thought that I was so overwhelmed by it all that I could not speak. I suppose I only really ruled out the possibility of a massive Morrison-inspired wind-up when other people starting ringing with their congratulations. Bath to Twickenham to England to Australia inside 24 hours. No one ever had such a weekend as that. It was all happening, but it was not happening.

I made a bitter-sweet call to Jayne. She, too, was emotional about the whole thing. We had just bought a house, a house which needed an awful lot of work on it during the summer months. Now, during those summer months, I would be away in Australia and she would have to organize all the hard work.

The phone went mad. There were scores of media calls, and the local paper sent a photographer. With amazing subtlety and vision, they worked out a 'photo opportunity' involving my status as a bricklayer. They sat me in a wheelbarrow with a bottle of champagne in one hand and a glass in another. I suppose their readers liked it.

The Lions tour was also slightly embarrassing. I had just turned down an invitation to make a ten-day tour of Spain with England 'B'. 'I have just bought a house,' I told one of the local papers. 'The roof needs a great deal of work on it and I cannot afford to be away.' I had to backtrack slightly to accept the invitation to the 53–day tour of Australia. In his first season of international rugby, I imagined people muttering, and already he's picking his games.

I suppose I should have felt some anxiety about it all. I had started the season in Pontypool. Soon, I would be in Bucharest, then Perth. It was all happening with amazing speed. This was all going too well. Surely, the run had to end. Perhaps I should have feared breaking a leg or driving into a brick wall. In fact, I spent very little time worrying about my good fortune. I simply thought that what had happened had happened, and that I should make the very best of it. So I did.

The Clan Guscott turned out in force for the trip to Bucharest. Mum and Dad flew over, together with Jayne, my brother Gary and his girlfriend; and also my grandmother and her brother. It was nice that so many came. The *Daily Mirror* worked out that the total bill had been £4,000.

Everyone was a little worried about the trip. These were pre-revolution days. Rumours surfaced that we would be followed everywhere by the Securitate and that our phones would be tapped; we were told officially to expect food shortages, and Twickenham arranged for food parcels to be taken out to sustain us. We flew Swissair to Bucharest and our hotel, the Bucharesti, was massive, dusty and dingy. I was rooming with Simon Halliday, and not the worst aspect of the whole affair was that I would be teaming up in the centre with my friend and club-mate, the player who had helped my game so much along the way.

We trained at the Steaua Club on the Thursday and Friday. It was warm and the pitches were hard and slick. We went through our team talks. Geoff Cooke, the manager, said very little to me. 'All we want you to do is to go out and play your natural game and show what you can do,' he said. The match was to take place in the August 23rd Stadium, a concrete bowl in Bucharest. Romania had already beaten Wales in Cardiff earlier that season, and in the centre they had Lungu and Fulina, both experienced campaigners.

When Halliday and I retired to our room on the night before the match, Halliday was sympathetic towards the new boy. He knew that Jayne was staying a few floors above in the same hotel. 'Why are you here?' he said. 'Why don't you spend the night with Jayne?' I thought about it. 'I'll stay with the lads,' I thought. Then I changed my mind and crept upstairs. As soon as I got there, it felt wrong. I crept back to Halliday. In the early morning, I woke and went back to Jayne's room. I offered her tea or coffee, which was ridiculous because I had known her for years and she didn't drink either. I went back to Halliday. I did not realize it at the time, but I was in a mild pre-match panic. Eventually, I went to find Kevin Murphy, our physiotherapist, in his room. I got a cigarette from him, sat down for a few minutes and became calm again. After a night of nerves I was ready.

When we got to the stadium the temperature was in the 90s. The England Under 21 team were playing in the hottest part of the day, and a small, blond youngster from the Midlands called Neil Back was in great form. The temperature had dropped a little when we took the field, but most of the players had already hacked off their sleeves to keep cool. I was not going to deface my first England jersey whatever the temperature, so I just rolled the sleeves up.

For me, in many ways, it was a continuation of the season, of the free-flowing style to which I had become accustomed. England won 58–3. Halliday and I teamed up well and I scored three tries, including an early one from long range which gave me a thrill. Simon Hodgkinson kicked 19 points, converting eight of our nine tries.

Chris Oti went one better than me with four. I never quite worked Oti out when we played together. I had a suspicion that he would rather have scored my tries himself, and the impression that he was not averse to the kudos of scoring was confirmed when Peter Winterbottom gave him a major telling-off for hogging the ball and not setting Winters up for a try. Still, it all could hardly have gone better. I can remember Halliday, typically, being pleased for me, and Mum and Dad and Jayne having huge smiles.

Roger Uttley, the coach, was also delighted. He cornered Gary, my brother, who looks a lot like me, and spent some time telling him how well he had played that afternoon. Gary played along for a while, then had to own up to Roger that, flattered as he was by the comments, he hadn't actually been on the field.

The presentation of the cap itself was low-key. For new caps at home games, there is a short presentation ceremony at the Hilton Hotel. In Bucharest the three new caps, Hodgkinson, Steve Bates and myself, were called forward by the RFU president, John Simpson. He plonked the caps on our heads. I had trimmed back the old Michael Jackson locks of old, but the cap still didn't fit. Hodgkinson's fitted perfectly, but he was built like a schoolboy anyway.

Still, at least I had a cap. Who cared if it fitted? The video of my career was apparently still in fast forward. It was only eight months on from Pontypool, but a world away.

6 The Hammer of Brisbane

The last acts of the year of innocence, Australia 1989

Early on a Saturday morning in July, 1989, my father emerged from the front door of his house in St Saviour's Terrace, Larkhall, on the hill above the A4 into Bath, carrying a sledgehammer. He went striding along the road towards the terraced house in Larkhall into which Jayne and I had recently moved. Apparently, there were few people about.

He reached the house and went in. There was no one at home. He marched into the kitchen, and proceeded to lay into a wall with the sledgehammer. He kept up a ceaseless battering, demolishing the wall brick by brick until, eventually, there was just a pile of rubble on the floor. He tidied up the mess and strode back to his house.

Before he had set off, he had been watching the live telecast of the second Test between the British Lions and Australia, played at Ballymore, in Brisbane. Towards the end of the Test I had been given the ball near the Australian line, chipped the ball between the Australian centres, ran on and regathered and scored under the posts. That try sealed our win. It levelled the series at 1–1 and set up a massive decider one week later, in Sydney. The win saved the tour. If we had lost the tour was dead. As it was, we went on to become the first successful Lions team for 15 years. We won the series.

When the transmission ended with a replay of the try, Dad was almost boiling with excitement and adrenalin. There was no outlet, no one around to talk to. It was too early. The only outlet he could think of was to smash to bits the wall which we needed to remove to extend our kitchen. Earlier in our lives, Dad and I had not been friends. By 1989, we were best friends. I think he was rather pleased about my try.

'I thought your thighs would be bigger than that,' said Finlay Calder, my room-mate, on the first night of the tour. They had roomed me, a baby of the party still in his first full season of serious rugby, with Calder, the tour captain, to help in the process of bringing the party together and, no doubt, so that Calder could assess me. We were in Perth, Western Australia, in the massive Burswood Resort Hotel.

'They are a damn sight bigger than yours,' I said. The challenge was on. We hunted round for a piece of string for a thigh-measuring contest. After due consideration I came out on top.

Finlay changed tack. He asked me who I would select in my team for the first Test match, then some weeks ahead. I chose myself, even though as a late replacement for Will Carling I must then have been fourth in line of the four centres. I chose Gareth Chilcott, my Bath friend. And on the open-side flank, Calder's position, I chose Bath's Andy Robinson, leaving the tour captain on the sidelines.

'Not me then,' said Finlay.

'No,' I said.

'You're very honest,' he said.

Nothing like getting in with the tour captain from the very start. It was probably what they call the innocence of youth, and, certainly, I was still in my youth as a player. I had reached a stage at which Jack Rowell seemed to believe I could handle things. He did not come up quite so often with advice about what I needed to pay attention to.

But I had only just finished my apprenticeship under Palmer and Halliday. I was still interested chiefly in having a good time. I was still ringing Chalkie and Peter on Sunday mornings to ask what we had done the night before, and if we could not piece together the full story we would meet at the Pulteney Arms on a Sunday to retrace our movements. People kept on asking me, before and during the tour, how I was dealing with the rapid climb from Bath to England to the Lions. The answer was that I was too busy doing it to deal with it. I just got on with it and, preparing for a major tour with the greatest players in Britain, I revelled in it all.

I had good company. Gareth Chilcott had ended the Five

Nations in the England team and was on tour. I reckoned that, because Coochie always mixed and matched with anyone, and because there was no chance of upstaging him in company, I could ride through the tour on his coat-tails. Andy Robinson was duly chosen, and so was David Sole, the prototype prop for the 1990s, so Bath men were there in force to look after me.

Some of the old hands on tour may well have mistrusted me and my reputation, and wondered if the new guy would let them down when the time came. I was too busy enjoying the prospects to worry about them, either. I noticed no undercurrents.

The Burswood is an enormous place with a foyer like an aircraft hangar. Unfortunately for the team there is also a large casino. When we were not training, we lived in the casino. Some of the lads lost their tour allowance in minutes, others lost several weeks' allowance in half an hour. Rory Underwood usually saves his allowance to take home, so at least he was immune from the heavy losses.

At the early training I was so relaxed, so comfortable with the ball. I was doing the things that were second nature to me – quick passing, being in the right place at the right time. Ian McGeechan, the coach, would come up and whisper: 'Keep that going, you're doing well.' Perhaps I still believed deep down that it could be as easy as playing outside Barnes and Halliday, with Lumsden speeding up outside.

It was my first time under McGeechan, a coach who was going to have the destiny of those Lions, and also the 1993 Lions, in his hands and so was to play a massive part in my career. At the time, I thought he was brilliant. He was very keen on getting our lines of running right, keen for us to take on our opposite numbers. But he hardly worked the backs to death. Now, with the perspective of two tours, it seems to me that he spends too much time concentrating on the forwards, not enough on the backs. As the 1989 tour rolled on, McGeechan realized that he could dominate in the forwards, and seemed to have decided that the backs could look after themselves until he had done every scrap he could to maximize that domination.

At the end of the tour, he told us about his frustration, that he had the forwards right but hadn't really had the time to tune up the backs, about how much he would have liked to take us on to New Zealand to complete the job of creating an all-round team. I tend to differ. I think that he coached the team in exactly the way he wanted to coach them. We underachieved in 1989 in the sense that the backs were defensive pawns, not an attacking force. But we won the series and I am positive that Geech settled for that.

Who could blame McGeechan, with the calibre of forwards he had under him? He tended to build things around Dean Richards, and especially on his massive strength and capacity for tidying up; on the power of Mike Teague, and on the kicking of Robert Jones, who played superbly, poking his kicks into the box. Geech is, at heart, something of a conservative, and Richards, Teague and Jones, with Rob Andrew (who arrived late as replacement for Paul Dean but quickly made the top team), could give him the safe base he needed. So whether or not he developed back play was something of an academic question.

Who turned out to be the kings of the tour? We were dead lucky with the management team, especially after all the horror stories you hear about managements on Lions tours of old. Clive Rowlands, the Welsh manager, was the identikit tour manager. He was exceptional. He was Welsh to the ultimate, and very emotional. He would greet the returning team in the dressing-room after the major victories late in the tour in a flood of tears. His theme, his rallying call as the tour went on, was: 'The Lion is getting bigger.'

Calder himself was an archetypal Lions captain. He was tremendously dedicated, his speeches were professionally delivered, he swore a lot in his team speeches, emphasized how much it all meant to him and how much it should all mean to us. He did not play well at the start of the tour, and many of the media party wrote that Andy Robinson should take his place in the top team. There was never the slightest chance. Robinson was not quite at his best, but in any case McGeechan would never have dropped Calder, and Finlay was too proud a man. It meant everything to him. After the initial bedroom measuring-up, I did not see much of Calder. He did not play a major part in my touring destiny, although his form did improve at the end of the tour.

Paul Ackford was an amazing figure on the tour. He broke the conventions of touring by having Susie, his wife, follow part of the tour. He would make a major contribution to team meetings, to training, and to matches. Then he would go off and spend time with

Susie. Naturally, he took the most ferocious stick about it, especially from Wade Dooley and the front five. It was not so much unkind, as pointed. Ackford would listen gravely. 'I agree, I agree,' he said, nodding apologetically, as we discussed the issue. Then he would get up. 'Sorry, but I've got to go now to meet Susie.' That was Ackford. It was a great shame that he matured as a player so late in his career.

Ackford was at his peak and he impressed me no end. In 1994, at Will Carling's wedding, I went up to Ackford and told him what I thought about him as a player. It is something I very rarely do, and I did wait until he had been retired for two years. 'You are the best lock I've ever seen,' I said. He thought I was taking the piss.

We also had Teague, who was to be voted player of the series. As a Gloucester man, Teague was a deadly enemy to the Bath contingent, although we all respected his play. But that was nothing to Australia 1989. I don't mean I was that shocked to see how incredibly Teague played on tour, but it was the best rugby he has ever produced. I am sure that the Scots on tour, the likes of Calder and John Jeffrey, didn't go a bundle on him at the start. They thought he was a typical England forward, slow and mauling; and I am equally sure that Teague, who trained fanatically, wanted to prove them wrong. The England management had never thought him fit enough. He proved *them* wrong, too. He was a colossal player.

The position of Roger Uttley, the assistant coach, was less clear-cut. I never really worked out the relationship between Roger and the England senior forwards when he was England coach; I was never really certain of how much respect Ackford, Brian Moore and the others had for Uttley as a coach. On tour, the Scottish forwards had it in for him at the first training session.

Roger set off to get a balance between rucking and mauling, but Finlay came down hard. He wanted a Scotland-type all-rucking game. 'We aren't going to play it this way, we are going to play it that way,' was Finlay's message. Uttley was undermined, and the rift never really healed, even though McGeechan and Uttley seemed to get on well and even though a balance between rucking and mauling was ultimately achieved. At the end of the tour, Finlay never mentioned Roger in his captain's report for the Four Home Unions.

I had told all the papers beforehand that to make the tour was the thing, that to make the Test team as well was not really on – all that rubbish. In fact I wanted dearly to play in the Tests, but I knew the other three centres, Devereux, Mullin and Scott Hastings, were powerful opposition, and, at the time, I could easily have accepted any two of the three being chosen above me. I was still in a state of euphoria, still the new boy glad to be chosen by anyone, anywhere.

John Devereux, of Wales, departed soon after the Lions tour for a successful career in rugby league, and enjoyed outstanding seasons in both England and Australia. At the start of the tour he was, unusually for him, fit. He was playing the rugby of his life. He was heavy, and had a terrific hand-off. You didn't want to run in his direction if you were playing against him.

Brendan Mullin, the Irishman, was a contrast. Oxford-educated, with angelic looks, he was a natural athlete. He was a runner and a glider. He could shift off line very comfortably.

Scott Hastings was the fourth centre. As a player he was nothing unusual. He was direct, without electrifying pace. The way he might turn a game, and might still turn a game even now, was to burst a tackle. To be frank, I tried to steer clear of him on tour. He had the knack of drawing attention to himself with some loud prank or another and it was wise to pretend that you were not with him and, in fact, didn't know him at all. Still, he was close to McGeechan, he was experienced, he was physical. At the time, I was none of those three things.

But I officially became a British Lion on a terrible pitch on a horrible night in Melbourne, when we played the second match of the tour against Australia 'B'. Jeffrey went a little berserk in the changing-rooms, stopping just short of headbanging. Mike Griffiths, the Cardiff prop, made strange retching noises as his build-up. People were climbing up the walls and hanging from the ceiling. As usual during the ritual, I did my best not to laugh. The ball never came to me, Devereux played extremely well alongside, we scraped in and the tour was off and running.

The first chance I had to play in the shadow Test team came against New South Wales, at the North Sydney Oval, and I was in the worst shape possible for the challenge. It was a vital match, coming a week before the first Test, and against the strongest opposition in Australia outside the national team. I was chosen initially on the bench and went out with the dirt-trackers in Sydney on the Friday for a little relaxation. I had two cans of Tooheys beer, then religiously turned my back on temptation and hit the Coca-Cola. It was tough going, with the others going strong alongside me. As the night wore on I cracked completely. I returned to the Tooheys in a big way, along with Mike Hall and a few others. We carried on at pace at a cellar night club, an establishment reeking of marijuana. A nagging voice inside kept asking: 'What if you get on tomorrow?' I managed to ignore the voice.

Later still, only just before dawn, the nagging voice piped up again. So I suddenly started drinking coffee by the gallon to try to sober up, then went back to my room, which I was sharing with Derek White, the Scotland back-row player. Unfortunately, things went downhill. The caffeine I had taken kept me awake. I had only just dozed off to sleep for the first time when there was a loud bang on the door. I opened the door a crack, peered out. It was McGeechan. I did my best to stand to attention, to sound bright and bushy. Brendan Mullin had withdrawn, I was in the starting line-up. Oh great, Geech, fantastic. Geech shut the door and left.

The word spread during the morning that Guscott had been out on the town. Kevin Murphy, the tour physiotherapist, had been knocking the rumours down as he worked on the players. 'No, Jerry wouldn't do that.' It was only when I walked into his room for my turn that he realized, from my appearance alone, that it was all true. I managed to get through. Craig Chalmers dropped a goal late on to win the match. We were not to lose outside Tests. If I had given the match away with some blunder, then my tour could well have shaped a lot different.

There was a happy evening a few days later in Dubbo, an outpost stop before the first Test, when it seemed that neither the drinking escapade nor some patchy form early in the tour had been held against me. The night before the team was to be announced, Roger Uttley took me aside in the hotel reception. I knew he had emerged from a long selection meeting.

'You'd better have an early night,' he said. 'You might have some good news in the morning.' I was sharing with Robert Jones, and was bursting to tell him. It was just as well that I did not crack. Early next morning, there was a tap on the door. Uttley came in, looking miserable. He couldn't apologize more, he said, he had been totally out of order, totally premature and so on. But I wasn't in the Test team after all. Even though Devereux and Hastings were unfit I wasn't in. Mullin and Hall were paired in the centre, the strongest evidence yet that I was not trusted by the hierarchy and that the Lions tour could prove a very downbeat end to a season to treasure.

Perhaps the closest I came to a disagreement on the whole tour, apart from the Finlay Calder Thigh-Measuring Dispute, was with Chris Oti, ploughing his own tour furrow on the left wing. Oti was his own man, something of an oddball. At times on tour it appeared that he didn't want to be there, especially when he realized that a Test place was out of the question with Ieuan Evans and Rory Underwood playing so well.

In the match against Queensland County in Cairns, early in the tour and with some of us desperate to fight our way out of the midweek team, we called a move in which Chris was supposed to come into the midfield on the dummy run, to be missed out and the ball to go wide. Oti came charging in as planned, but then, when Rob Andrew hammered the ball across his path to the men outside, he tried to catch it and knocked on. I dished out a medium-sized bollocking for his lack of concentration.

A few minutes later, Rob was kicking for goal. I went back to the wing to cover, and found Oti lurking there, instead of lying up infield to follow the kick. 'That's a strange position,' I said. 'How are you going to chase the kick?'

Having won the match, we showered and changed. I was walking across the pitch to put my kitbag on the coach prior to the post-match function when Roger Uttley called me aside. 'Can I have a word?' he said. 'I hear you and Chris have had a few words and Chris isn't too happy about it.'

I was incredulous. I stood back and looked at Roger. 'Are you serious, or is this a wind-up?' I was not going to be fingered for it. I called Chris over. I asked him was the report correct, had I upset him?

'You shouldn't have said the things you said to me, you should have let me get on with my own game,' he said.

'So you were right to try to catch that ball when you weren't in the move? And you were right to stay back and not follow up the kicks?' I demanded.

'That isn't the point. Let me play my own game,' he said.

I looked at Roger. I was furious that this had been turned round on me. 'There, that's what I'm up against,' I said to Roger. I walked away and left Chris to it. Eventually, he became injured and went home. Whatever was getting to him went with him.

It was only after watching the first Test in the Sydney Football Stadium and seeing the Lions being thrashed that my ambition suddenly surfaced, that I really started to chase the Test position. We were completely outplayed by Australia, we were never in control of any part of the pitch, and we lost. The tour had one lower point to reach, when we played Australian Capital Territory in Canberra in the week, and at one time trailed 0–17. We came back strongly and won well; and all the players not involved lined up outside our dressing-room to applaud us in. It was quickly forgotten that at 0–17, only a little earlier in the afternoon, we were probably a few minutes away from the tour dying of shame.

Now we were back on the road, and so was I. We gathered at a team meeting in Canberra for the anouncement of the team to play Australia in the second Test at Brisbane. On the other side of the room, I saw Gareth Chilcott with his thumbs up. I was in the Test team. It was one day before my 24th birthday and eight months since I had started my first season as a Bath regular at Pontypool. Rob Andrew was in for Craig Chalmers, Scott Hastings was alongside me in the centre. Teague, who had missed the first Test with injury, was fit to take his place. Wade Dooley had taken the place of Robert Norster at lock.

It was a sign that a penny had dropped somewhere among the selectors. It was just one week and one match since I had been left out of the first Test in favour of a new and patched-up combination of Mullin and Hall. I never found out who had originally held out and who had now caved in. And I could not have cared less.

The reaction at home was remarkable. My parents were inundated with media requests for their reaction, and it seemed that everyone who had ever played with me or coached me was called in to add their own reactions. I had messages from all sorts of people offering congratulations. For the first time, I had a sense of the reaction of people at home in Bath. Like all the Lions, we wanted to win for them all. But also for ourselves.

To add to my experience in the big time there was another first – my first major stitch-up from the press. Mike Porter, a travelling British radio reporter, asked me for an interview. I did not know it at the time, but he had something he wanted to ask me which he hid among the normal interview questions. He started by asking me how I was enjoying the tour, what did I think about being in the Test team, how would it go, etc. I was flowing along in perfect interview mode.

'And what do you think of Australian referees?' I stayed in the same carefree mode. 'I wouldn't trust the referees here to take charge of Bath's mini-rugby section,' I said, diplomatically. 'They are so one-eyed and they are crap.' The piece was sent home, was duly quoted back to all the major Australian papers, and I was hauled over the coals by Clive Rowlands in a big way. It was a lesson learned.

Brisbane is a relaxed city, and Ballymore, the Test stadium, is the nearest thing you get to Twickenham in the Southern Hemisphere for off-pitch activity, with all the partying and hospitality tents. In the build-up there was one difficult experience when we went for a team haircut. I always ask for a No. 4 cut on top, a No. 2 around the sides and then for the hairdresser to blend it all in. The Brisbane barber/butcher started at the front, then ploughed his way straight though my hair from the front, and the whole cut developed into a skinhead. The others were scalped too. Scott Hastings, typically, had to stand out. He had a part of his head shaven, leaving lines of hair. He looked like the first-ever Watsonians Red Indian.

The week of preparation between the Tests had pulled the party together. Rob Andrew was now installed at fly-half and was more relaxed than I have ever seen him before or since. He was not an original selection for the party, so had nothing to lose. Robert Jones was playing brilliantly at scrum-half, and his quick pass had helped to transform Rob Andrew's game. Gavin Hastings was at his best at full-back, and the change in the pack was also significant. Norster, one of the most experienced players in the party and something of an idol, was devastated at being left out. But the inclusion of Dooley, as it turned out, was one of the final pieces of the jigsaw, one of the counters to Bill Campbell and Steve Cutler, Australia's second-row giants.

It was a harsh, exciting match, and although we played well and to plan, we just could not get our noses in front. Towards the end, we were losing 12–9, and the tour was slipping away despite our improvements and the authority of our pack. Then, we set up another move which ended with Scott Hastings bowling out a long, bouncing pass to Gavin and Gavin scoring down the right. We were in the lead. And there were just four minutes left.

Then came what a newspaper described as 'the richest moment enjoyed in British rugby for 15 years'. Robert Jones had been told to harass David Campese with high kicks, and he had taunted the Australia defence, and Campese in particular, all afternoon.

Now, he chipped a perfect kick over the scrum. Campo dropped the ball under pressure, Calder charged up the field with it. He laid it back and Rob Andrew passed to me going left. Both Walker and Maguire, the two Australian centres, came up to take me. On the tour, I had been watching a good deal of Australian rugby league on the television and had noticed how, on the sixth tackle, they either put the ball up into the air and chased it, or they put a little kick through. I saw some space between and behind the centres; I had the confidence to take the chance which opened up. I chipped the ball left-footed between the centres and went through after it. I never even had to bend down to pick it up, just to crouch a little as the ball bounced up. I scored under the posts.

Everything went wild in my mind. Robert Jones picked me up and I saw the rest of the Lions celebrating back down the field. The easy conversion meant that we led by two scores inside the last two minutes, that the Test was won and the series saved.

People who have played with me will tell you that I do not show much emotion on the field. This time, it was difficult to remain calm. If they had made a film of the moment, the historical background to the try would have included images of Dad taking me to Bath mini-rugby at the age of seven; of my being dumped in the mud first time out; then of rising through the Colts, the thirds and seconds, of becoming a Bath player. It is no exaggeration to say that, after the try, all my rugby life flashed before my eyes.

It was just as memorable at home in Bath. Jayne had gone to my parents' house and they sat down in the early hours to watch the match together. She also had a thrill from it, as she said later in an interview. 'I have only seen Jeremy express emotion on the rugby field twice. The second time was when he jumped on Stuart Barnes after the winning drop goal against Harlequins in the cup; the first time was the try in Brisbane. We were in Slim and Sue's lounge, and when Jeremy scored we were jumping up and down and hugging each other. It was incredible. Then the phone started going mad, even though it was almost in the middle of the night. We were trying to get rid of them so that we could watch the replay.'

The evening in Brisbane was spent basking in the glory. Finlay went to the press conference. 'People have always been telling me about Jeremy, Ian McGeechan has kept on telling me how good he is,' he said. 'I was always a bit suspicious. Until today.' I was delighted for everyone. Clive Rowlands, predictably, was in tears, hugging everyone. Roger Uttley was on an even keel, savouring the victory and also the fact that we had never become the rucking machine that Finlay ordered. And back at home, my father took the hammer and walked down the road and smashed the wall into tiny pieces.

It was not simply the victory which inspired wild reactions. During the test, which was littered with disagreements, Steve Cutler of Australia was kicked in the head by David Young, our tight-head prop. That was the signal for a major punch-up between the forwards. There was also a lightweight contest between, of all people, Robert Jones and Nick Farr-Jones. They made up with enthusiasm what they lacked in punching power.

The Young incident and the fact that Australia had lost provoked the biggest furore I have ever experienced. The Australian media went berserk, calling us savage Poms, strong-arm Poms, disgraceful Poms. There were editorials in the big papers. Meanwhile there was a week before the deciding Test back at Sydney, and we spent it up at Surfers Paradise. It might sound glamorous, but when we got there, it was winter, and Surfers was shut and deserted. It was a ghost town, a shocker. The bars were empty, there was no life in the clubs. We did go to a factory and pillaged those big Australian coats. That was it.

But the storm was still raging. The hue and cry reached unbelievable heights, and was clearly intended to put us off our game. It was caused by the increasing panic in the country, shared by everyone from Bob Dwyer, the Australian coach, downwards that our forwards were getting stronger and stronger and exposing the home forwards.

The most frequent allegation was that the violence was premeditated on our part, that it was all a repeat of the notorious '99' call first originated by the 1974 British Lions in South Africa. There was one item that *was* premeditated. We realized that Farr-Jones was the key to the Australian operation, and in the second Test we had Robert Jones niggle at him a little. At the first scrum, Robert stood on Farr-Jones's foot and gave him a nudge, and Farr-Jones reacted violently.

There was nothing else, or at least nothing was discussed in the team meetings. The David Young incident was ridiculous. Only David can explain what was on his mind when he kicked Cutler. No one can even begin to condone it. But it was not part of a campaign. As you might expect, the team line was exactly the same as any team line in top rugby – if they start anything, stand your ground.

And the most transparent thing about the whole fuss was that it was caused chiefly by Australia's defeat. If they had won they would not have whinged about rough play. As for us, the controversy took us all back to the match against Queensland, where Mike Hall, freshly arrived from the United Kingdom after sitting his exams at Cambridge, was kicked about twenty times at the back of a ruck. He had all the breath kicked out of him. Welcome to Australia, Mike. We didn't hear much about that incident in the Australian media, or much about an incident in the third Test when David Campese, of all people, stamped on David Sole's upturned face. It took us only a few days after the second Test to dismiss the whole campaign, and to laugh at it.

The intensity of the build-up to the third Test got through even to me. Until then I had felt mildly detached from all that rhetoric. Now Finlay came into his own. He was pushing it into us. We had come this far. There was no turning back now, otherwise it was all for nothing. He emphasized how much it meant – to us, to the whole squad, to families and friends, and to everyone who had helped us through our careers. We could see in our mind's eye all the people at home, desperate for us to win.

It was also the most powerful coming together of the party. There are factions on all tours; for example, the dirt-trackers who fall out of Test contention can sometimes drift away from the main party, as some of the Scots forwards did at the end of the Lions tour of New Zealand in 1993. Sometimes that can even cause dissension.

But the midweek team on this tour had been expertly led by Donal Lenihan. 'Donal's Donuts' had their own sense of pride. I know. I played for them. They had a laugh, they had their own T-shirts. They backed up the Test team all the way.

There was perhaps some possibility of a Norster-led faction after Rob had taken his demotion from the top team so badly. He was in a black and uncommunicative mood for a day or two. Then, when the dirt-trackers were on their way back from a function in Brisbane, Norster stopped the coach. They all got off, invaded a club called the Toucan, and let their hair down with Rob leading the singing. He was hurt, but he swallowed his pride.

And the change in atmosphere among ordinary Australians was marked. Instead of them telling us: 'We're going to thrash you,' there was more respect. I remember the staff of our Travelodge hotel in Sydney becoming quietly converted to our cause, perhaps even rooting for us.

Geech drove us on. It was all built, as usual, around Dean Richards, Robert Jones, Mike Teague and Rob Andrew. We knew all our strengths and weaknesses, where Australia would be strong and where they could be attacked. The training went as smooth as silk and we ran out down the tunnel into the cauldron of the Sydney Football Stadium as well prepared as we could be.

History shows that we won 19–18. It was a great experience, but only afterwards. We were too busy fighting for our lives in the intensity to worry about glory. And I had my worst moment of the tour near half-time, when we were leading 9–3 and our forwards had already taken charge. Finlay Calder had a great match, as did Teague and most of the others. But then Lynagh and Campese brought off a scissors in midfield, Lynagh went inside me when I really should have stopped him easily, and he handed a try to Ian

Williams. Behind the posts, I was almost horror-stricken. I still cringe about it.

We went ahead again, chiefly thanks to what has become known as the greatest blunder of modern-day Test rugby, by David Campese. He tried to run the ball out of his own left-hand corner after Rob Andrew had missed with a drop kick. When Ieuan Evans closed on him, he chucked the ball out to Greg Martin, the full-back, who was not ready for it and had his back half-turned as Campese ran. The ball went loose and Ieuan Evans dived on it for the try.

The storm of abuse from Australian people which came down on Campo was astonishing. It took up a whole chapter of his book. At the post-match dinner that evening he came late and left early, obviously still shattered. I did not share the general view. Campese tries things – that is part of his genius. If Martin had been thinking as quickly, he could have taken the pass and cleared. Of course it was risky by Campese, but I would put some of the blame on Martin too. If he had been alive to the possibilities, he could have gained 30 yards.

With 16 minutes left we were 19–12 ahead, and our forwards were still playing superbly. But the closing stages were almost a nightmare. It was total panic. They tried to run the ball at us from everywhere. Two penalties by Lynagh brought them back to 19–18. It was last-ditch time, chasing shadows time. Every time we closed down one attack the ball seemed to shoot off somewhere else, bringing some more tackling and some more panic as we tried to hold our lines.

The final whistle blew at last. We all hugged each other and the rest of the guys set off on a lap of honour around the field, to wave to the crowd and especially to our supporters who had travelled so far. I am not into the laps of honour. I walked down the tunnel, waving to people who were hanging over shouting congratulations. I sat down in the changing-room and stood with my head against the wall. I drank some Pepsi, then the boys came in.

Clive Rowlands, as ever, was in floods of tears. Some of the boys joined him. It was not so much the bouncing around I remember, as the exultation inside. There were celebratory group shots for the photographers. Steve Hampson and Andy Gregory, the two Wigan rugby league players who were playing in Australian rugby league that season, were welcomed into the dressing-room to join the fun. They seemed as pleased as we were.

There was a week of the tour remaining, with a provincial match in Newcastle against New South Wales County and the final match in Brisbane against ANZAC, a composite team of Australian and New Zealand internationals. At that time, too, we gathered to discuss an invitation we had received to go to South Africa *en bloc* for the celebrations of the South African Rugby Board's centenary. Finlay stood up at the meeting and said that he did not think it was right to go, but that any individual who wanted to take up the invitation was welcome. Everyone declared that they wouldn't, and that seemed to be the end of it. Suddenly, some time after we returned to the British Isles, some of the Welsh, together with Teague and Jeff Probyn and Paul Rendall, decided to take part after all. I have heard all the rumours about major payments, but even among the players, if you asked about the rumours, all you got was the careful, political answer: 'We are only going to play rugby.'

McGeechan came up to me in the wild evening after the third Test. 'You've played enough,' he said. I had the final week off, and departed on a bender of epic proportions. The only thing left to negotiate were the jibes of people who said that we hadn't been on a true Lions tour because we hadn't been to New Zealand or South Africa. Bollocks, we said to them. The only people who said that were people who weren't following the tour.

The other problem for me to handle, when the final whistle blew to end the third Test and the season which had begun ten months earlier with a Bath tour, was the realization that nothing could really be so good again in my rugby career. And, in some senses, nothing ever was so good again.

'Well done, Son,' said my father when I came home. My family were overjoyed; and the season had finally ended. It was a season like no other, of course. There was no point in even dreaming about bettering it for sporting adventures and for freedom to run with the ball.

I had never had a second to contemplate these achievements along the way. As I said before, and as I told every interviewer during the season who was mystified that I was taking it all so calmly, I never had time to sit back and wonder. There was always the next step.

The reckoning did eventually come, back at home in the summer of 1989, and when it came it was weird, and difficult. I could not accept coming back to ground level after the excitement of the long flight. As the new season approached, I announced that I would not play till Christmas, not even for Bath; that I needed the recuperation. I did drift back early in the season. I was at a loose end. There was nothing else to do. But I was very disturbed to find that the feelings were different, that nothing felt the way it felt before.

My Bath Saturday rituals had always been the same. I used to wake up and tingle with the anticipation. I could never eat because of the butterflies in my stomach. Richard Hill used to drive down the hill to pick me up, and we would talk about the game on our way to join the others for our lunch and team meeting. Then we used to go to the Recreation Ground, go out and play for Bath. You could not beat the feeling.

I felt strange from the first game back. I was different, both as a player and as a person. I tried hard to grasp hold of something that would bring the old feeling back, not realizing that something had gone for good. It was the reckoning.

The biggest shock was that I did not feel the same in Bath's dressing-room. I made no contribution, I drifted in team meetings, and I played little good rugby for Bath during the season. Towards the end of it, with murmurings in the team growing, I was dropped for the semi-final of the cup against Moseley at The Reddings. It came on the heels of the defeat in the 1990 Grand Slam decider at Murrayfield. I had heard that some of the Bath players too were unhappy about my commitment and attitude.

Stuart Barnes rang me with the news of Jack Rowell's decision. 'Jeremy has been dropped because he has not played well enough for the club,' Jack had said. It was obviously a blow and a strange feeling, something I disagreed with. It was difficult to confront Jack with it. When I saw him next, in typical Jack mode he tried to defuse the situation. 'Don't worry,' he said. 'You'll be back in for the final.'

The press had a field day. 'Dropping Guscott opens the way to professional ranks,' said *The Times*. The *Today* newspaper wrote: 'Guscott may answer London calling,' suggesting that I would now make a supposedly lucrative move to Harlequins or Wasps. Lots of rugby league men, among them Doug Laughton and David Oxley, advised me in print to go to rugby league. I had to disappoint them all. While Bath won through to the final, I played for the second XV on the Rec. Then they picked me again, and we beat Gloucester in the final.

At the time, there was no one to talk it through with. Jayne and I hardly ever discuss rugby. I couldn't go to Jack Rowell because I never wanted to show signs of weakness in front of him. In any case, Jack tends to put you right then remind you that he did so for the rest of your career, so that was something to avoid as well.

Finally, my sporting life began to settle down again. It stopped being all a blur and took on features. Gradually, enthusiasm re-appeared. Not quite the old, youthful enthusiasm, but at least an adjustment, an appetite for more rugby. Everything had come to me so quickly and it was difficult to slow down. Perhaps I realized, too, that I had just enjoyed the time of my sporting life and some price had to be paid.

7 Dying Dreams of the Grandest Slam

The ill-fated 1990 season with Carling's England

Scotland is undoubtedly my least favourite place to play rugby. I don't mean to give the impression that I hate the Scots. But I do detest playing in Edinburgh. The pitch at Murrayfield had a brilliant playing surface, until it declined dramatically recently. The city itself seems nice. If we did not have to go there to play rugby I could even become a fan of the place. But it seems that when England go there to play we are hated from the moment we touch down to the moment we depart. It makes you want to arrive late, play the match and fly out early. The reception from the public and media seems to date back to historical grudges. They seem to have a major problem with the English.

The rivalry between the England and Scottish players reached a peak in 1991. The Scottish squad, who had just been wiped out by New Zealand in the play-off match to decide third and fourth place in the World Cup, arrived en bloc *at Twickenham for the final, England against Australia. They all wore Australian scarves. They might have seen it all as a big joke, but we thought it was an appalling gesture. Some of them tried to apologize afterwards. But the damage was done.*

The relationship between myself and Edinburgh first began to go sour in 1990. England had won next to nothing in rugby for decades. We had become something of a joke in the 1970s and 1980s. But in that international season, my first in the team, we had entered a new era. We played brilliantly. We thrashed Ireland, France and Wales and played some of the best rugby seen for years.

We came to Edinburgh looking for the Grand Slam. It was a disastrous day, a crushing, numbing defeat, and it was a match which changed the whole course of England rugby for years to come. For some, the wounds remain to this day.

When I came home from Australia as one of the Lions' conquering heroes, I believed that at last, my traditional pessimism about selection would be banished and that I would sail into the England team to continue the fast start I had made in Romania.

At least, that was the theory. In my mind, I soon started to talk myself out of the team. I had only played one match for England, and that only when captain Carling withdrew. But Carling was back for the autumn of 1989, when we were to kick off the season against Fiji at Twickenham. Halliday was available. I contemplated, as usual, the worst scenario. Let's see. Carling is bound to be in because he is captain; Halliday has done nothing wrong in an England jersey: I've had it.

At the squad session before the match against Fiji, and before the start of yet another English attempt to win something worth winning, I waited for Geoff Cooke to come up and say: 'Well, Jerry. You played really well in Australia. But . . .' Whenever he started to edge towards me I assumed that the bad news was coming.

I got in. Halliday was left out. It was a bizarre feeling, the first time I had got ahead of the guy who had helped me and whom I had looked up to for so long. I remember thinking that it was a crying shame we had not both been chosen. I would have loved the opportunity to play twenty games alongside Halliday for England, to try to recreate at international level what we had created for Bath. Indeed, before the selection, many people had said that the club partnership should be chosen, that Halliday and I were in form. Still, there was my first match at Twickenham to think about, playing alongside Will for the first time.

I had been to the stadium itself only twice before. At 14, I went up on a coach with my father and Gary in a party from Bath RFC to watch England play Wales. It was also my first real experience of Chilcott. He sat at the back of the coach in the middle seat, with his huge tree-trunk legs splayed out. He was wearing a sinister Crombie, and with his sinister cropped hair and moustache he looked, well, sinister. I could not believe the sheer numbers at Twickenham. I was almost shell-shocked by it all. We were poured into the packed terraces, and the crush became so enormous that we youngsters were manhandled over the heads of the crowd and sat on the grass in front of the fence.

There was a lone Welshman there, scruffy and drunk. He kept taking sips from a bottle of vodka and a bottle of whisky. Eventually, Dusty Hare had a penalty to win the match from the West Stand side. The Welshman couldn't look. When he heard the roar, and he knew the kick was good, he slumped to the ground, felled by a mixture of grief and alcohol. I was almost sorry for him.

In the Fiji match I almost felt sorry for me, too. We beat the Fijians, but not before they completely lost their tempers. The main object was to get rid of the ball then curl up while running and bring your knees up to stop the Fijian nutcases hitting you high and late in the neck and head. Noa Nadruku and Tevita Vonolagi were sent off.

Poor Simon Hodgkinson at full-back bore the brunt of it. They took Hodgy out whether he still had the ball or whether he had passed it five minutes before. It was a disaster for the Fijians, for whom Twickenham was like Mecca. They scored some decent tries when they tried to play rugby, but they were seen in an atrocious light because of their antics. Still, for me at least there was a happy ending. I was becoming concerned during the match that I hadn't scored myself. Eventually, after one of Rob Andrew's very rare breaks, I did.

Life as an England player grew in pressure and commitment. England had thrown away a great chance of a championship by losing in Cardiff at the end of the previous season, and there was a real sense that 1990 was to be our year in the Five Nations. After years of appalling selection, appalling results and low morale, there was a sense of expectation growing in the country as a whole.

A regular feature of the England planning was the annual New Year training camp at Lanzarote, in the Canaries. For several years we made camp at Club La Santa. It was my first introduction to scientific fitness measuring and testing, and my first dip into team politics.

There were grid tests, muscular endurance tests, the infamous VO2 max tests, body fat ratio tests. At least I learned how to cheat at the tests from an early stage. You could do ten press-ups, rest while Geoff Cooke and his men looked the other way, then do another ten when they looked back. In the VO2 max tests, in which you have to reach the end of each length just as the bleep goes off, you could arrive at the line just before the bleep, making the return run slightly shorter and easier.

My results were poor, and I began to worry. The management kept on insisting that the tests were just a guide, to help the individual player to identify the areas on which he might work. They were not a selection aid for the team, they said. I wasn't so sure. If you were found to be really off the pace, or really fatty, they'd have the perfect excuse.

At least I was quicker than Carling and Halliday, though not as quick as Rory Underwood and Chris Oti. But my VO2 max results were worse than all the other backs, and my body fat ratio was higher than most.

Then, disastrously for my chances of retaining my position, I realized that, in the Lanzarote complex, Carling and Halliday were sharing a room. I thought all sorts of dark thoughts. Will and Hallers in a twin! You can always read a hell of a lot of team psychology into the rooming lists. I convinced myself that the rooming had some global significance. I was out of the team for the forthcoming Five Nations, and the two room-mates were in together.

I also felt some insecurity on account of my position in the squad. I was still the new boy. I have always paid attention to what people think of me, even though I may give the opposite impression. On the Lions tour, I never felt that I had to make an impression. Nothing was expected. Back with England, I now had achievements under my belt, high profile ones. I imagined, possibly with justification, that the squad would have a preconceived idea of what I would be like – something of an arrogant upstart, perhaps. There were indeed some petty jealousies. There always are. I deliberately played it low key. I listened to what others were saying, and tried to blend quietly into the squad that way.

Gradually, your affinities begin to build. My affinities have almost always been with the forwards, rather than with any sort of clique formed by the fast backs. I am told that Walter Payton, the great American football running back, always socialized with his linemen rather than with his colleagues in the backfield.

It was the beginning of a warm friendship with the likes of Dean Richards. Not that Deano said much. He still doesn't say much, but whether he is speaking or not, I enjoy his company. But it was not just the forwards who were friendly. I found from an early stage, too, that Rory Underwood was easy-going, would never do anything to upset you, in fact would do anything for you. Rory and I were to become room-mates through seasons of international rugby.

Yet the relationship which most people, including myself, were intrigued about (and still are) was that with Will himself. In the early stages, there wasn't one. We might talk over a few things on the training field, but there was no immediate rapport off the field at all.

Perhaps it was because I saw him as someone I was competing against. Perhaps, too, it was my masterly, subtle comment when I arrived for the first England session of the season: 'Now you've had it. The best player's arrived!' Will did his best to wind up a smile, but never quite managed it.

Also, of course, he was captain – to all intents he seemed to be captain for life. I admit I even suspected then that he was only playing because he was captain. Meanwhile, not only at Bath but also in some areas of the media, the Halliday/Guscott partnership was being pushed. From Will's point of view, that probably represented a threat. At the time of and ever since the Lions tour, I was not exactly short of publicity, of newspaper features and media attention in general. To some extent, I suppose, as we looked at each other, each of us was muttering under his breath: 'You lucky bastard.'

Will was also a totally different player to Halliday. For a start, he played inside centre. The ball did not reach me as often as it did at Bath, where we played left and right. Will would usually take the ball back into contact in our early games together. I would be itching to explode, to tell Will to move out and let me take a ball in for a change.

Even if Halliday was slightly predictable, even if everyone knew what he would try to do, no one could do anything about it. Will was and is more of a New Zealand style of player, from the same mould as a Craig Innes, if not quite as aggressive. When Will did go off line in those early games, he was difficult to stop. He revealed that strong hand-off and low centre of gravity. Halliday and I had developed an understanding. He knew that if he went through a gap, I would be there outside him. He knew without looking. Carling tended to look inside, rather than outside. The early months of the new centre partnership, both on and off the field, were always interesting and never easy.

He was certainly a central figure in the squad, alongside Geoff Cooke and Roger Uttley, the coach. Since the previous season they had worked hard on confidence, and continuity of selection. I got the impression from some of the older hands that Cooke and Carling allowed players to express what they thought, whereas previously the players were seen but not heard. Throughout the early part of that season, from the Fijian game and Lanzarote to the build-up to the opening of the Five Nations against Ireland at Twickenham, they drummed into us that we had to win something. Unless we did, all the work counted for nothing, and we were nothing.

Lanzarote gave me my first close-up view of Cooke. I was quite impressed. He took charge, set the programme and was a good organizer. As a coach, however, he did not impress me, and eventually he was to give up most of the coaching duties in favour of Uttley or, later, Richard Best. I remember in some early sessions Cooke talking to us about back play. Looking at him, I could not help remembering that he had never played international rugby, and telling myself that he didn't know what he was talking about. I realized later where he was coming from, and the value to the team of his management style.

Still, to his everlasting credit, and regardless of the rooming list at Lanzarote, Cooke picked me in the centre to play Ireland and the international road suddenly became a fast track . . .

And on the subject of a fast track, it was always fascinating at Lanzarote to see which other athletes were working out there. During my first visit the great Jamaican sprinter Merlene Ottey was there. She had the next apartment to those two equally outstanding athletes, John Olver and Mark Linnett, of Harlequins and Moseley. Olver and the rest of the lads kept on at Linnett all week that he should borrow Merlene's yellow Lycra training gear, which she put on the balcony. Linnett eventually cracked, borrowed the yellow Lycra gear and paraded around the complex wearing it.

It is easy to forget that in the first half of the match against Ireland, there were few signs that England were breaking out of the era of frustration. By the end, people were talking about a whole new era. We won 23–0. I made a break and saw Rory wide on the right. I floated the ball to him as I saw the heat approaching in peripheral vision. Rory still had it all to do, but his pace and finishing were incredible. He scored a try that no one else in the world would have scored. It was also his 19th try for England, which gave him the record formerly held by Cyril Lowe. Soon afterwards, Will went for the outside, broke cleanly and passed it on to me. I was running in a straight line, David Irwin of Ireland came close, but I managed to jerk out of his way with extra pace. I scored. Will had already scored himself, and it was a highly encouraging day. It did wonders for our confidence. Deep down, I felt excited by the whole experience.

After the match I was collared by the BBC. I accidentally began one sentence, live on *Grandstand*: 'Much to my surprisement . . .' On *Rugby Special* next day, they ran the same interview but had blanked out the '. . . ment' – much to my surprise!

That was nothing to what every English rugby fan was feeling in Paris a fortnight later. For me it was the first time in the Parc des Princes and the first Paris Experience. We trained at the Racing Club, and there were more photographers there than there had been spectators at some games I had played in. The session before the match went incredibly well, and we found that the Adidas ball was superb to handle.

We had not won in Paris for eight years. Now Will and I were up against the famous partnership of Philippe Sella and Denis Charvet. Charvet looked a little podgy, as if he had had his best days. He was no longer the will-o'-the-wisp of former years. Sella was still an immensely powerful player, always in the right place, always with skills to create space. Unless you can get outside Sella you are history. If you come within five feet of him to the left or the right he will hit you like a moving telephone box.

There was also the great Serge Blanco to plan for. We drummed it into ourselves: don't give him an easy ball, make him run for it, send him into traps he can't run out of.

I knew how irresistible the French could be, having played against them for the 'B' team. It is like playing against the All Blacks, but far more exciting. Both sides come in wave after wave, but whereas the All Blacks come in predictable waves, the French can come straight or to the left or the right.

Despite everything, despite the physical ordeal of playing in Paris, something strange was creeping into us, something called confidence. We were even relaxed. Rory and I gave in to chocoholism. We ate four or five Mars bars each. We went on to the Parc in a day of howling winds and howling people. The noise in Paris is always more of a howl than a roar. Even in defence it is exciting to play there.

But we did not defend too much. We gave one of rugby history's best performances to beat France 26–7. The forwards played brilliantly, Simon Hodgkinson kicked some great goals in the wind, and Rory scored near half-time after chasing a chip from Rob Andrew. In the second half, Denis Charvet tried to chip over our heads. The ball cannoned off Will, I followed it, kicked it on, picked it up on the bounce and scored. At the end, Serge Blanco, another French legend taking the day off, was left for dead by Will for our third try, and, now the singing of the English in the stands was drowning the French howls.

The media barrage after the match was amazing. 'Rugby Rambos slam the French,' said the *Sunday Mirror.* Apparently, I was now one of the greatest superstars in the history of the world. Alex Murphy, who had tried to sign me for St Helens, popped up in a newspaper interview. 'Jeremy Guscott could be rugby league's first millionaire,' he said. Good old Alex, always with his feet on the ground.

We behaved riotously at the post-match dinner. Forfeits consisted of downing a bottle of wine in one. John Olver, the bench hooker, was ill at his table. Then we went proudly on into the Parisian night, to the Crazy Horse, the Moulin Rouge, the Lido. The Crazy Horse trod a thin line between sophisticated entertainment and a haunt for dirty old men. All our wives and girlfriends were there, uncomfortable with the show, while the players leered and cheered, almost past caring.

The next leg of the charge for the championship meant an awful lot more to others than it did to me. Cooke wanted to beat Wales more than he wanted to beat all the other teams combined. Many of the older players, like Richard Hill and Mark Bailey, had suffered from Welsh domination over England; England had not won there since 1963, and even though the match was to take place at Twickenham, there seemed to be a fear that the Welsh would raise their game and put one over on us.

My view was that it was just another game. We at Bath had played Welsh teams, week in, week out, for most of our sporting lives, and beat them more than they beat us, so we never developed a complex. I never felt that a Welsh rugby player was better by birth. And to be frank, they were then so poor, so lacking in spirit, that anyone who did have a complex needed to see a doctor.

We beat Wales with some outstanding combination between forwards and backs, but without really hitting top gear. It ended 34–6, with four tries. Will scored one which should never have been. He went through tackle after tackle. The killer came when Rory intercepted during a Welsh attack and ran 80 yards. I chased him all the way, shouting encouragement. He flopped down over the line. Having gone all that way I had to do something. I walked up to the prostrate Rory and bent down to drag him to his feet as the crowd went berserk. 'Fucking leave me alone,' said our hero, still shattered.

Wales? Whatever they used to be, they weren't any more. You could tell, during and after the match, that there was dissension in the ranks, that the players were dejected. Later in the evening, there was no holding back as they expressed their feelings. They seemed very parochial, very club orientated, as if the national feeling had completely gone.

The elation in the England team was something you could almost touch. Meanwhile Cooke and Carling kept drumming it in – we had still won nothing. But the whole country, rugby followers or not, were talking about us. One of the Sunday newspapers called the back-to-back wins over France and Wales 'the two best consecutive England performances for years, perhaps ever'.

Scotland were also unbeaten, having won three out of three. It was to be a proper Grand Slam shoot-out, with the big prize at stake for both teams. Scotland's progress had been sketchy. They had scraped a lucky win over Ireland in Dublin, beaten a woeful French team in Edinburgh, and beaten an even more woeful Welsh team, then in the grip of a Neath obsession, in Cardiff. They had scored five tries in their three matches, while we had scored 11.

But it was none of this that was to prove the key factor. The Scottish players, media and public became obsessed with the idea that we were approaching the match, one of the biggest occasions in British sport of the year, in a state of supreme arrogance, as if we had only to walk on to the field to win. It was rubbish – none of us thought that. But the Scots seized on every scrap from the London papers which they could use to fuel their obsession, and it suited their hierarchy not to deflate the obsession in any way.

The build-up was tense. We stayed at the Peebles Hydro, in the Borders, with its superb facilities, plus a crummy little pitch-and-putt course. 'Come on lads, we can create history here' was the theme. Brian Moore was very, very prominent. Every time I saw him, he was telling another group of players what we were going to do, when and how. He had all the questions and he had all the answers. I didn't feel there was anything a forward could tell me about playing Test rugby in the threequarter line anyway, and eventually he wore me down. I was tempted to say, 'For Christ's sake, Brian, shut your mouth.' I didn't discuss it with the other players and I have no idea what they thought.

We could easily sense the anti-English sentiment as we took the field. There was a great roar for Scotland and for their gesture which has now become famous and copied – David Sole, the captain, led his team on at a sedate walk. Many people seemed to see The Walk as some decisive psychological gesture which put us all off. I didn't give a monkey's how they came on.

But there were other signs of how fired-up the Scots were. I remember Scott Hastings being in a trance, as if with a film over his eyes; he was sweating and looking straight through us. 'He's not here,' I thought.

We did establish some order when I scored down the left after a move launched by Mike Teague and carried on by Richard Hill and Carling. But we also gave away a crucial try in the second half, Mike Teague knocking on at a scrum and Tony Stanger following up to score when Scotland attacked from the next scrum. They swarmed over us, they were given a free ride by the referee and they were the better side. We tried to attack near the end, but there was a breakdown in communication between Will and Brian, with both trying to make the decisions when we were awarded penalties. The whistle blew to signal a Scottish victory, and the end of our massive pre-match hopes. It was 13–7 and a Grand Slam for Scotland.

I left the field just before the end. When the players came in, I was sitting with an ice-pack covering a dead leg. The result was no surprise – I had listened to the crowd as they sensed our hopes collapsing. The dressing-rooms at Murrayfield are huge. The players sat scattered around, heads buried in their necks, as if in shock.

After a while, I looked around and wanted to shout: 'It's only a game!' I wanted to get my kitbag and get out of there, but no one seemed able to move. Perhaps those who had been around for much longer, who had seen this chance of glory blown, felt it more deeply. Teague was feeling dreadful about his knock-on. Richards kept telling him not to dwell on it. Roger Uttley looked miserable, and admitted later that he was absolutely devastated. He had fallen out with some of the Scots on the Lions tour, so it was doubly bitter for him.

Jayne later recalled the scene when the players went to meet their wives and girlfriends afterwards. 'Some players really seemed to take it to heart. Some of them seemed to be crying, and some of the wives seemed to be in tears. Jerry had hurt his leg, so he came in limping. I started laughing and so did Jeremy. Then I decided I should maybe be more reserved, because it all seemed so important.'

At the dinner, Scott Hastings had returned to the planet and was normal again. But even the Scots appeared to be in shock, as if they could not quite believe it themselves and could not let themselves go to celebrate.

And that was, in one sense, the end of the innocence of that England team. We had played superb rugby in winning our first three games, and had expanded the style. The massive, crushing weight of the defeat at Murrayfield concentrated minds. Thereafter, partly consciously and partly not, Cooke and the hierarchy resolved that we had to win a championship – that was the only priority. If that meant that we ground it out, abandoned all of our wide game and bored our way to the title, then so be it. Out of the despair of Murrayfield was born a bloody-minded determination. If we had won, we could have been free and clear, with the title under our belts and ready for an all-out attacking assault. It was not to be. That dream died at Murrayfield.

The season dragged to a conclusion. I regained my place in the Bath team after being dropped for the cup match against Moseley, as described earlier. Bath roasted Gloucester in the cup final. There was another showpiece match at Twickenham in aid of the Rugby for Romania fund. I scored a try from long range. Peter Jackson of the *Daily Mail* wrote: 'Jeremy Guscott brought Twickenham's profitable Sunday showpiece to a dazzling climax with a try outrageous even by his standards.'

There was a trip to the Hong Kong Sevens with the Barbarians, and the *Daily Mirror* snapped up a photograph, taken at the post-final banquet, of us dressed in women's swimsuits, staging a send-up of a beauty contest. It must have been a send-up, because Brian Moore was chosen as the winner. That summer England toured Argentina. Without me. I stayed at home and drank my way through the summer. And Jayne and I were married, at St Saviour's Church, in Larkhall. We went to Florida for a fortnight on honeymoon. I became the man who had everything – except a Grand Slam.

8

Red Rose Speedway

The Slams, and steps to world domination bar one

Richard Hill got to his feet in the calm and purposeful atmosphere of our team room in the hotel. He started slowly. 'I've got to make the right calls, I've got to keep an eye on proceedings. I've got to make the kicks tell.' Then, he saw red. He had had enough of the tactical stuff. 'And if I get hold of Robert Jones I'm going to rip him apart.' That was it. Suddenly, Hilly was in full stride. His speech became an almost savage diatribe in which all the years of frustration at the hands of the Welsh finally poured out. He went on and on, slamming all the slights at the hands of the Welsh, swearing and cursing.

It was a desperate moment. Here we were, awaiting what was for some the biggest game of their careers, with the crippling run of Cardiff defeats to avenge, and in the middle of a scientific psychological build-up – and suddenly the main object of the whole meeting was not to collapse in hysterical laughter. I was right at the back. I could see Brian Moore's shoulders begin to heave at the front. I could see that John Olver was on the point of exploding. Tears were rolling down my cheeks. At the front, Will and Geoff Cooke were fighting desperately to control themselves. Other players were almost bent double, clutching their stomachs.

We were slamless and back in Lanzarote, in preparation for dodging the fitness tests and for the 1991 Five Nations, for a summer tour of Australia and then for the World Cup in the autumn – just a quiet sort of time, really. We were a sadder, wiser, but more experienced team. We could look back on a decent autumn. We beat the Barbarians at Twickenham by 18–16 in a game that never really took off as Barbarians games are supposed to; and those people who had toured Argentina in the summer and been defeated in the second Test in Buenos Aires had their revenge. We beat Argentina 51–0. We crushed them. I scored two tries, Hodgkinson broke the English scoring record with his 23 points. Rory, who was deadly, scored a hat-trick.

The most memorable aspect of the match was not the tries. It was a punch from Federico Mendez, the 18-year-old Argentinian prop who, amazingly, was still a schoolboy at the time of the match. An altercation grew around Jeff Probyn and Mendez and for some reason, Mendez ran up to Paul Ackford and laid him out with a right cross. Ackford eventually got to his feet, but his legs were rubber and he was dragged off.

The traditional sympathy from the rest of the squad flowed soon after the game. We never ceased to remind Ackford that he had been put off the field by a mere schoolboy. 'Schoolboy lays out man of 6′ 6″ – that will be the headline in the papers,' it was suggested to him.

Hodgkinson would also pass for a schoolboy. He was a good all-round player and he was winning lots of games at the time with his goal-kicking. He was so small and neat that he would not have looked out of place in a junior school team.

But I had always been spoiled by my full-backs. I had played so much with Audley Lumsden at Bath and I knew that, once Barnes and Halliday had put me through, Audley would have the gas to come up outside for the pass. I used to look at Hodgy, who had nothing like that kind of pace, and ask myself whether he would be up there when I made a break.

The traditional Lanzarote reminders that we had yet to win anything were becoming a little tiresome. True, but tiresome. We laid down our intention to win the Grand Slam in 1991, to get something on to the record books. We said that it did not matter a damn if we were as dull as ditchwater. We would be methodical. Our game would be mapped out in advance, and it was clearly understood that we would proceed from one position on the field to another in preplanned play. There would be a lot of Richard Hill's boot and a fair amount of Rob Andrew's boot, too. That set the tone for the season, because we went through enormous training sessions which were designed to programme the game into our mental computers.

It might not sound the sort of game to appeal to me, or to some of the other backs, at all. But I could understand it. I had lived through Edinburgh. To be frank, if we won a Grand Slam I didn't care if I never touched the ball. We knew before we even set out that we would take stick from the press for being a boring team, and the press were not to disappoint us. We knew that on that score, we couldn't win. But we also knew that above anything, the English rugby public would be elated with a Slam.

The path to the Slam seemed a little easier this time. We had to play the two best teams, France and Scotland, at Twickenham. The two weaker teams, Wales and Ireland, were to be met away from home. And so the Cardiff spectre duly reared its head. England still had not won there since 1963, and it seemed to loom large in the minds of too many Englishmen. Once again, those of us who never cared a damn about playing in Wales had to look on as the whole build-up was geared to demystifying Cardiff for those who were still scared.

We trained in the week before the match at Kingsholm, Gloucester. We were going about our lawful business when suddenly, the loudspeakers burst into life, blaring out 'Land of My Fathers', the Welsh national anthem. When it finished, it rewound and started again. It was played time and again. It may have seemed to some a psychological master-stroke by Cooke, to get us used to the passion of Cardiff. To me, it was just a bloody noise.

We drove right into the heart of Cardiff two days before the game. This was so that we would experience the full pressure in the centre of the city, rather than staying in a vacuum outside. On the coach across the Severn Bridge, the sound system sprang to life. It was time for another dozen rousing choruses of 'Land of My Fathers'. By the end of the week, I knew the anthem better than most Welshmen.

We had our final team meeting in the Crest Hotel the day before the game. It was a classic. Will spoke briefly, then, as usual, went around some of the senior players asking them what they felt England had to concentrate on.

'What do we have to do tomorrow, Brian?' Will asked Brian

Moore. 'We have to present the ball well, make tackles,' said Moore. All the usual stuff.

'What do we have to do, Richard?' Will asked Richard Hill. Now Hilly and Wales have a history. He has suffered most from the years of Welsh victories. He was even thrown out of the team after the battle of Cardiff in 1987, when Wade Dooley poleaxed Phil Davies, and four players, Wade Dooley, Graham Dawe, Gareth Chilcott and Hill, were suspended from the next match. And that was why Hill lost it in the dressing-room and started raging at the whole history of defeat and degradation at the hands of the Welsh nation. It was a major performance.

Somehow, we got the meeting back together before everyone collapsed in hysterical laughter. Next day, in the dressing-room, we started the communal warm-up. Will deputed a few individuals to take some exercises. Hilly started the stretching, then, suddenly, he started to go again, started the calls to war. This time, Will hastily intervened. 'Thanks for that, Hilly,' he said. 'Right Rob, you do the hamstrings.' The laughing died down again.

The truth is that after all those years of suffering in Cardiff and all the ruses used to try to sort out our mental approach, the spectre was demolished better by a few moments of hilarity. We lined up for the national anthems. 'Christ, not again,' I said to someone. I supposed we were desensitized to it, so the trick had worked.

I can let the *Daily Telegraph* sum up the match itself. 'Tedium takes edge off the banishment of the Welsh ghost.' We won 25–5, with a try from short range from Mike Teague and seven penalties by Hodgkinson. Paul Ackford and Wade Dooley had big games. I chased some kicks, made some tackles. Geoff Cooke was overwhelmed at the result, and went round the dressing-room with his congratulations.

But John Mason said in the *Telegraph*: 'England's efforts were about as exciting as watching the tide turn in Swansea Bay.' We were delighted with the win, we were unapologetic, we were on our way. Wales were clearly on their way to nowhere. In the end, and even though they took an early lead, the Cardiff fortress fell easily. Anyone who felt cheated of entertainment could always go out to Swansea Bay to watch the tide turn.

However, the match was only sandwiched that weekend

between the more important matters. It was a supreme irony that we had won at last and yet most of the papers next day, and on the Monday, hardly mentioned the match at all. There was another furious controversy.

Before the match, the BBC had been approached to ask for a contribution from them in exchange for the co-operation of the players in interviews around the match. The BBC refused. On the Thursday and Friday before the game, the squad raised the suggestion that we would simply not do post-match interviews of any sort, as a show of strength. The underlying reasons also concerned our frustration that the RFU would still not clarify what we were allowed to do in commercial deals, and some of the players also felt that certain journalists were harassing them with a barrage of calls. Geoff Cooke wanted to take the players' view but did not want it to get out of control. 'Let's be sensible about this,' he said. But some players hammered home the message.

I was unaware that a final decision had been made as I showered after the match and quickly left the dressing-room. British Gas, my employers, were sponsoring the game. They had asked if I might pop up to their hospitality suite afterwards to chat to the directors and some of our customers. It was an open-ended arrangement, there was no pressure, but I was perfectly willing to spend some time with them. I walked outside en route and saw Richard Hill giving a quick radio interview, in spite of the ban.

I spoke to the directors, some salesmen and some customers, then walked back to the hotel to prepare for the dinner. The hotel lobby seemed to be full of part-crazed pressmen scuttling back and forth. Tony Roche, of *Today*, came up. 'I suppose you're not going to talk to us either,' he said. That was when I realized that the agreement must have hardened in the dressing-room and that we were supposed to carry out the threat. I linked up with Jayne, who was as bewildered as me. Not that it bothered me much.

At the dinner, other sentiments took over. There was a strong anti-Neath faction in the Welsh squad complaining about the coaching of Ron Waldron, then in charge, and about the large number of Neath players in the team. It could hardly have helped the Welsh mood that the wine bottles on the table, produced specially for the event, had the score embossed on the labels. It was an unwanted reminder that Wales had conceded their biggest ever defeat in Cardiff. Waldron sat up on the balcony. His ears must have been burning. So was Kevin Phillips's stomach. Mick Skinner took Phillips on in a drinking competition, and Phillips quickly became a wreck. Neil Jenkins, the Welsh fly-half, asked how they got the cream in the profiteroles. The Bath contingent immediately marked Neil down as a raconteur to stand alongside our own Andy Reed.

The embers of the no-talk story were fanned. Dudley Wood told the press that he was incensed by the players' action. We had just signed up with a company run by Bob Willis, the old England fast bowler. It was a short-lived arrangement, and the fact that Willis had been involved in the approach to the BBC gave Wood the opening he needed to attack us. 'Nothing an agent does surprises me,' he said. Cooke was hauled over the coals by the RFU. There was even some talk of him losing the managership.

I have to say that the line that it was all a protest against harassment came later, an excuse to cover the tracks left by the request for money from the BBC. I have been called by many pressmen, but never harassed. All you have to do is to say that you don't have any comment and please don't ring again. I didn't see why the three line whip on the team needed to be imposed. Poor Hodgkinson had just beaten the world record and should have been able to look forward to many column inches of tribute laced with quotes from himself. But he was gagged, and the record passed almost unnoticed.

The match which really meant something for me was the next one, Scotland, The Revenge. We set up ourselves once again to be bland, methodical and structured. The final score was 21–12, but it was never as close as that. Peter Winterbottom and Dean Richards set up our only try, scored by Nigel Heslop in the right-hand corner after the ball had gone across the line. Hodgkinson kicked some more goals, Richards had a tremendous match, Ackford and Dooley were dominant in the line-out and the job was done. Andrew kicked into the corners to keep them pinned back. There were the odd murmurings in the press about lack of style. Tough. 'The style isn't pretty, but it gets results,' said Ian McGeechan, the Scottish coach. 'After last year's game they are conditioned to win and to cut down the mistakes.' Spot on.

So we had to beat Ireland for the Triple Crown, and we could ignore for the moment the fact that a new-look French team were also cruising along unbeaten. The Irish were having a poor season, but we all knew that previous form would count for nothing if the Irish had a chance to stop our momentum. There was a bad omen before the game. We decided to have a team haircut in Dublin. It was a risk. All I can say is that they obviously did not make a speciality of cutting Afro-Caribbean hair.

With eight minutes of the match remaining, the haircut had rather skipped from my mind. We were trailing 6–7, we were taking a few wrong options, the Irish forwards were outstanding and we could get none of the control we had enjoyed earlier in the season. Brian Moore said afterwards: 'We thought it might be Murrayfield all over again.' I disagreed, because I always thought we would win.

We did. Dean Richards made a drive, and Andrew and Hodgkinson sent Rory Underwood away. He still had it all to do, but he cut through and scored. Mike Teague scored again near the end, and we won 16–7. It was probably the most important of all Rory's tries. It meant we had won England's sixteenth Triple Crown – the first since 1980. At last, we had won something.

You could tell how much it meant because even Rory took alcohol that night. He was seen in public with a glass of champagne. It was a great night. After a round of night clubs, with all the team in a buoyant mood, we adjourned to the team hotel. Richard Hill's party piece is 'Ruby, Don't Take Your Love to Town'. He has sung it so many times over the years. This time, he was so drunk that he forgot the words. We had enough senses left to absorb the news that on the same afternoon in Paris, France had thrashed Wales. It meant that for the second season in succession, the final match would be a shoot-out with both teams going for the Grand Slam. It did wonders for rugby's profile.

It was a fantastic day, too. France scored by far the best try I have ever seen, partly because I misjudged the move in defence. Both teams played some superb rugby – France had to. England's forwards were outstanding, Hilly and Andrew kept turning the screws with kicks. And England, finally, won the Grand Slam. Scotland was almost forgotten; after seasons of threatening to win something, then winning nothing, we had won everything. People started talking about us as possible world champions, not that anyone in the England camp was looking that far ahead. The sense of relief afterwards was incredible.

Yet again, we knew that we had to restrict France and Serge Blanco, so that they only had the ball in certain areas where they could do no damage. Rob Andrew would kick into the box and to the posts, Richard Hill would chip into the box. We also tried to play as much rugby as possible on the right of the field, because we felt we were a better team moving right to left and would score more tries that way.

That was the theory. When Blanco caught a missed kick from Hodgkinson behind the French line there was nothing on. When the move was developing, still deep inside the French twenty-two, I came across with Rob Andrew inside me. I could have left Blanco and gone for the man outside but I was worried that Blanco would run round Rob Andrew, who was inside me. He certainly had the pace to. I came in for Blanco, who got his pass away. Lafond and Camberabero took it on, Sella and Camberabero again handled as the move progressed upfield. Then, Camberabero launched the perfect cross-kick, Philippe Saint-André came up the middle of the field and picked up the ball and scored at the posts. It didn't matter how disappointed we were. It was impossible not to admire the try.

We would not match that sort of try but we stayed calm. The forwards re-established their season-long dominance. It was 9–9 after half an hour, then we scored our try. Mike Teague did wonders to cross the advantage line after being caught from a scrum. When the ball came across line, I was running close to Will so Rob missed me out and passed on to Hodgkinson. Hodgy flicked the ball on to Rory, who was still marked by Jean-Baptiste Lafond. He only had a few yards to work in. He straightened, then twisted away to the outside. He shoved away a weak effort by Lafond and ran on to score. We were still 21–13 ahead with one minute of normal time to go. Franck Mesnel scored in the dying stages to make it 21–19. That gave us some anxious moments.

When the whistle went, I threw my arms up in the air, hugged a few people, then everything became dark with onrushing supporters. We sprinted off, guzzled champagne in the dressing-room, posed for some delirious pictures and, basically, went crazy. Blanco made a nice speech at the Hilton. So they told me next day.

The newspapers went overboard. They all seemed to choose one key man from the triumphant season and started to prognosticate on our chances in the World Cup, which was then less than six months ahead. Most of them singled out Carling but in a sense, he had been innocuous during the season. All the tactical responsibilities had been taken by Hill and Andrew and, for me, Hill was the central figure of the whole season, whether with his kicking or tactical control.

Geoff Cooke had a major influence off the field; and Roger Uttley, the coach? I've no idea. Roger tended to leave the backs to themselves and disappeared with the forwards. To me, he was just the big ugly bastard who looked after the pack.

As for the forwards, even though Brian Moore seemed to take most of the media space, the key forward for me was unquestionably Paul Ackford. As a lock he was years ahead of his time. He had so much to give and his understanding of his position was light years ahead of any other lock in the game. He was so strong and so tough mentally. I once told him that I didn't think he challenged strongly enough when the opposition threw the ball into the line-out. 'What do you know about it?' he said. It was a shame that he went into the media after the World Cup. He could express himself so well, and I saw him more as a coach. The more videos you watch of Ackers, the more you grasp what a complete player he was.

Moore was certainly high-profile and he did some things extremely well. It was a problem to assess him, because I have always thought Graham Dawe the better player. Moore was aggressive during the season, but to me he did not seem as hard as Dawe, and the likes of Uli Schmidt of South Africa or some of the French hookers of the era. He was certainly a showman, however, and was the self-elected spokesman of the squad in the endless arguments with the RFU.

The team changed in character, too. When I came into the squad we were split into forwards and backs. We often trained separately, we had different philosophies. We took the piss out of each other. By the end of the Grand Slam season we thought as one. The team was built around the half-backs and the back row, but the forwards wanted to know what moves the backs were making.

Personal goals were put to one side. We had played terrific rugby in 1990, and if I had the choice, that is the style I would have preferred. But I was as anxious for success as anyone. I was in agreement with the conservative policy, even though it meant that I lost some of my individualism and, for the first time in my career, stopped scoring tries at the same rate. I tended to go out not to make mistakes, because no one wanted to be the player who gave away the Grand Slam. It might all have been different but for Murrayfield 1990. But in any case, our Slam gave an incredible boost to the game in England. Interest was at an all-time high, sponsors were battering down the door at Twickenham to get into the game. It may not have been a stylish Grand Slam, but we gave back to English rugby a self-respect which it had not enjoyed for years.

The World Cup of 1991 was obviously the biggest month in the history of rugby. I have always put British Lions tours ahead of all other experiences I have had in the game, and I would have to sit down quietly to assess my second World Cup, in South Africa in 1995, to make up my mind whether the tournament would take precedence over the Lions in my own list.

Even though the English group matches all took place at Twickenham, the backdrop was different. Instead of making camp at the Petersham Hotel on the top of Richmond Hill, we stayed at the Tylney Hall Hotel, in a beautiful location outside Basingstoke. There were training facilities nearby, and there was a golf course next to the hotel grounds. Jon Webb distinguished himself with his tee shot when we had a golf day there just before the tournament. His drive disappeared out of bounds, so he teed up again and no one thought any more of it – until a van pulled into the car park of the golf club with a hole in the driver's side window. The driver calmed down when he realized who we were, but it must have seemed to him like a bullet coming through his window. They also caught me on the dummy golf ball. I swung on the first tee and the ball exploded in a puff of dust.

And as for the rugby, the squad itself was fit and confident. The recent tour to Australia and Fiji had been disastrous from the point of view of results but, as Geoff Cooke kept telling everyone, results were not the real point of the exercise, and it was all of fantastic benefit for our World Cup plans. I don't know how many were convinced.

The first section of the Fijian leg was like living in paradise. We had already been beaten by Queensland and New South Wales when we moved on Fiji and to the Sheraton, on the seafront near Nadi. We were treated like royalty; there were watersports and cocktails, everything we needed was on the complex, except the training fields.

It was a rude awakening to move on to Suva, the capital, for the Test, after the midweek team had lost to Fiji 'B' at Lautoka. Suva was less glamorous, and the Fijian team, who were typically big and hard, caused us problems early on. We did win the Test by 28–11, Rob Andrew scoring his first try for England with a sizzling burst from six inches. Jeff Probyn and Rory Underwood also scored and we put in a big finish. The weather was also in our favour. The day before the match, the temperature had been in the 90s. But heavy rain fell overnight, and the temperature at kick-off was no worse than on an English spring day.

It was still too much for Mike Teague. He had been suffering from a nasty viral infection and a bad stomach. He decided to play, but when we got together at half-time, he looked terrible. He was pale, gaunt and sweating. He looked at us. 'Lads,' he said, 'I've given my all. I can't go on.' Normally we would have felt sorry for him, but the B movie script he used in telling us came over so hilariously that we almost fell about laughing in our huddle. It was just Teague being honest, Teague to a T. He tottered off and Mick Skinner arrived for the second half.

We almost had severe problems off the field in Suva. We had been invited to Mad Harry's Nightclub. When we arrived, we were warmly welcomed by the manager but a bit taken aback by the gigantic transvestite who was there too. It was certainly one of the most obvious transvestites I have ever seen – huge Adam's apple, moustache and stubble. You had to work hard to ignore his fluttering eyelashes.

We did come badly unstuck in the Test against Australia at the Sydney Football Stadium. We tried to expand our game on the fast pitch. It was quite successful for a while. I scored a try in the first half. I had some space out on the left and was running down the touch-line. Willie Ofahengaue came across, and it was obvious he was going to try to dump me into the crowd. When he was ten yards away he began to lower his head for the final charge. I checked, and almost stopped. Willie went past and I scored. Some of our other moves came off pretty well, too.

But we were new to that style of game. Australia had been playing it for a long time and they scored five tries, to win the match 40–15. It seemed to me that every time they worked themselves into a try-scoring position, they scored. Every one of the back-row moves from scrums seemed to work.

At Basingstoke as the World Cup tournament approached, our confidence grew, with a more familiar pattern of play on the blackboard – based around the old faithfuls, Hill and Andrew. I also trained religiously; I actually followed many of the training charts which Twickenham sent us. Richard Hill and I worked together throughout the months leading up to the tournament. It was a stage on which I really wanted to play well; I realized that if I brought my fitness levels up then I could do what I do more often. Practically the only reversion came when some of us celebrated Mike Teague's birthday with a vengeance at a pub near Basingstoke.

Certainly, there was a tremendous sense of dedication and purpose in the team. We were European champions, the tournament was to take place in Europe, and if we kept going we would play most of our matches at home, including, if we stayed that long, the final. The planning of Geoff Cooke and Roger Uttley, together with Will Carling, Don Rutherford of the RFU and all the fitness advisers, was meticulous. The aim was nothing less than to make us world champions. We have to live with the fact that we came near enough to achieving that ambition, that the ultimate prize was there for the taking. And we did not take it.

Naturally, after the months of build-up, you are desperate for action. It does not matter how beautiful your surroundings, they can still be a prison if you are confined there long enough. It was a hard slog in training; there was a mountain of media interviews to get through;

there was a mountain of PR work and pictures with children. All that was fine, but wearing.

It was vital that we won the first game, against New Zealand, so that we would finish top of the group; the group runner-up would have to play a quarter-final in Paris against the French, assuming that they won their group. The World Cup was to be the swansong for Serge Blanco, so it did not take a crystal ball to work out that France would be fired up on Serge's behalf.

And the prospect quickly became a certainty, because we lost to New Zealand. I had the impression en route to the game that things would not go well. Wherever we went in the World Cup, with the exception of the toilet, it seemed that a TV camera was pointed at us. ITV were covering the event, and one of their cameramen, who was a nice guy, dogged us for the whole four or so weeks. On the bus to Twickenham for the New Zealand game, it struck me that all the growling and grimacing was simply going through the motions for the camera, not the real thing. It seemed to me that the boys were putting on a 'thinking deeply about the game' act whenever the lens was shoved in their face.

If the New Zealand game had been a pointer for the rest of the tournament, then the whole thing would have been a disaster. It was a terrible game, ruined by penalty awards, and we never got to grips with New Zealand at all. Michael Jones scored their try and we lost 18–12. We then beat Italy by 36–6. I scored two of our four tries, one an individual effort which has been replayed a fair bit. I should never have got there. The commentators said that I weaved in and out like a magician. In fact, I ran across and across, and only straightened at the very end. I should have been tackled. We went on to beat the United States by 37–9, with Halliday given a run in the centre alongside Carling – just to keep the old boy's hand in. We managed to give all the squad a game except poor David Pears and Dewi Morris, who never took the field in any World Cup match.

So we qualified second. France beat Canada, Romania and Fiji to win their group and the quarter-finals were set. We finally broke camp at Basingstoke, spent a few days in Jersey with our wives and girlfriends for a welcome break. One afternoon, after returning from golf for dinner, we decided to extend the evening to take in a night club. When we got back to the hotel, we saw an unbelievable sight.

Peter Winterbottom was standing in the bar in an almost impossible position. He was rigid from toes to waist but almost at right angles above that. He was beyond paralytic. He was talking to people, pointing his finger at them and saying 'I love you.' Next day, owing to a mixture of hangover and embarrassment, he never even surfaced. It was the first time many of us had seen the hard man of the back row in such a state. Dewi Morris captured the incident for posterity on a camcorder.

Then we set off for Paris – and everything that Serge and company could throw at us. And they threw quite a bit. It was an incredibly intense match, and we could thank our forwards for a fantastically gutsy effort and the whole team for an outstanding performance under pressure. It was the day when even the supporters of the Southern Hemisphere teams realized we were contenders. It was the day we started to believe it ourselves. I made a break to give Rory a try in the early stages, but there were times when France came after us in waves. Will scored a try at the end to seal it. It was a fantastic victory. I celebrated for two whole days. There was also a major fuss after Daniel Dubroca, the French coach, manhandled Dave Bishop, the referee, in the tunnel after the game. The newspapers went to town on the incident. In the England camp, we could hardly have cared less. We were in the semi-final, against Scotland. The Scots had played well in their semi-final to beat Western Samoa.

We had to win at all costs at Murrayfield. We are seriously unwelcome there. I felt even worse after our first night in the city. I lost the spoof when we were having an Indian meal, and had to eat the dish of chilli pickles. But this time, there was not quite the ill-feeling before the game that there had been in 1990. We were ready. They still had their back row of Calder, White and Jeffrey, but our control in the forwards was complete. We won 9–6. 'A colossal effort by a superlative pack,' said one paper. Afterwards, we were heavily criticized for not expanding our game and for giving Scotland a chance which they did not deserve on the run of play. Indeed, Gavin Hastings had an easy penalty to put Scotland in front inside the last quarter, and I accept that if Scotland had won we would have been kicking ourselves for years. As Gavin went through his preparations I was talking to Rory about our next move when the penalty went over. But when I turned round he had missed it. Rob dropped the goal which won us the match only seven minutes before the end. I can also remember Will's leadership. At one stage of the match he brought us together. 'Right,' he said. 'We've got to step up the pace.' Immediately after he said it, Scotland upped the pace and put us under real pressure. Good timing by Will.

It was a great feeling to be in the final, and to have beaten the Scots to get there. The Scots responded by arriving at the final wearing Australian scarves. We were not amused.

The media barrage about 'boring England' rumbled on, although at least some of the papers picked up the triumphant mood among English rugby supporters. The tournament was made as well. It needed England to get through to the final, so that interest and commercial activity stayed at fever pitch. Australia had played some brilliant stuff, especially when beating New Zealand in Dublin one day after our semi. As a spectacle, it outshone our game. It all gave David Campese the ideal opportunity to have a go at us for being boring, and put up the backs of the players who could not take his sniping. I did not give a damn about the accusations, and Campo never got under my skin.

The week was exciting, but it felt that even time for proper preparation was limited. We were back at our regular home from home, the Petersham Hotel, and training at the Stoop Memorial Ground. The telephone was ringing in the team room all the time; the media were queueing for interviews. It took Geoff Cooke ages to get rid of a reporter from the *Mail* who had gatecrashed. There were hordes of photographers every time we left the hotel. I have never been involved in a week like that, for hype and pressure, in my life.

And in that mad week we lost the final. History shows that we lost by 12–6 and that Australia became world champions. What it does not show is that England had enough of the match to have won with something to spare.

The media certainly had a hand, with their blanket criticism after the semi-final. It is a shame we do not have the Irish nature. Which Irishman, in the team, in the media or in the country, would have given a stuff if Ireland had got through to the final playing boring rugby? Ireland played no great rugby in the tournament, they were knocked out by Australia, the better side, in the quarter-final, and yet everyone hailed them as heroes. In the same way the public there go bananas when Jack Charlton's soccer team returns home after yet another World Cup failure. It is typical of the differences. If the public in England had that same attitude towards English teams then we would all be twice the teams we are. I think the media pressure subconsciously told, and that we were driven towards playing a more expansive game than we really wanted.

But there were also sound technical grounds to change the style which had given us a Grand Slam and which had taken us into the final of the ultimate tournament – or so we thought. Our hierarchy reckoned that we would have to change tactics because we could not expect to dominate the line-out, with McCall, Eales and Coker in the Australian team. And indeed, they seemed to think that it was doubtful if we would win our fair share of possession at all.

We worked out that we had to make the most of our possession. We planned that the half-backs would pass the ball on. We even worked on extravagant new moves. We lined up in training with me standing at full-back so that I could be one of two deep runners – Rory was the other. Jon Webb lined up in the centre. We tried that formation twice in the final itself. Jason Little read it perfectly each time and tackled me on both occasions. So much for that.

The whole match had an unreal air. Right from the start, it was obvious that our fears about possession were not coming true. Dooley dominated John Eales in the line-out, and we won plenty of good possession from all phases. The statistics show that we gave Australia something of a beating in the forwards. Yet we did not switch plans. We desperately needed to nurse the play a bit, but the half-backs kept passing it on, we kept spreading the ball.

Richard Hill and Rob Andrew became a little locked in; there was a Plan A, but there was no real Plan B. It is easy to criticize Will as captain for not changing the tactics, but you also have to remember that very few teams actually do change tactics substantially in a match. You are either a rucking team or a mauling team; a kicking team or an attacking team. It is difficult to switch. The All Blacks do sometimes switch their game, but that usually consists of nothing more than playing their traditional game much quicker.

I was not objecting to all possession, but the Australians' defence was excellent. We had always thought of Jason Little as the weak link in the midfield, but on the day he was outstanding. We almost got Rory away once or twice, but Australia scored their try when Tony Daly went over from close range, and in a bizarre whirl of attack, we went down to defeat and finished as second best in the world.

Many of the players were desperately upset, especially Mike Teague and a few of the forwards, who had given their all. It does not live with me. I was disappointed, a little bemused by the way we played. But I threw it all out with the waste paper.

At the dinner that night, a farcical affair with thousands of officials attending and with the players shoved up into the back of the room, a guy came up and asked me to sign his menu. I was in the middle of dinner so I said, politely, that I would be delighted to sign if he came back a bit later.

'Do you know who I am?' he said. 'I am a reporter from the *Sun*, and I'll write that it was you who lost the final.' Something along those lines duly appeared in the *Sun* – the rugby-lover's bible.

England players from past years will be furious to hear me say it, and so will players England met in the Five Nations of 1992; but our Grand Slam that season, the first time any team had managed back-to-back Grand Slams since England did it in 1913 and 1914, was a formality. We were still on a high after the World Cup; had tried to forget the chance we missed in the final. Only Paul Ackford had actually retired after the World Cup, even though there had been rumours of several others leaving. We all felt that the middle of the season was a strange time to retire, given that we had all worked so incredibly hard on fitness.

Our forwards were so dominant in Europe that we could afford to come slightly out of our shell. There were other changes. Roger Uttley had departed, and Richard Best, who had been in the wings for some time, now stepped up. So did Dewi Morris. Richard Hill was made a scapegoat for the World Cup final, and ejected from the team, which was totally unfair. Martin Bayfield, who had first played in the Test in Sydney in 1991, came in alongside big Wade. We were a little wary that Ackers was no longer there. But soon, in the momentum of the season, we forgot the departed. You just get on with it.

So we were all back at Lanzarote in the New Year of 1992. We still liked to give the impression that some of the newspaper articles were true and that we were indeed totally dedicated to training and never touched a drop. Some of the writers actually fell for all that. At Lanzarote one morning, neither Skinner nor Teague arrived for the start of training. They staggered along later. Teague looked terrible. 'We've been on it large,' he said. They had to undergo the normal punishment. They had to run through a line of players holding tackle pads and be assaulted all the way along.

It was a red-letter trip because Jon Hall had fought his way back into the squad after his injuries. It was also the first opportunity to assess Best in the top role, especially now that Cooke had retreated from his early days when he used to fancy a bit of coaching along with the administrative duties. It was a role Best was to hold right through until the summer of 1994, when Jack Rowell pushed him out and took over the coaching reins.

At first, I got on extremely well with him. He was quite open. He used to say that there wasn't much he could teach a bunch of players like us. He tried hard to get the forwards to think quicker, and to become more complete footballers; to improve the presentation of the ball from the forwards to the scrum-half; to get everyone to grasp the difference between good ball and bad ball.

Best's trademark has always been a blast of abuse for wrongdoers followed by orders for them to run around the posts as a punishment. He tried to embarrass and even humiliate players to make his point. I always refused point blank to run around the posts. I could see nothing more childish. Once at Twickenham in training, someone passed me a ball around my laces. I dropped it and Besty told me to run around the posts. I told him to send the guy who made the bad pass. From then, he tended not to pick on me in case there was a scene, because he knew I'd say no.

He became more confident as the seasons went on. He had the capacity to make you think about the game; he would demand that the training drills be done under pressure, close to match conditions. He was good with small groups, good running little workshops. To the backs he had little to offer from the technical point of view, and although he had a fresh approach when he came in, he did not seem to retain that freshness. He was a casualty of Jack Rowell's new regime in 1994.

His first Five Nations match was at Murrayfield, nearly two years on from the infamous day. We were reminded of that match when it was relived on TV, in the papers and in our nightmares. We were reminded of it when we returned to the huge dressing-rooms and recalled with a shudder the image of the team silent and shell-shocked. Elsewhere in the world on the rugby circuit, I have dozed off in team meetings and occasionally drifted in training sessions. In Edinburgh, I paid close attention to everything.

As well as the other changes, we were now entering a Five Nations with Simon Hodgkinson departed and Jon Webb reinstalled at full-back. Halliday had also forced his way back on the wing. I looked forward to the extra dimension Webb could offer us in pace from the back, even if he did seem to have become a little sidetracked. He had applied himself so much to his kicking that the other side of his game had fallen into some disuse. He used to run great lines, come through into the line at pace and run on to score, but he was in some danger of neglecting that element.

He had also become incredibly analytical. Indeed, Stuart Barnes and I told him at Bath that he had started to analyse things too much. Nevertheless, you felt safer with him there because he was bigger than Hodgy, and his kicking had come good. It would be difficult to say at the time that you felt safer with Bayfield. He was taking the place of a legend, and was so slight that you thought he might snap at any moment. He looked like a giant Bambi. Still, he was 6′ 10″ and the Scots line-out forwards weren't. So there.

We were never in real trouble in any of the four matches. In every one of the games, I turned to Will with around 20 minutes to go and said that I had never imagined how easy it would be. Scotland had lost Finlay Calder, and also John Jeffrey. Under their free and easy rules of eligibility, they had brought in Neil 'Eddie' Edwards of Harlequins. They ran on to the field this time, to complete the differences.

We had a bit of trouble with the Scots pack, who once pushed us over our line for a try. But not much. Rory scored down the left, and in the second half a great run by Halliday sent Dewi Morris over. However, we never really established authority until Dean Richards arrived. He had been left on the bench in favour of Tim Rodber, but when Rodber left with spinal concussion, the difference in the England pack was incredible. The final score was 25–7. I loved every last point.

Against the Irish at Twickenham, we turned the clock back a year or two. We won 38–9, Webb scoring in the opening seconds, and finishing with a tally of 22 points. Rory, Hallers, Dewi and Webb (again) added further tries. Ireland were weak. When we finished with them, they were even weaker.

The fuss that broke after the quarter-final match in Paris in the World Cup was nothing to the storm that followed the next meeting only a few months later. This time, England gave one of their great forward displays. We crucified the French pack, scored four tries and won 31–13.

The French lost more than the match. 'French rugby crashed in flames,' as a London newspaper said. You could see it in their eyes that they were going, and towards the end they went completely. I did not see Grégoire Lascubé treading on Bayfield, but Steve Hilditch, the referee, sent him off. The French became ever more lunatic. Jeff Tordo, their flanker, had come into the front row to take the place of Lascubé. You could tell as the next scrum formed up that the French were going to dive in head first. Jeff Probyn took the precaution of lowering his head, so that he took the butt on the top; the scrum broke up in fighting and Vincent Moscato, the French hooker, followed Lascubé down the tunnel. The atmosphere at the dinner that night was frosty. Not that we cared.

For years, other teams had traded on the weakness of England forwards. They had worked out that you could punch the lights out of the England forwards and they would not retaliate. But in the 1990s, with the likes of Skinner and Dooley around, and with Ackford's influence remaining even after the man himself had departed, they were a different bunch. Geoff Cooke always argued strongly against individual action. He used to say: 'Don't do it, don't do it. If you are caught it might end your international career. Sort it out collectively.' In that match, France were still trying the cheap shots. It was a mental battle, which we won.

We were back at the Petersham for the final match of the season, needing to beat Wales to win the Grand Slam, and not even optimistic Welshmen thought they would stop us. That was the indication of the new confidence and strength of the team.

John Olver, who had endured years on the bench, had recently been joined by Neil Hynes, the former Orrell loose-head. They roomed together. Two days before the match, they entered their room together and there, gleaming on the bed, were two shirts in wrappers. In fact, though they looked good as new, Olver had sent them down to the laundry earlier.

Hynes's eyes lit up. 'Where did you get those from?' he said. Olver explained that on request the hotel would obtain a couple of shirts from a shop in Richmond and send them up – and that they could be charged to the Rugby Football Union's bill. All you had to do was to give the receptionist a call.

Olver carefully primed the receptionist. Hynes rang down, asked for two shirts to be sent up and charged to the RFU bill. Olver explained the wheeze to Cooke and Carling and sat back to await developments. At breakfast next day in the team room, Cooke stood up and asked to make an announcement. A serious matter had come to his attention, he said. Once again, there had been a case of a player abusing the facilities and putting items on the RFU tab. He explained that unless the culprit identified himself, all team expenses for the weekend would be stopped.

Halliday, not in on the joke, exploded. 'Olver!' he shouted. 'It's fucking you again. You always have to ruin it for other people. Stand up and admit it!' Olver had to get up and defend himself. The word had spread to a few more players, and Webb and Winterbottom both started to crack. Cooke pulled himself together and reiterated the demand. The breakfast gathering broke up, gradually. Hynes pulled himself together, went up to Cooke, admitted the crime and apologized. Everyone collapsed. Hynes still did not grasp the wind-up. He was seen eventually disappearing up to his room to apologize to Olver for grassing.

By this time, home wins over Wales were routine. We beat them 24–0 and the whole occasion was much more flat than it had been when we won the first Grand Slam against the French. Carling scored in the opening minutes after a high kick. Skinner and even Dooley also scored tries. The Welsh went out to play a negative game, to keep the score down, but they didn't even manage that.

The atmosphere between the teams at the dinner was very good, but it was obvious that the old morale was still missing from the Welsh ranks. The international season ended with England dominant and with most of the players well able to take the march on into the future. Talk of a Grand Slam treble, the first ever, began in the media. We secretly began to dream about it ourselves.

9
Blinded by the Laws
In the pocket of decline; Carling's England, 1992–94

The high point came when Dewi Morris threw out a bad pass. Barnes had to reach high for it and it pushed him on to the back foot. Suddenly, he made an amazing break out of nothing. He shot up in the middle of the field in the sort of move Bath followers had been thrilling to for years. He was helped by the very fact that the bad pass had drawn the defence on to him. All he had to do was step to wrongfoot them and he was away. Easy for him, though perhaps not for lesser players.

As far as I was concerned, it was a matter of reacting and anticipating. I came up wide to his left and it was then a question of when he decided to pass and whether the pass would be perfect enough for me to stretch for it. Perfect? It was the best pass he ever threw. Left was his best side. He is not so good at passing to his right, but then who is?

I was in full stride when I took the ball. I did not have to chop and change. I was in my flow. Scott Hastings was there, trying to recover and catch up. I left him behind. I contemplated chipping the ball over the head of Gavin Hastings because Tony Stanger, Rory's opposite number, was still there marking his man. I kept running and held on, and held on, hoping that either Gavin would fall over or that Rory would change his line on Stanger.

Suddenly, Stanger came in towards me. I could hardly believe it. When he came I slipped the ball to Rory, and Rory scored. The crowd erupted, of course. They had seen so few tries of that sort from us since 1990.

I can't have had all my wits about me, because when I was running back I thought that it was Tony I had put in for the try, not Rory. I thought that Tony's reaction was rather muted when I went up to receive his thanks. I was winking at him, thinking he would be overwhelmed by what Barnesie and I had done for him. Then I worked out that Rory had scored. It all happened at a million miles an hour, but also in a special kind of slow motion. Welcome back, Stuart.

At last, when we prepared for the start of the 1992–93 season we no longer had to thrash ourselves with the fact that we had never won anything. We had two consecutive Grand Slams, we had the momentum, we were looked upon in European rugby with the same envy that Wales were looked upon in the 1970s. It was tremendous to be part of it all.

The mental picture had changed as we planned. Now we had to find new goals and new motivations. The planning for the season was simply to win the Grand Slam again – not just to repeat, but to 'three-peat', as they say in America. It had never been done before, so a place in history was reserved for us if we did it. We came out with all the old rubbish about taking one game at a time, but it was difficult not to think beyond that.

If you looked at the Five Nations season, it seemed that Wales were still weak, Ireland were showing no signs at all of getting their squad together; France were rebuilding, true, but in any case, we were down to play them at home at Twickenham, where they are never happy and sometimes overawed; and the Scots appeared to be beatable at home without too much trouble. They were still struggling to replace the experienced forwards who had left the game in the past two seasons. So were thinking about the 'three-peat' months ahead. It was impossible not to.

People asked me if the inner hunger was still there now that we had achieved some success. Who cared? It made no difference to me what we had done or not done. My motivation was not affected by what had just happened. I like being part of successful teams, and when you have tasted that success you want it to continue and you work for it. That is always the Bath attitude. It is not so much a feeling of power, or superiority. It is just nice to win.

In the event, all those hopes came to nothing. The team lost momentum, and although we beat Canada on a sunny day at Wembley, and beat South Africa in a dark monsoon at Twickenham, we hobbled through the Five Nations and finished in the middle of the table, below France, the champions, and even below the Scots on points difference. Enough of the players kept their form as individuals to make selection for the British Lions tour of New Zealand at the end of the season – that tour was unquestionably one of my major goals for the season – but the assurance had gone.

Even in the season after, when I was on the sidelines waiting for my groin injury to clear up, and even though England beat New Zealand in a tremendous battle at Twickenham, we struggled still. We won in Paris, but we were lucky to beat Scotland in Edinburgh; we somehow managed the incredible feat of losing at home to Ireland, and even though we recovered slightly to beat Wales, we did not score enough points to stop an average Welsh team winning the Five Nations.

By that time, all the predictions of our keenest supporters and all the fears of our keenest enemies – that we would dominate the Five Nations for years and years to come – had crumbled to dust.

Our most difficult opposition was not met on the field. It was a group of men in suits – the International Rugby Board's laws committee. For the start of the 1992–93 season a new law was brought in which was meant to keep rugby flowing. The law stated, basically, that if the ball failed to emerge from rucks and mauls, then the team which did not take the ball in was given the scrum. Beforehand, the team that was moving forward was given the scrum.

The storm of opposition provoked by the law change brought about a partial climb-down two years later when the turnover law, as it became known, was reduced to apply only to the maul, no longer the ruck. My own view is that the laws threatened to make the game a clone of rugby league, moving us towards a smaller pack of running forwards to make inroads, to try to create some space for the backs. That was the theory. In an ideal world they might have worked. But rugby will never be an ideal world, and no team does have eight Ben Clarkes or eight Steve Ojomohs to call upon.

And the laws seemed to have the opposite effect to the one intended. They certainly created a heavily populated pitch. David Campese's reaction was to say that he had never been tackled by so many prop forwards in his life. When the ball came back he found them all hanging around because they no longer had to commit themselves to the rucks and mauls.

But whatever its merits or otherwise, the law was there, and there was nothing we could do except work at it and adapt. And that was where the English momentum died. We could not adapt; or at least, it took us two years to do so. The law meant that the ball was in play for longer, so we could not plan our game with the same rigidity. More had to be done off the cuff, and the forwards had to change their style and their attitudes. Geoff Cooke and Dick Best had to thrash out a new-look England to take the place of the pre-programmed England.

Not to put down England forwards, but the reason why England will never be a consistent force in the game at the same level of achievement as New Zealand is the mentality which exists among English forwards. To me, their job is to win the ball, present it in a certain way and then do it again and again. The new laws put a premium on such play. But generally, English forwards have always been set-piece oriented and slow to adapt.

But even if a new breed of forwards like Clarke and Ojomoh were coming through, before we could thrash out our new approach we had to find out what on earth our new approach was. The England squad in that early part of the season was more like a debating chamber than a focused operation making clear decisions.

In the sessions when we gathered to put together our new game plan, too many of the forwards always seemed to have too much to say (they would probably say the same about the backs). It seemed to me that a New Zealand coach would come to the meetings with his strategy worked out. He would say: 'This is what we are going to do.' There would be no comeback, no democracy. If the coach isn't good enough to take charge in that fashion then he shouldn't be there in the first place. With everyone having their own opinions on how we should get round the new law, how it could be handled and how it could be turned to our advantage, there was a kind of mayhem. As a rugby nation, we are bad at the whole business.

The talking shop went on and on. Martin Bayfield was now established in the team and a few of the older forwards, like Jeff Probyn, Wade Dooley and Mike Teague, were beginning to think about retiring. Perhaps the old dogs were put off a bit by the new tricks. But at every team gathering that season, we would have our discussion as a squad. Geoff Cooke would close the meeting, outlining the programme for the next day, and we would get ready to disperse.

But then, Besty would ask the forwards to stay behind a little longer. Every time we trained, the forwards would be asked to stay back like schoolkids in detention. It was only much later in the season that Numbers 9 and 10 were asked to attend those exclusive forward meetings too, which suggested that they were having difficulties with their interminable thrashing-out procedures.

Brian Moore and Dean Richards were among the major influences, and Peter Winterbottom, who had never been used enough by Cooke, was often consulted too. If Brian was ever made England captain then he could die happy. Even as pack leader at the time, he could call all his little meetings. My opinion is that Dean Richards should always have been our pack leader. I may not be too close to the forward battle, but he is always the central figure, and the memory of what he did to the whole course of the match at Murrayfield in 1992, when Tim Rodber went off and Dino took it by the scruff of the neck, should have convinced anyone. There are very few forwards around in the game today who can make that sort of difference.

In the whole season, however, despite all the discussion, we never adapted to the new laws and we never got over the hurdle of having too many voices discussing how to do so. But we did not have the excuse that it was impossible to do. At Bath, we did have forwards who could adapt and a few strong characters, especially Jack Rowell, who could lay down the law for everyone else to follow. We scored a hatful of tries that season, we broke all our points records. I could not understand for the life of me why Cooke and Best did not take some of what we achieved at Bath and put it to effect in England colours.

We have always played a running game at Bath, especially in the forwards. That season, Nigel Redman turned back the clock to become 21 again. He was everywhere, a lifeline to the whole team. People like Redman, Graham Dawe and Andy Reed could get about the field and make the runs; they were mobile and adaptable. We also had the players like Jon Hall and Andy Robinson who could stop the flow of the other team. In the England team, at least we had Dean Richards, who could have stemmed the flow of most things; but we never tried to plant elements of the Bath approach.

It was still a joy to play for England that season; the team spirit remained high even though new faces were gradually easing their way into the exclusive club atmosphere we had formed in the Grand Slams. It was a shame that we drifted off course because of a few people in committee rooms and what could be called an English disease of non-adaptability.

The season began with a dummy called Will Carling. Our match against Canada was moved from Twickenham, where rebuilding of the East Stand side was proceeding, to Wembley. The press made a big deal of the temporary switch. Madame Tussaud's brought to one of our training sessions their latest waxwork, of captain Will. It was an excellent likeness. I wondered aloud to the press if that version of Will would pass to me more than the real one. They duly reported it and put it in their papers, and Geoff Cooke had a word with me, but only in passing.

The surface at Wembley was fantastic. It was cut short, far better to play on than Twickenham's jungle-length grass. It was only at the start of the 1994–95 season that the RFU finally announced that they were going to crop the grass shorter. It was long overdue.

But although it was an experience playing at Wembley, it felt unfamiliar, and therefore not essentially like a home match. We beat Canada 26–13, with two tries from Ian Hunter, one by Peter Winterbottom and one by me. I was goalhanging down the left wing and I managed to squeeze over in the corner in the tackle. Canada played well, but it was difficult to get properly motivated. Will and Geoff have always worked very hard on getting the mental side right, and at getting the team into the correct psychological frame for the task to come, whatever it might be. But if you know before the match that you are almost definitely going to win, then that mental edge is harder to find. Tony Underwood had begun a campaign to make the Lions party at the end of the season and he was buzzing around the field to good effect. Some of the others were off the pace on the day. We let Graf, the Canadian scrum-half, in for a try and it all left us with lots to work on – and still talking about the elusive formula to crack the new laws.

South Africa made a tour of France and England that autumn, but it was still too early in their come-back to international rugby for them to be a brilliant side. And with their forward-dominated game they had even more trouble than England in adapting to the new style required by the laws. They had managed to draw the Test series with France at 1–1 before they arrived in England, chiefly because France played disastrously in the first Test; but they had lost four of their other matches in France. They improved after arriving in England. They won their three non-Test matches. But they lost the Test itself.

We were 16–8 down and our forwards were in some trouble. But they sorted themselves out and we came back strongly. In the end the South Africans could not handle the pressure – especially the pressure of Rob Andrew's high kicks in the dark and the wet. Rory and Tony Underwood had already scored a great try in the first half; Will and Dewi Morris scored a try each when South Africa panicked under the falling ball, and I scored without a South African in sight when Rob chipped the ball over the midfield. I ran on to a perfect kick and caught it on the full for a satisfying try.

By this time, the Lanzarote trip was a piece of cake for us old hands. Yet there was a disappointing aspect this time because we actually went to the usual La Santa complex over the New Year period, and therefore couldn't spend New Year's Eve with our families – for many people it is the best party of the year, and it caused a certain amount of bad feeling that we were forced to miss out.

We spent some time in a square in Lanzarote, watching as the New Year celebrations began to get into top gear. All the poppers went off and Stuart Barnes and I looked at each other. We had not even had a drink to celebrate. No words passed between us. Then we looked towards a night club on the edge of the square. Jason Leonard was there too. He caught the direction of our glances. Still, no one had said a word. 'I'm coming too,' said Jason, interpreting perfectly.

It was a major night. We arrived back at the La Santa complex at 4.30 in the morning. That day, it was the annual VO2 test. Barnes was disgusted to learn afterwards that I had achieved a PB for the test; he managed a PW, a personal worst.

The Five Nations saw us stagger along. All the assurance of the past two seasons had largely disappeared. We were extremely lucky to beat France at Twickenham. We gave Philippe Saint-André two tries through defensive mistakes, notably when Jon Webb dropped an easy ball to let him in for the first; we also defended badly for the second. A high kick was dropping behind our line and Saint-André jumped up among a herd of English and caught the ball and scored. All that we managed was some kicks and a lucky try, scored when Ian Hunter grabbed the ball after it had come back off the post following a kick at goal by Rob Andrew, and his momentum carried him over the line for the try. Jean-Baptiste Lafond tried a drop goal that could have won it for France, but the ball cannoned back into play from the crossbar and we held on to win 16–15.

Practically the only good news was that Martin Johnson, the young Leicester lock, played well, even though he had come in for Wade Dooley only on the day before the game. He even had to have a dinner jacket altered at the last minute to fit so that he could attend the dinner. Johnson was left out for the rest of the season when Wade was fit to return; and with hindsight, I think he should have stayed. Big Wade had done a fantastic job for us over the years. But he was affected by the new laws as much as anyone.

Our season came completely off the rails in Cardiff. It was nothing to do with the traditional problem. The bogey had gone. We no longer feared the place irrationally. But from the start I sensed it was one of those games we simply were not going to win. The Welsh were still relatively weak, with a new front row. But they had the spirit and the togetherness back. They tackled like lunatics. They were not unbeatable, but they wanted it more than we did.

Nothing seemed to be happening for us; there was the odd break or half break, there would be some support, but then things would fizzle out. Wherever we went we were tackled. We found lots of ways not to score, and had what looked like a good try by Dewi Morris disallowed. Dewi had a good match against his own countrymen, but towards the end he was brought down just short after he beat six or seven defenders. In the breaks, Will told us that we had been in this situation before and got out of it before. If we kept our concentration we would escape again.

In fact, we were leading 9–3 near half-time. Jon Webb had kicked two penalties and I dropped a goal with my left foot which I secretly treasured. Then, just before half-time, Emyr Lewis, the Welsh flanker, got the ball going right. I came up to take him, but as I moved in he surprisingly kicked the ball downfield down the right wing. I was unconcerned. Webby was back there. Rory was back there. Barnes and I often gave Webb a ribbing for daydreaming and being caught out of position, and this time he was indeed a few yards adrift, too near the centre of the field.

However, Rory Underwood was on the scene and he had ages to get back and get rid of the ball before Ieuan Evans came on the scene. He had an easy toe-poke into touch, for the line-out and a regrouping of our defence. For some reason known only to Rory, he reacted painfully slowly, meandered back and, suddenly, Ieuan was on him. Ieuan kicked the ball on from under Rory's nose, hacked it over our line and fell on it for the try. The match turned on that moment. Neil Jenkins kicked the conversion and there was no scoring in the whole of the second half.

Any illusions of invincibility were shattered – and not only because of our problems with the laws. As the appetite of the Welsh pack indicated (not to mention the wild celebrations throughout the country after the match), we had become the team everyone else was desperate to beat. The other teams felt that we had been lording it for far too long.

The joke around at the time was that Rory was signing for panto, so that all the audience could shout, as they might have shouted to Rory on the field had they been English, and seen Ieuan Evans approaching: 'He's behind you!'

The greatest selection debate by far in my time in the England squad was quite obviously about the rivalry between Rob Andrew and Stuart Barnes for the fly-half position. Andrew had, by this stage, won nearly 50 caps in the position and he was to go on to surpass the half-century comfortably. At this stage, Barnes, despite all his years of brilliance at Bath, had never been given a start at fly-half in any Five Nations game. I think that even those who supported Rob's case believed that was unfair.

Barnes finally got his chance. He and Geoff Cooke had never seen eye to eye. Barnes had said so many times that he was no supporter of the rigid, kicking-based game plan. He had also dropped out of contention for England selection on two occasions in the past and was feeling more impatient than ever. But Andrew was dropped after Cardiff and in all honesty, even if it was by no means all his fault, then you have to say that he did not manage to set the game alight with the ball he received. It was still strange that he got all the blame and strange that this moment was the one chosen to re-launch our Stuart.

Rob did not take his dismissal sitting down. I believe that the best thing to do when dropped is to keep quiet, to keep playing the best you can. But he came out in public. He appeared in the papers, requesting a top-level pow-wow with Geoff Cooke, and carried on for some days about the injustice. I couldn't understand it.

So Barnes was in, to take on Scotland at Twickenham in the match that would either revive our season or, if we lost, dip it into crisis. There was so much to think about. It is no secret that he and some of the squad were not exactly close friends, as he himself revealed in the press after his retirement. I think he felt something of an interloper in a close-knit squad.

I wanted him to have a great game. If he didn't, it would make nonsense of everything that had been written about him, and everything he had said in the press about himself. In that sense he was the only one who was going to lose. Also, he is a friend, a close one. Plus, if it did go well, then we in the backs might see more of the ball. I never objected to taking part in our pre-planned game on the way to the Grand Slam, but that did not mean that I was not eager for a different approach. I had played with Barnes for years, long enough to know that with his style, that approach could become reality. As an all-round team, England did not exist at the time.

I do think Will felt a little threatened when Barnes was around. Will is a strong voice, he has strong opinions and a good way of putting things across. I knew that he and Cooke talked a great deal about style, and tactics. Here was Barnes coming in, a man used to running the match as he saw it at the time. Will would have to change some of his thinking or be seen to be in conflict with Barnes. As for Cooke, he is an excellent organizer and would therefore be happier with someone like Rob, who is easier to organize. To bore to victory was fine by him.

The rest is history, even if history may have captured the game wrongly. We beat Scotland 26–12; both Underwoods scored tries, I scored a try, the England backs were seen in the best light we had been seen in for a long, long time. Twickenham was delighted, the season was back on the rails, and the centre of attention and praise, naturally, was my friend from Bath. 'It was the rebirth of Stuart Barnes, the man who never should have been away. It was the rebirth of England and the return of excitement,' said one newspaper account, breathlessly.

The try set up by the Barnes break, by my long run past Scott Hastings and past the obliging Stanger for Rory (not Tony) to score came soon after half-time. I had scored a try down the left wing in the 28th minute, after Barnes had already set us moving well. After Rory's try, Tony had his moment. Rory came inside to draw the defence and made enough space for Tony to run around him and score down the left. It was the try that sent Mrs Anne Underwood dancing in the stands, and after the TV camera picked her out, she became almost as famous at the match as Barnes.

But not quite. And the amazing thing about it was that I doubt if he had the ball in his hands all that often, and I probably had the ball in my hands only about seven times. But the difference was in the positions I was in when I did touch the ball. If Rob had taken that high pass from Dewi he could have cut back and kicked high into the box and done it very well. But only through Barnes, of the fly-halves around at the time, would the move have ended in a try.

Everyone in England thought we were back on the march. If we were, then it was a short march. Two weeks later, we were thrashed in Dublin by the fighting Irish. This time we saw very little of the ball and it did not really matter who was at fly-half, Rob or Stuart. There was nothing anyone could have done. To finish in mid-table was a failure; apart from the dizzy day at Twickenham, the season was one to forget.

So too was the 1993–94 season, which I watched from the sidelines. England beat New Zealand in a match of incredible intensity, with Phil de Glanville at least ensuring that my jersey was passed on to a Bath man (kept warm for me, more like). It was a power-play victory won against an All Black team that was undisciplined, notably when Jamie Joseph went out of his way to stamp on Kieran Bracken. It was great to see Nigel Redman play such a fantastic match, and be singled out by Laurie Mains, the All Black coach. The back row of Rodber, Richards and Clarke were outstanding too. But it was a game based totally on power: there was little back play, with Rob, reinstalled to the fury of Barnes, deep in the pocket playing to a set plan.

History will show that the optimism was, again, misplaced. Jon Callard saved us at Murrayfield, kicking a goal in the last second to win the match by 15–14, after the Scots had, themselves, apparently won the match with a drop goal by Gregor Townsend which sent Murrayfield mad. The good news was that Jon Hall had finally forced his way back into the England team for the match. He was out again for the next match, made a scapegoat unfairly; but it was a great achievement in itself to get back.

The most disastrous day of recent years arrived soon afterwards when we showed that our dreadful form at Murrayfield was no fluke. We lost to Ireland 13–12, scoring no tries and conceding one to Simon Geoghegan. Our back play was again non-existent; Rob was so deep in the pocket that he was almost behind the dead ball line; and our back row seemed totally unbalanced, with Tim Rodber alongside Steve Ojomoh (his first cap) and Neil Back. Now the 'boring England' critics had the field to themselves. At least in the Grand Slam seasons we had the excuse that we were winning.

The forwards rescued the season in Paris, and although yet again we failed to score a try, Rob did kick superbly and we won 18–14. We kept the Indian sign on the French and our record in Paris is remarkable – none of the other home countries has won there since Wales in 1975. We beat Wales easily at Twickenham, 15–8; there was the rare sight of an England try, a good one by Rory Underwood. Tim Rodber scored another when Wales threw the ball into a line-out straight to him. Afterwards there was the strange sight of the Welsh team walking up to receive the Five Nations trophy from the Queen. They took it on points difference, having already beaten Ireland, Scotland and France; on the day, the points difference was ours. If we had scored one more try we would have taken the title but, given our poor performances, that would not have been cause for rejoicing.

England had no respite. Still without me, they ploughed their way through a tough fixture list in South Africa, won a great victory in the first Test at Loftus Versveld and, perhaps predictably, lost a little steam in the last match and were beaten by a South African team playing out of its skin in Cape Town. It was a fierce and controversial tour, but at least it gave Jack Rowell, newly installed, the chance to get to know his players – although whether any of the players got to know Jack was another matter. He certainly shook up the clubby atmosphere that had developed; when the 1994–95 season opened he spoke strongly about the need to wake up players who had spent a long time in the England team, and who were, perhaps, mentally coasting. Jack ejected Dick Best after the tour, allowed Les Cusworth a look-in as backs coach, but otherwise took on all the coaching responsibilities.

So if the team was in transition when I first played for my country in 1989, then the team I was hoping to return to in 1994–95 was back in the same situation. In one sense, nothing had changed; in another sense, given our record, everything had changed. It was a sheer delight to be part of an era when England had their best results ever. But I had not yet had enough of it.

Stuart Barnes announced his retirement from all rugby in the summer of 1994 after being ignored for the major matches on the tour of South Africa. He departed for the BSkyB commentary box and a new career in the media. I was one of the first to tell him that I could not grant him an interview at that stage.

It meant that never again would I have to answer the thousands of questions about Andrew and Barnes. Who was the better player? Which would I chose in my England team? Did I, as a friend of Barnes from way back at Bath, actually speak to Rob at all? I can't say I've missed the questions since Stuart left. Not at all.

I felt for him when he retired. If I were him I would have felt victimized. He left the game as the unluckiest fly-half in the world because he was never given a proper chance to show what he could do at the top level. He won only ten caps, but four of them came as a replacement. He started a Five Nations match at fly-half only twice.

Leaving aside the debate about the merits of the two players for a moment, if Barnes had been allowed fifty caps for England he would now be a legend of the game. The other regret is that he left before we could have a season together at Bath with some of the pressure off. I would have loved to have one season with him without all the crap surrounding playing for England – disappearing immediately after games for squad sessions, etc. – and then call it quits. It is sad that we are not going to do it.

As a wasted talent there are parallels between Barnesie and George Best. Barnes was a magician. He must have been a nightmare for the opposition No. 7 to play against. Even when you had Barnes cornered, he would be away as if through your legs, and gone. As a club fly-half, he sparked everything. Like any good club, however, Bath have simply carried on, moving Mike Catt to fly-half. But that is not to say that they haven't missed him. Given the opportunities, he would now be ranked among the greatest international fly-halves.

His greatest strength was his speed off the mark. He also had the ability to move left or right on the burst, a range of movement which made it difficult for the opposing flanker to cover him. I can remember hardly a single occasion in all the times I played with him when he was caught by the No. 7 from a set-piece. If the flanker marking him was a little slow, Barnes would soon realize it, get behind him and release his centres.

As far as the different techniques go, Andrew could take the ball up to the opposition No. 7 and release his inside centre, just like in the old coaching manuals. Barnes had that extra ability, to get past the No. 7 and go another 15 yards, creating disruption and apprehension in the defence; instead of having three backs to continue the movement, you would have the whole line.

The biggest difference to outward appearances is that Stuart stood flat, close to the opposition defence, while Rob stands back in the pocket, whether it be at the line-out or scrum, to give himself more time to kick with less danger of the charge-down. Barnes likes to leave the decision which side to attack till the last second. With the understanding which Stuart and I built up over the years, I could react to him and stay on his shoulder. Rob finds it far more difficult to make that final change of direction.

Rob is very dedicated, meticulous and probably the fittest back in the squad. Forwards today like the element of pre-planning which he brings, because they know where they stand. He loves to get stuck in. His cover tackling is excellent – as is Barnesie's. He does not like the charging second rows coming at him too much. But I haven't come across too many who do.

Rob Andrew is very good at what he does, and he takes out a strong idea of how he is going to play. If every other wheel is moving smoothly around him, then he is outstandingly effective; if something gets out of line – perhaps a bad pass from his scrum-half – he has never quite had the running ability to change the game and to get out of trouble. He is the ideal man for a forward-driven side, which is exactly what we were when we won the Grand Slams.

For a centre-threequarter it is very difficult to get your lines of running from Andrew. Barnes was a ferret, probably slightly quicker than me off the mark, but by the time he had exhausted his burst and come near to the end of what he had got, I was usually just going into the flow. If I want to get that sort of flow when playing with Rob, I have to stand around 30 yards back, or perhaps about 20 yards deep and 20 yards wide so that he does not eat up my space when he decides to run with the ball. When he does run with the ball, as he tried to do in 1993 when he felt that Ian McGeechan, the Lions coach, would be looking for a little running from him, we had to shout 'straighten up, straighten up' as he went along. Rob stands deep at about 45 degrees to his scrum-half and then if the rest of us are at about 25 degrees from Rob, it is ages before the two back lines come together.

As far as their kicking went, they both used to annoy me. They both kicked as well and as badly as each other. It is perhaps unfair to compare them with Grant Fox and Michael Lynagh, whose percentages when kicking at goal were much higher. But those are the people they must be compared with because goal-kicking is so important. And neither of them had that consistency. They both probably had more bad days than good days, if you count a good day as the day when you put over all the kicks that really matter.

Barnes could launch a 60-yard touch-finder when he caught the ball right, and Rob transformed his own kicking remarkably when he started consulting Dave Aldred, the kicking guru, recently. He has never been quite so happy in his game when he is also the team's front line kicker. I don't think there are many players around who can put with the disappointment – both their own and that of their team – when they are missing crucial kicks at goal, and still concentrate on their games.

It is blindingly obvious that Barnes is a completely different character. His exploits with wine are legendary and did him no good in the puritanical world which England like to think they inhabit – they don't, but they still think they do. It is not a drink problem, he just enjoys it. He is a good friend, I have enjoyed his company, although we have also played a full part in the traditional Bath winding-up ceremonies. We even had a blazing row on my stag night and have had the normal Bath disagreements since.

Rob is not that heavy. He must be every woman's ideal son-in-law. When celebrating the night away he can change into a horrible little schoolboy, but he quickly recovers next morning. He is perfect for the image of rugby – he is rarely controversial, although he has been a leading figure, alongside Brian Moore, in fighting for the rights of the England squad and in pursuing our Playervision campaign.

People might expect an edge between Rob and me, because both of us knew that, as a Bath man, I was a Barnes man at heart. But there has never been any problem, we have always been friends. Perhaps he may even have escaped the lash of the Guscott tongue more than most. I did go for him once. In the first Test of the 1993 Lions tour at Christchurch, he kept on shouting 'No penalties, no penalties.' He went on shouting it, till it got on my nerves. In the end, I just yelled: 'For Christ's sake, Rob, shut up.' I have also given Rob the look that Rory Underwood has sometimes given me. It is the look that says 'Why didn't you pass that ball out, you prat!' But I have never interfered in his tactics, never demanded that he stop kicking and start passing the ball out. I left that to Will.

When you consider the question of who was the better player you have to remember that there is no one-word answer and that, in certain situations, Rob can do a great job. You have to consider the way you are going to play. If I had Barnes as my fly-half, I would have changed the forwards and the whole approach and moulded the team around him. You cannot have half measures. I would have given him the tactical control and the captaincy. I would have changed everything to suit him, then let him loose.

And if Barnes is seen as a victim of the selectors and the England management, then he is also the victim of an English style and English attitude. When you play with a flat line you are playing football, you are demanding that all your team are thinking on their feet. The England game and especially the England forward game is not geared to that kind of thought pattern; Geoff Cooke was geared to a far more cautious game.

To introduce a Barnes into the traditional English set-up would be like saying to a shopowner who has sold clothes all his life that now he is suddenly going to start selling fruit. Certainly if Barnes had been in control when we played so well in 1990, he would not have allowed the tactics to revert and the team to retreat into ourselves. He would have had faith in the approach, and one defeat would not have shaken him. It is futile, however, to look back now and try to say how many games would have ended differently, for good or bad, had the fly-halves been changed. England in my time have won many more games than they have lost. And as I have said before, I love everything that goes hand in hand with playing rugby for England. But if you are not involved in the game continually then you start to wonder when you are going to touch the ball; when people come up afterwards and say that it was 25 minutes before you saw the ball.

Then you start to wonder about style, and enjoyment; and about players who can play to the style that would give you most satisfaction. Stuart Barnes was the most enjoyable and satisfying player to play with that I have come across in the game. The final irony is that Rob, encouraged by Jack Rowell and Les Cusworth, now stands up much flatter since Barnes retired.

If people have always bombarded me with questions about the relative merits of the two fly-halves, it was nothing compared with the interest shown in my opinions on my co-centre. Up to May 1995, Will Carling had led us to three Grand Slams, to the World Cup final; he holds the world record for the number of times he has captained his country, he is already England's most-capped centre by a street. He is the most discussed rugby player ever and one of the best-known figures in British sport, even in households where rugby is never discussed. Not a bad profile for a young man.

After all the games we have played together and all the meetings and post-match social occasions we have attended, it is strange to report that I do not pretend to know Will, as a close friend or schoolmate would know him, at all. Obviously, any captain has to keep a certain distance, and I know that, until his marriage to Julia in the summer of 1994, Will preferred the company of a few close 'house-mates' and to keep away from the public gaze. Simon Halliday was closest to him of any regular squad member.

Sometimes, Will can be besieged by members of the public wanting an autograph, a photograph taken with him, everything. It is simply not that easy for him to fraternize in public. I remember a few of us going out for a drink after we played Canada at Wembley a few seasons ago. It was a rare event. I don't believe Will is shy, but he cannot let his hair down in public. He knows the importance of the office of England captain and the need to portray the correct image.

He is a private man. I don't know what he thinks, what he has for breakfast, where he goes for a pint. My relationship with Will is a sporting one, and the same would go for most of the England squad. If he has close friends, then they are outside the squad. I have dined with him on tours, roomed with him, had an enjoyable meal with Will and Julia during the 1995 Lions tour; with Julia there, following part of the tour, and with Will playing in the midweek team rather than the Saturday team, I saw very little of him. We did not discuss at length the fact that he was not made Lions captain or that he did not make the Test team, although he showed his character towards the end of the tour by trying to keep the midweek team together when it was obvious that some of the forwards had almost given up. Jayne and I were honoured to have been invited to his wedding. It was a great day, although my favourite memory is of encountering Bill Carling, Will's father. He was enjoying himself but obviously had one eye on the purse strings. 'Thank God I never had a daughter,' he said.

As I have already written, we got off slightly on the wrong foot when we first played together in the England Team in 1989. With typical judgment, I walked in and effectively told Will to move over because the best centre in the world had arrived. It was just a minor bit of psyching-out. There was also the suspicion at that time, especially in the media, that Simon Halliday and myself were the best centres available; and because I had never had the chance to play with Will and assess his game close up, and because Halliday and I had been through so much together, I admit I did nothing to knock this opinion down.

Will had his own close tie-up in the England squad. It was unprecedented for a team manager and a team captain to have enjoyed such security of tenure as Will and Geoff Cooke enjoyed, but they both were long-term appointments; Will, in fact, was Geoff's long-term appointment. Their close relationship never bothered me, although some of the other players resented it slightly and others, like Jeff Probyn, came out strongly against it. Geoff Cooke always said that Will would only be picked if he was playing well enough; although it was always extremely difficult to see Geoff dropping Will. Jack Rowell retained Will as captain on succeeding Geoff.

Will proved himself to me as a player in 1992, when he had a tremendous year and played superbly against Bath for Harlequins in the cup final of that year. I think perhaps his style has changed a little since then and he has not played quite so well. We used to give a fair old ribbing to Jim Fallon, the Bath wing who signed professional for the Leeds rugby league club, for his habit of sticking out his jaw (we used to call him Lockjaw) when in possession and tucking the ball under his arm. Will has gone slightly that way, become more of a New Zealand style of player.

It is simple. When he turns outwards, he is a great player. He has so much ability in all parts of the game. When he turns back inwards, as he tends to do, he sets up the ball extremely well but he is not nearly so effective. It is a small adjustment to make. His record when he started was excellent – he made a try for Halliday in his first match as captain, against Australia in 1988. He made a try for me against Ireland at Twickenham in 1990. I don't think he has felt threatened by me as a player since those early days and my brash arrival, especially since our roles have been different. It was good to see Will attacking again in 1995.

In the context of what has been sometimes a limited relationship we have always got on well. He took the trouble to ring me frequently when I was injured, and if he did not consult me about playing matters as much as he consults the inner circle such as Rob, Dean and Brian, then it is probably because I have not put myself forward in team meetings as often as I might have done.

He also grabbed the reins of the team in 1990 after the Grand Slam match at Murrayfield. In that game, Brian Moore was effectively running the team on the field. He was so much closer to the action and took some big decisions as to whether we should run penalties. The confusion seemed to be obvious from the stands. As a result of that Carling now comes running up to grab the ball and to take charge of proceedings more overtly.

Rugby, of course, is part of Will's business. He has taken what he has learned as England captain into his business life. In the motivational training schemes which he runs for major companies he draws on what he has done in an England jersey and tries to relate it to the business world. He has obviously carved out a highly lucrative career in tandem with Jon Holmes, his agent; and like me, he has encountered a certain amount of jealousy. If you had told either of us several years ago that rugby would become so big that players would become personalities outside the sport, then we would have laughed. When I started, Billy Beaumont was doing a few advertisements and *A Question of Sport*; now the opportunities are infinitely greater and, not surprisingly, Will has taken full advantage. To call him the Henry Cooper of sporting commercialization is a little harsh, however. He is far better looking.

He is not the first captain whose motivational skills have left me a little cold, and he will probably not be the last. Various behind-the-scenes videos have been produced which have given him a reputation as a mystical motivator. He certainly has good communication skills, but there was nothing mystical about his speeches. On the night before a match, in past years, he would say that we should all be thinking about the game, that families and wives should be blanked out of our minds, that we should be thinking about our roles. He would then ask Brian for a round-up of his tasks for the match. Dewi would be asked to chip in with a résumé of his role. I was hardly ever asked. I knew what I was going to do. I didn't have to discuss it with all and sundry. The whole experience was something of a trial for the experienced hands, although to be fair to Will it is always something you should make an effort to tap into for the sake of the team.

Will did also introduce into the squad a framework in which everyone could have their say, which was a great advance – although too much democracy in a rugby team can be confusing.

It can also feel a little like a Carling roadshow. So many cameras follow him around that it is difficult for either him or others to shoo them away. I can remember cameras trailing us throughout the World Cup, even in the last stages of the build-up; and in the end, we had to make representations through Will to have them removed occasionally, just for some privacy.

What no one can argue with is his record in the England jersey and his composure under some of the fiercest pressure any England rugby captain has had to endure. He and I may never have become bosom buddies, because neither the circumstances nor our characters were set up like that. He may not have realized his full potential on the field – there is still time. But we could not have spent all those Saturday afternoons together without forging a mutual respect.

10
Catching the Plane, Missing the Boat
With the British Lions in New Zealand, 1993

'Come on, John. Look at me. Look at me.' Eventually, after what seemed ages even though it took only micro-seconds, John looked. And then he was dead and beaten.

It had started when Sean Fitzpatrick, the New Zealand captain, made a schoolboy error, spilling the ball forward as he tried to drive up the field, then driving at it, sweating and cursing. But our forwards accepted his gift. Thanks, Sean.

The ball came to Dewi Morris, and as he ran a few yards to the blind side, I came up on his left, calling loudly for the pass. When Dewi handed it on to me, I had Rory Underwood outside and John Kirwan, the New Zealand wing, marking Rory Underwood, came racing up. When people sitting in the stands sense a space opening, they begin to rise from their seats. Here there was just a fraction of daylight.

I knew that Kirwan was in two minds. Should he ignore me and keep going, head out for Rory and gamble that I would make the pass? Or should he come in to tackle me? All I had to do was make him look at me, hold on to the ball until he made the first gesture and the first movement of turning in for the tackle. As soon as I saw the look, as soon as I saw him half turn in, I passed the ball to Rory, and Rory had the foot of space he needed.

Kirwan tried desperately to readjust, diving desperately to flap with one outstretched hand at Rory's ankles. He missed. Rory sprinted down the touch-line. When he reached the line, he decided to celebrate with a full-length dive, the type now fashionable among leading players. When exam-

ined on video later, it was one of the scruffiest dives ever executed. If he had landed one of his RAF aircraft like that he would have been drummed out of the Services.

But he scored. We gave him none for artistic merit, five for a try. In the stand, the Lions management and reserves were dancing with joy. We could not be caught, and the second Test, arguably the most important match played in British rugby history, was won.

Someone wrote that a British Lions tour is a cross between a medieval crusade and a school outing; and as definitions go, it is perfect. One day, you can be fighting for your life in a massive sporting contest. The next day, you can be riding the white waters on a giant inflatable raft, giggling like sport's oldest infants.

I have never been particularly bothered by rugby's traditions, but I am the greatest fan of the Lions. A Lions tour gives you something extra, something higher than playing for a single national team. To become a Lion is to be guaranteed a place in history. You become part of what happened on previous tours, you become associated with previous greats. And, since victorious Lions tours are so few and far between, there is the chance to come back with stories of glory with which you can bore people to tears for decades to come.

In the season before the 1993 tour, I realized the possibilities for my own standing. I sensed that in some parts of the game I was thought of as an attacking player, almost a flashy player. New Zealanders know rugby back to front. They are expert in analysing others, and their perception of me was, almost certainly, as a player who could run but who was not an all-rounder, not a strong defender.

It was my personal goal to go there and prove otherwise, prove that I could do other things. In fact, prove that I could do the lot. And there is no better or more ferocious environment. If you prove yourself in New Zealand, you have proved yourself. For good. Full stop.

When I toured with the 1989 Lions to Australia, I was too new to it all to grasp the wider implications. But now I realized that British Isles players can only become true legends through Lions tours. They have produced many Welsh legends – Gareth Edwards, Barry John, Mervyn Davies. Even Irish legends – Tony O'Reilly,

Willie-John McBride. But there are so few Lions legends from England. I didn't want to be too diffident about this. If there was any legend status going spare, then I wanted some.

Of course, there is no chance of proving anything unless you are chosen to go. There were still the old anxieties. Even though I was in every single one of the selections made by rugby writers, even though my family and friends simply carried on making plans for my absence, I still had the odd disturbing wave of doubt.

After England had beaten Scotland at Twickenham in March 1993, two weeks before the Lions party was to be announced, Stuart Barnes and I told ourselves we had nothing to worry about. Barnes, at last given a chance as England's starting fly-half in the Five Nations, had practically torn Scotland apart with some typical breaks, and he and I had, as one paper put it, 'conjured brilliantly together'. We had to play Ireland in Dublin on the eve of Lions selection. They had been hopeless for years.

'We're definitely there, even if we have a nightmare against Ireland,' we agreed. Unfortunately, we did have a nightmare against Ireland. So our prediction was to be put to the test.

Geoff Cooke had been appointed manager of the tour, and was therefore chairman of selectors. Before the England team dispersed after the retreat from Lansdowne Road, where we were hammered by an emerald blur, he said that all tourists would be informed of their selection over the telephone on the Sunday.

On the day before the Ireland match, I had sat with Mike Slemen, England's assistant coach, and thrashed out our Lions party. All over Britain and Ireland, in pubs and clubs and workplaces and homes, people were doing the same, endlessly weighing up the alternatives, even running sweeps on the eventual outcome. You also have to bear in mind that the selectors from Ireland, say, might hold out for a quota. When we had almost finished, Geoff Cooke came over to us.

'What are you doing?' he asked.

We showed him. We looked up and down the list. He made some tut-tutting noises, shook his head a few times, gave back the list and walked away. At the time, it came across as a light-hearted tease. But at home in Bath on Sunday evening, with the day wearing on and still no call, his gestures took on all sorts of high significance. Jayne became anxious too.

All of that Sunday, tortured little groups of players anxiously compared notes. There was one contingent of hopefuls in West Wales; another in Bath; another in a pub in Wandsworth. For all we knew, there were similar little groups all around the rugby-playing communities.

'Have you heard anything?'

'Nothing at all. What about you?'

The group in the Wandsworth pub – Jason Leonard, Brian Moore and Peter Winterbottom – became so frantic for news that they cracked. They decided to ring Dick Best. Even though Best, the tour's assistant coach, was not officially a selector, he would have the Knowledge, the inside line on the selection. After about four calls, Best himself cracked. He demanded to know who was gathered in the pub. They gave him the three names.

'Right,' he said. 'You lot have nothing to worry about. Now get off the phone.' Phew.

Next morning, Ben Clarke had still heard nothing. He telephoned Barnes, then at his desk at the Stroud & Swindon Building Society. Barnes, gloomily believing that he had yet again been dumped by selectors, loosed off a savage volley of abuse at the selectors and life in general. We found later that the selection meeting had simply overrun, and inconsiderately – or sadistically – selectors never bothered to ring around.

The Big Issue remained the same. Will Carling. For years previously and for most of the 1993 Five Nations season, he had been such a warm favourite to captain the team that betting had almost ended. Yet his chances began to slide. After the defeat in Cardiff the Red Rose itself began to wilt. People started to worry themselves sick about the possibility of a party composed chiefly of Englishmen being managed by an Englishman and captained by an Englishman. People spoke of the affinity between Scots and Kiwis, and between Gavin Hastings and New Zealand rugby. Slowly, Will's chances began to evaporate, even though he himself had done nothing to diminish them.

I never discussed the issue with him, but I had a feeling that Will had a feeling it was slipping. He even said so in the build-up for the Scotland match, which everyone had set up as a shoot-out for the Lions captaincy between Carling and Hastings. (If it was, then it was Gavin who was shot.) 'I don't think I'm going to get it,' Will said.

Did he jump, or was he nudged? Eventually, the story emerged that he had withdrawn his candidacy, and was looking forward to a summer as one of the lads, out of the spotlight. That he was tired, which he definitely was. But surely, he must have taken soundings and surely, if those soundings still sounded like a chance, he would have fought on. I don't think you turn down the captaincy of the Lions if they offer it to you.

There were 16 Englishmen in the eventual party, and the only England regulars not to be chosen were Jon Webb, the full-back, and Jeff Probyn, the tight-head. Webb's position was teeming with contenders, and Gavin Hastings and Tony Clement were chosen instead. Fair enough. Webb had a lot of medical commitments in any case and chose to retire from the game.

Probyn's position was not teeming with contenders. Probyn and I are close. I knew how vastly he was respected by fellow donkeys for his scrummaging and tidying up and burrowing. If I were sole selector he would be in. But the key forwards in New Zealand are also fast-moving forwards, runners and handlers. So I could also see why they left him out. Until the tour started. The two touring tight-heads were to be Paul Burnell and Peter Wright, and if the selection looked peculiar at the time, it was not half as peculiar as it did at the end of the tour.

There were seven Scots, five of them forwards. This was not too comforting. As a body, Scots forwards arouse about as much awe as American cricketers and Jamaican ski-jumpers. There were five Welshmen and, from Ireland, just Nick Popplewell and Mick Galwey, who had scored Ireland's try against us on the Saturday. 'What is Galwey like as a player?' people asked, since I had played against him only a day or two before. I had no idea. Galwey had simply been part of the emerald blur.

But, as the congratulations and the calls from the media poured in, who cared? Selection? Players? The captaincy? These were merely technical things, merely matters of sport. I and all the others chosen were in for a shot at legend.

The first obstacle was not dressed in Black. It was a vast rigmarole of form-filling, measuring-up, kitting out and medical and dental checks. We were given two blazers, three formal shirts, Lions ties and bow-ties and a wide variety of Lions pullovers, leisure wear tracksuits, training tracksuits, boots, training shoes and casual wear. At the dispensation of kit, with gleaming piles of pristine gear standing expectantly, we found that two pairs of the shoes had gone missing. Hardly the atmosphere of trust needed between men who are to spend the next two months in proximity to each other.

There were players I did not really know at all. Popplewell and Galwey were mysteries to me; so were Burnell, whom I had met briefly, and Wright; I did know that, while Burnell was not everyone's idea of the terrifying prop, he was durable. I knew the Welsh players extremely well, and regarded the likes of Robert Jones and Scott Gibbs as friends. I knew that Richard Webster, the Swansea flanker, would mount a strong challenge for the role of butt for tour humour. He did not disappoint me. I also expected him to prove a hard-core forward, and he came up with the goods there too.

The tour officers were elected. Players' courts are part of every tour. Their main function is to produce a peer-group decision, usually viciously unfair, to penalize some excess of behaviour – say, excessive drinking – with imaginative penalties – say, excessive drinking. Popplewell was elected judge, which was predictable. On almost every tour, a prop who regards himself as having above the normal intelligence quota for a prop is appointed to deal with a group without the courage to rid him of his notion. There was a story that Popplewell had turned up at Weybridge for a pre-tour training session, looked around the assembled English, Welsh, Scottish and Irish and asked what time the French would be arriving! After further votes, Stuart Barnes was appointed prosecutor, Brian Moore clerk of the court, Peter Wright defence counsel, and Dewi Morris was to be in charge of collecting fines.

Ian McGeechan, the only man in Lions history to coach two Lions tours, was clearly the central figure from the time we assembled at Weybridge to the time we left New Zealand at the end. His strategy was crystal clear. He said categorically that we would try to beat New Zealand at their own game, at the fluid, hard-running style they had perfected. And they should have perfected it. Every team in New Zealand from the minis to the national team, every provincial side and every forgotten dog club team, has been playing the same style for as long as anyone can remember.

McGeechan looked for dissent, for players who might incline to a more British approach, perhaps for some words about brilliance of back play, individual genius. There was not a sound. Players like Peter Winterbottom and Dean Richards were right behind him. And fair enough – British-style rugby, with high hopes and fairy tales, never did much down under.

I had already decided to keep a low profile in the team meetings on tour. I suppose I had a dread of half the party muttering to themselves, 'What the hell does he know about it?' if I spoke up. People have told me that I should take part more.

We had to break camp at Weybridge because some of the England players were involved in important league matches that day. Bath had to beat Saracens to take the Courage title again, and even though we were behind inside the last ten minutes we finished strongly and won. The champagne flowed in the dressing-room afterwards, and fuelled by champers, we made a rash decision. Behind the Saracens clubhouse someone had rigged up a giant crane for bungee-jumping. They took you up on a moving platform.

I announced that I was going to jump. The dressing-room went quiet; everyone had heard and I realized I could not back down. The news went around, crowds gathered and Barnes, Ben Clarke and I lined up. My parents were at the match, and when they were called to the scene they could not believe it was me up there. Barnes is afraid of heights, so was in a panic. We all landed safely and pretended that it was a piece of cake.

Captain Gavin quietly went around the squad getting to know everyone, but I did not expect him to keep as low a profile as he did. He was inconspicuous early on, which was surprising. I half expected a few British (or Scottish) bulldog speeches. It would have done nothing for me, but I expected it anyway. But there was nothing, only Gavin being quietly Gavin. I sat next to him on the long flight. We talked about how we could combat them, how we could get all 15 players involved.

We touched down at Auckland's international airport. There were a few customs checks, a few cameras, and the management,

Cooke, McGeechan, Best and Hastings, went off to take part in a press conference. I had always wondered what on earth they all talk about in these endless sessions between management and media. Both sides have given me the answer – nothing. It is all just a ritual of obvious questions and obvious answers, all neatly noted. The Auckland conference was apparently merely a warm-up for the Platitudes Trophy. We re-embarked, this time on an aircraft several divisions smaller, made a bumpy flight to the north-east coast of New Zealand and landed at Kerikeri. It had one tarmac strip, one taxi, one hut.

There were a few Red Dragon flags waving and a few embarrassed groans from the Welsh players. Robert Jones was amazed that, wherever they touched down in the rugby world, there were always Red Dragons flying. Popplewell, who had toured in the previous summer with Ireland, who conceded huge scores, warned us that we would receive calls from Kiwis bearing the same surnames, demanding to know if they were related to us. Robert Jones went pale at the prospect.

We were installed in a seafront hotel in Pahia, in the sub-tropical Bay of Islands, where we had the first of an endless procession of unremarkable meals. Throughout New Zealand, it was always the same things – boring pumpkin soup, chips, cod pieces, cauliflower. Variation-free, vision-free, even taste-free.

Yet it felt like a rugby tour. After a slow start, the interest in the tour was overwhelming. The intensity was high. In Australia in 1989, there had been times when, it seemed, only parts of the country even knew we were there. In New Zealand, every last Kiwi, old and young, and every last farmer's wife, followed the tour avidly.

And we settled into the peculiar rhythm of a tour. On match days there were the flashes of glamour and glory and pressure and tension and sheer effort. In between there was the endless grind of daily training. Then there were all sorts of activities generously laid on by the people of this generous country – golf, jet-boating, goat-shooting, deep sea fishing, clay pigeon shooting, white water boating. The policemen in the party would receive invitations from local police; Rory of the RAF was entertained at New Zealand Air Force bases.

Mixed in with all this were the humdrum hours when nothing was happening, when we hung around hotel lobbies and airport lounges, when we fell back on endless card games and books, waiting for something to happen. My moods tend to change by the day anyway. Here, there was ample scope for moodiness.

Webster began his bid to win a Test place on the open-side flank away from Peter Winterbottom. On a clay pigeon shoot, Webster had, for some reason, got hold of a pump action shotgun. Now Webster is hyperactive, excitable, and definitely not the sort of man to be near when he is holding a pump action shotgun. That is like giving whisky to the Red Indians.

Webster took a few shots at a few clay pigeons, and was celebrating a hit or two, holding the gun in one hand, when it went off. It discharged violently into the ground and, as Webster and the gun recoiled, there was an explosion of flying turf and lumps of mud from a position about six inches from Winterbottom's foot. Winterbottom was reasonably calm in the shocked silence. It was only afterwards that the narrowness of his escape hit home, when he realized how the lack of a foot would have jeopardized his chances of making the Test team.

It was in New Zealand that Popplewell began a habit of sleeping the night in other people's beds. In one town he was found dead to the world in Dewi Morris's room and in another, sleeping peacefully in Ben Clarke's.

Coach McGeechan set out his stall in the Bay of Islands. He is famous for being meticulous, and if meticulous means spending endless hours either in team training or team meetings, then he was on the meticulous side of meticulous. The team meeting concept was something which, for me and others, had become a monster long before the end.

There was a team meeting almost every day of the tour. Each hotel had a room designated as the team room. It would be a common room for the Lions, with a table laid out with a few jugs of orange juice and other soft drinks; even a few cans of beer. There was always a television and a video. Always a video.

Every day, we would file gravely into the team room for the team meeting. We would discuss that day's training, the last match, the next match. We would watch videos of our next opponents. The captain and the pack leader for the next match would say their piece.

McGeechan, Cooke, Best – and any one who fancied saying a piece – said their piece.

At least they eventually found how to edit the videos; at first, we had to sit and watch a whole game. At least, too, they eventually said that only the team and reserves for the next game had to be present.

Even so, the meetings became boring and repetitive. I felt that we spent too long talking and worrying about the opposition and not long enough talking about ourselves. All the home teams played in the same style anyway, so once you had laid plans to play one, you had laid plans to play them all. The team meetings turned the tour into a treadmill.

So did the training. The sessions were daily and endless. We would even venture out on the morning of matches for some extra bits and pieces – perhaps on to a patch of parkland or waste ground near the hotel. It took some of the soul from the play. To have endless sessions at the start of the tour, when we trained at the Kerikeri and Kawakawa clubs, was understandable. No problem. They would soon tail off and become shorter and sharper. Wouldn't they? They never did. Geech was trying to get a message through, but I was bored inside two days at Pahia.

But some of this still lay in the future. We left Pahia to travel down the road for the first match, against North Auckland in Whangarei. I was chosen, alongside Scott Hastings in the centre and under the captaincy of Barnes. And no matter how hard he tried to hide it, the honour excited him no end. Barnesie and I worked out a few things in order to make an impression and it is no offence to Rob Andrew to say that I dearly wanted Barnes to make the Test team. We were friends and, apart from that, he was a better player. He started off the tour with his usual drinking habits – steady supping of red wine. Once we reached the half-way stage and he was out of the Test team, it was a regular thing to see Barnesie boarding the coach for training in the morning wearing Ray-Bans, after the kind of session we referred to as 'Two Quiet Ones (followed by Twenty Loud Ones)'.

The first game is always an ordeal. Barnes led us on, we started badly and our legs felt the way legs should feel at the end of a long tour.

I could not believe how tired I was. We eventually won 30–17, scoring four tries (Scott Hastings, Clement, Rory Underwood, Guscott) to three, although to say we subdued North Auckland would not be true. They began at pace and ranged from fast to even faster.

Our first try was a classic, set up by Barnes. Tony Clement came up into the line and passed back inside to Barnes, who made a clean break straight up the middle of the field. I came up on Stuart's right and Rory came up on his left. I shouted loudest. Barnes passed to me and I had the full-back, Warren Johnston, to beat. Johnston was slow and big, and I could not have taken the flak in the team room if he had caught me. He didn't. After the phoney war it was good to have a match under the belt.

It was pleasing to win, and to score. And it was a big night. Partly thanks to the England team's PR machine, the impression has been given that top rugby players have grown abstemious. I can't speak for the others, but this Lions team had some champion drinkers. Webster, Jason Leonard, Nick Popplewell and Damien Cronin were of world class and, with respect to Damien, at the end of the tour he looked like it; and although a mere back I like to think I could live in that company.

The hotel, a faded establishment in the centre of Whangarei, laid on a Karaoke, and surprise, surprise, Webster was the first entrant behind the microphone. Eventually, I took over behind the bar in the absence of the proprietor. When he returned, he was not pleased at all.

Nor was poor Ian Hunter, who had dislocated his shoulder and was out of the tour after one match. In the excitement of the tour taking off, it was a reminder that it only took one injury for a player's tour to be over.

I have no problem whatsoever with New Zealand's rucking. They stop players killing the ball and it is accepted by their referees. The biggest rucking I ever had was in a match against Scotland at Murrayfield. It happened in a flash as their forwards went over me in a wedge, with studs flying. No problem. It can sometimes be excessive, and then it is up to the referee to sort things out, because a deliberate kick in the head is something completely different.

The rucking controversy, 1993 version, began against North

Harbour, in a match played in the suburbs of Auckland at the soulless Mount Smart Stadium, which we won 29–13. Dean Richards caught Frank Bunce in the head as he came into a ruck; soon, the home forwards were rushing in to retaliate and a huge punch-up began. One of Frank Bunce's promotional activities with the rugby union there is a campaign called Play Hard, Play Fair. Dean Richards had been given a shirt bearing that motto, so it was highly ironic when they clashed on the field.

I thought our reaction was brilliant. It showed everyone in New Zealand that we had come to compete. We would not be vigilantes, but we would deal with things, we would look after one another. All the Lions stood next to one another and traded punch for punch, which was good.

Apart from the flying fists, it was the hands of Scott Gibbs, and his passing and his handling skills, which made the biggest impression on me. We scored four tries, through Tony Underwood, Rob Andrew, Richard Webster and a brilliant effort by Ieuan Evans. North Harbour scored one try, and their famous backs never showed. Through our fists and Scott's hands, and through a handy all-round effort, the tour was on the road.

We had shown talent and in the next match we were absolutely forced to use it. We played the Maoris at Athletic Park, Wellington. I appeared for a six-minute cameo, replacing Will Carling as partner for Scott Hastings in the centre. At one stage we were 20–0 down, and Ben Clarke had to bring off a brilliant tackle to stop another try. It was also obvious that Peter Wright and Damien Cronin were off the pace, because they occasionally laboured yards behind the play. Allan Prince and Steve Hirini scored their tries, and even early in the second half, there was no revival in sight.

When it came it was brilliant. Ieuan Evans scored a typical try, weaving down his wing to score from almost nothing. Almost immediately afterwards, Ieuan set up another try by running the ball flat across the field, linking with Will Carling and Scott Hastings, and Scott sent Rory Underwood down the wing for the try. We were back. Gavin Hastings scored the try which put us in the lead near the end. No doubt the relief of our supporters was tinged with anxiety that parts of our game were not working properly, but by

Simply the start of two world-class celebrations. Above: the fizz flies as England celebrate the first Grand Slam for eleven years, and France are beaten. Right: Manager Clive Rowlands, heart on sleeve and can in hand, orchestrates the hysteria after the defeat of Australia in the Third Test in 1989, the first Lions tour series success for fifteen years. (17, 18)

Some coaches who tried to get their messages through to me, with varying degrees of success. Above: Roger Uttley and Ian McGeechan getting to grips. Right: Geoff Cooke, not the magician of his publicity, but a superb organizer. Opposite page top: Richard Best, deserving respect, although not three laps of the pitch. Opposite page bottom: One coach who did get through: Jack Rowell – complicated, clever, unreachable. (19, 20, 21, 22)

The 1993 Courage League title is safely in the bag after the win at Saracens. High-level celebrations, still in playing kit, with take-off, flight and landing safely accomplished. (23, 24, 25)

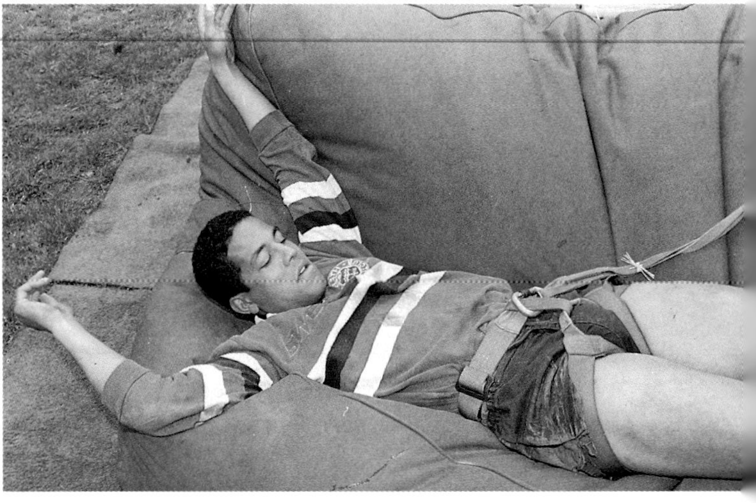

Trying to put Scott Gibbs, a close friend and a brilliant centre, in the clear playing for the 1993 British Lions against Auckland. (26)

As the 1993 Lions tour progressed, we kicked more and more. I joined the club in the victory over the All Blacks in the Second Test in Wellington. (27)

At the centre of celebrations for my third Grand Slam with England after victory over the Scots at Twickenham. (28a)

There are now too many donkey forwards in midfield. Here I feel the full force of Phil Kearns, the Australian hooker, in the emotional quarter-final. (28b)

Handing on rare possession in Pretoria during the play-off against France. (28c)

Scenes from another career. Promotional shots taken for various uses, and hanging off the cliff while filming *Body Heat* for Central TV, which I presented with Sally Gunnell. (29, 30, 31)

now, New Zealanders were beginning to sit up and take notice, and talk about the stars of our back division.

The legend of the Wellington Three was born in Wellington during that visit. Before the match, some of the players not involved went to an Irish bar, the kind which had sprung up in several places in New Zealand. Robert Jones, Richard Webster, Dean Richards and Jason Leonard were the ringleaders, and it was a major night. Dean, Jason and myself were the last people back and were crashing around the hotel making serious noise as we disappeared towards our rooms.

Next morning at the team meeting, Geoff Cooke complained about noisy players. He asked those responsible to see him after the meeting. Needless to say, none of us went. Loyally, I decided not to grass up the others. Till now. The Wellington Three are revealed.

However, there was another mystery. Poor Popplewell was badly affected by homesickness. He kept hinting that he would have to go home. I have found out since that on the same night as the Irish Bar Excursion, Mike Teague and others decided on a Cheer Up Poppie night, and their group came steaming into the hotel at an unearthly hour as well. They all looked at each other when Cooke made his complaint next day. Perhaps my Wellington Three were not the real culprits after all.

Lancaster Park, the home ground of Canterbury, has a beautiful surface. When we arrived to walk the pitch before the match against Canterbury it looked as beautiful as ever, flat, the grass cut short and emerald green. It was only when we actually walked on it and started to sink that the trouble became obvious. Heavy rain had saturated it completely, and when the game started, players falling or being tackled sent up sheets of spray.

We won easily, 28–10, with tries by Galwey, Guscott, Tony Underwood and Andrew. Four minutes from the end, Stuart Barnes came on for Rob Andrew. Almost immediately, he made a typical break. He stepped inside, then out, and was clear. I went through with him, as I always do. He passed to me, the try was almost assured and it could only have been good news for Barnes's prospects. For some reason, I stopped looking at the ball and looked up to see where I was going. I dropped the ball. Barnes looked at me with an expression which, on reflection, may have been reproachful. To say the least.

Further down the South Island, our progress hit the buffers when we played the match which affected the tour thinking for ever. The thrashing we received from Otago helped to draw us back from the expansive game we had been playing. After Otago we played miserably against Southland in Invercargill, the next stop before the terminus at the end of the world. Then we lost the first Test. So much for progress.

The Otago match was the real ground-breaker. We were in no trouble. Ieuan scored on the right after Barnes broke and missed me out with his pass. We were comfortable. But suddenly the match slipped. Wade had a poor game in the middle of the line-out, and the ball stopped emerging. When we did win it, Otago swarmed all over us, managing to strip the ball away. Off they went with it. Backs always know when the game is drifting away – we spend all our time tackling and chasing.

We lost momentum, and we were to lose our ambition as the conservatives took over. Some of the senior forwards began to insist that we cut out mistakes, played more to the percentages. That Otago result put our backs to the wall, and the reaction was strong.

Gavin Hastings had become more vocal by this stage. When we were checked in at the Christchurch hotel in preparation for the first Test, he began to talk about the overwhelming importance of winning; insisting that we had to win for our families, wives and friends 12,000 miles away. It had no effect on me, but it may have been what the other lads wanted to hear. It is part of the routine, but I never miss those speeches if they don't happen.

Yet the tension was rising. Will Carling and I were the centres, and Rob Andrew was at fly-half. Stuart Barnes was not considered – he had been cut on the head by an accidental kick from Robert Jones in a scrappy win over Southland. Our forwards failed to sort out Southland when they tried to put the boot in.

If it was possible, we trained even harder in Christchurch. We watched videos of the All Blacks, and Will and I paid particular attention to Frank Bunce and Walter Little, our opposite numbers. I knew that Bunce was a very heavy tackler, and I knew that I probably wouldn't have to tackle Little at all. Invariably, he turns back inside towards the forwards.

However, Inga Tuigamala would need tackling, and neither of us was desperate to have him turning back inside towards us. It is totally unfair – anyone weighing over 16 stone should be ordered to play in the forwards and to leave us alone. Change the laws.

We spoke to Ieuan Evans about his job of marking Tuigamala. McGeechan had noticed that the teams which played him best were those who sat on him, left him no space in which to run or even to move. I spent the first Test shouting to Ieuan – 'Get in. Get in. Don't give him room.'

On the Friday, a few of us were sitting outside the team room, on a balcony overlooking the packed public areas of the Park Royal, our hotel. All the preparations – apart from the final team talking – were done. A group of Kiwis walked straight past us and into the team room, which we always regarded as sacrosanct. It was sometimes our only refuge from thousands of punters.

Mike Teague walked in after them and asked them what they wanted. 'This is our team room,' he said. They replied that it was a part of sporting history and they wanted to look around. The team room is hardly a cultural Mecca – just a few bottles of orange juice and a video and some chairs.

My sense of rugby history let me down again, because one of the intruders was an old All Black. His name meant nothing to me. 'If you were an All Black then you'll understand the concept of the team room and having privacy,' I said. Off they went, with ruffled feathers.

Match day, Test day. I got up at 10.30. We put on our tracksuits, wandered to a small park nearby and went through a few more things. Undertrained we were not. We had another meeting at 1.15, then a smaller one when everyone bar the 15 starters left. McGeechan spoke, so did Dick Best, so did Gavin Hastings.

We boarded the coach. Gavin had said that there was too much chit-chat on the coach to games on the tour. The implication was that we were not focusing well enough. Different things work for different people, and perhaps Gavin was over-reacting. But the coach was deathly quiet (apart from the engine). As usual, there was an

ITV cameraman wandering around sticking his lens in your face. That sort of thing gets on my nerves. It is unnecessary.

McGeechan singled me out. He said that I was the person for the big occasion. This was the stage for me. I should show the Kiwis what I could do. But I never really got the chance. It was a day on which the preparations counted for nothing and we lost, 20–18. It was a nervous and a poor game. We played nothing like as well as we should have done, and we were robbed by the referee as well.

Brian Kinsey, the official, had taken charge of the Test matches when England toured Argentina in 1990, and he left a nasty taste in English mouths then. He was not welcome back. The match turned on two decisions by him. Near the start, when the All Blacks were throwing everything at us, Grant Fox put up a high kick. Bunce and Evans jumped for it and they came crashing down together over our line. Bunce looked the strongest on the ball, but Ieuan definitely had his hands on it too. Kinsey was yards away from the play, but gave the try anyway.

But within a few minutes of the end of injury time at the end of the match, we were leading 18–17. Gavin kicked six goals, including a tremendous kick to put us in the lead. We had held them out with ease when they tried to attack, and they had one more chance at the end. Even their own crowd had begun to react against them.

Then, Dean Richards caught Bunce to stop yet another attack. He took man and ball, turned Bunce round and the maul collapsed. Dean could have let Bunce go and lose the ball or go down together. They went down together and Bunce came down facing our side. It seemed the perfect tackle. There is no way it would ever have come out on their side unless Bunce had turned over illegally in the tackle.

The only possible decisions were a scrum to the Lions for the turnover, or a penalty to the Lions. He gave a penalty against us. Gavin came up to remonstrate, Dewi Morris was furious. If I was Kinsey, I would be extremely embarrassed to look at that incident again. We are training harder and harder in rugby at the moment. We are devoting more and more time. But Kinsey reminded everyone that referees are not keeping up. They are standing still and letting down the game. The way they appoint referees to big games should be overhauled, because players are being let down by refereeing standards and interpretations.

In the dressing-room, the reaction was that we had lost the game because of the referee. It was not sour grapes. It had been a very poor game in which both teams made far too many mistakes. If we didn't deserve to win it, then the All Blacks didn't either. It all hinged on the referee and, because of him, we now had to try to come back from 0–1 in a three-match series. From that point on, we were always trying to play catch-up.

You could tell how serious it all was. The management gave us a day off training on the Sunday. It was just as well, because the sorrows had to be drowned, and the game had left us with casualties. We flew to New Plymouth next day for the match against Taranaki. I slept through the flight from take-off to touch-down. After we landed, the lads told me that it had been an horrendously bumpy trip.

So was the tour itself, by now. We beat Taranaki, 49–25, with Barnes in charge and playing well. The hotel and food in Taranaki still left a lot to be desired, but New Plymouth pulled out all the stops to make us feel welcome. Bull Allen, the All Black squad prop, was the local hero. He seemed a well-balanced bloke, too. But he tried to make too much of an impression and probably got in his team's way.

Scott Gibbs played well against Taranaki, completing a lightning recovery from his injury and stretchered departure at Southland. When the team was announced for the match against Auckland – obviously a trial for the second Test – Gibbs was in. Carling was dropped and, predictably, the media pack hounded him. I congratulated Scott. Will and I never discussed it. There was very little I could have said.

I also found trouble off the field in New Plymouth. After a major night of relaxation, I dimly remember crawling into a taxi which was already full of Lions, and my foot striking the dashboard as I did so. We also made some noise in the hotel corridor. Next day, I was called to Geoff Cook's suite. 'You lot had a night of it last night, didn't you?' Cooke asked. Apparently, he had received a bill from the taxi driver for 400 New Zealand dollars for damage to his dashboard. The driver had called round at the hotel in the morning. 'He said that you were the only one he recognized.' I wonder why.

And by this stage of the tour, the senior players in the party, especially the senior forwards like Dean Richards and Brian Moore, were becoming more conservative in their outlook. So were the coaches. Slowly, we had been turning away from our initial policy of moving the ball and relying on the speed and skill of our backs. We lost the Auckland match 23–18, even though we scored a penalty try and another Ieuan Evans special. We seemed to sit back and allow them to come at us in the second half. They were a good side but they were not unbeatable, and yet they beat us. With good ball, our backs had scored a great try. But we did not seem to be trusted after that.

Then, any support from the midweek team began to collapse completely. A considerable drinking school had evolved in the team. They were thrashed and humiliated by Hawkes Bay and Waikato. And when the chips were down, some of the Lions forwards were worse than pathetic. My memories of watching the second half at Hawkes Bay are of the poor Lions backs having to tackle the Hawkes Bay front row as they ran riot. I felt anger at some of the people who were not giving their best, and I felt very sorry for those who *were* trying – Barnes was trying to get into the Test team; Carling was trying to get his tour back on the road; Webster was another who played his heart out.

To come off the field not having played as hard as you could is a disgraceful thing for a British Lion. Some of the Scottish forwards were yards off the pace and out of their depth. I never saw a front five player make a tackle in the whole match. At our traditional post-match debriefing session, Barnes, the captain, blew his lid. He said that players were shirking their responsibilities, were running away from confrontation, were letting down the traditions of the British Lions. It was quite a speech, and he was expressing the feelings of the majority of the squad. McGeechan both backed him up and cut him short. He stepped in smartly, and said: 'I think Stuart has said what we all know.'

We flew back to Wellington from Napier after the Hawkes Bay shambles, for the match which would save or end the tour, the second Test. I expected long training sessions. I was not disappointed. The session we had in Wellington, a closed affair away from the cameras and media, was the longest I have ever been involved in. It must have lasted at least three hours, and we must have covered every blade of grass on the training pitch at least three times.

We started with every possible situation that might arise in the match. First, we walked through what our reaction would be; then we ran through it. We went through everything you could possibly imagine. It was far, far too long and it showed that the element of pre-programming was taking over from any reliance on spontaneity.

Some of the players prefer it like that. Rob Andrew already knew most of it, because that sort of thing is what his game is based on. Dewi Morris was worried about communication between Rob and Dean Richards, worried about who was going to call what, and where. The tension mounted when Gavin Hastings reacted angrily to the fact that some young children had arrived to watch the closed session and were bantering from the touch-lines.

McGeechan apologized afterwards for the length of the session. He said it was necessary for everyone to know what he was doing. To be fair, the talk was all that the tour was over if we lost the Test.

Was Gavin's tour over? He had pulled a hamstring against Auckland and come off – leaving Will to face the music out of position at full-back. Now, with the Test approaching, Gavin was taking almost no part. On the Thursday, he was simply jogging about. He could not even contemplate any kicking. The tension was bad enough in any case, but we started to become anxious. 'Come on, Geech,' I remember saying. 'Either he's going to play or he isn't. I don't want to have a brand new full-back come in two hours before the match. And I don't want Gavin outside me if he's going to be 15 yards behind when we look for him.' I was aggravated by it all. So were others. Rob Andrew was trying to find out; even Rory Underwood was less relaxed about the fuss than usual.

On the Friday morning session, there was a major meeting on the pitch involving all the management, our popular medical people, Dr James Robson and Kevin Murphy, and Gavin and Tony Clement. I knew that Tony also had a niggling injury, though understandably he was keeping quiet about it. Later, McGeechan tried some kidology. 'He just wants some of you to tell him he should play. That is what he needs. He's all right really, he's just unsure inside.'

'Come on Gav,' I pleaded dutifully. 'You can bloody play.' He played. The atmosphere before the game was incredible. The stakes were enormous. But after the fuss and the hard work of the previous two weeks, after the upheavals and the saga of the Hastings Hamstring, all I wanted to do was get out there and get stuck into it.

After a couple of minutes I wished we had never bothered to talk Gavin round. He dropped a high kick coming at him out of the sun and Eroni Clarke scored near our posts. We would not have been half as worried, however, if we had known then that it was to be their only score of the match.

People told me afterwards that it was one of the greatest days in Lions history. I'll have to take their word for it. We won 20–7, but if it sounds like an easy victory it certainly wasn't. My memories are of tackling, tackling, trying to close down Timu and Tuigamala. And of chasing kicks, because we kicked almost all the time. Martin Bayfield dominated the line-out, and our pack held on brilliantly in the line-out and especially in the scrum, where once they pushed back the All Blacks a crucial few feet just when the All Blacks were gathering themselves for a pushover. Brian Moore was rightly proud of that. I remember the noise of our supporters, which amazed me. It sounded as if the crowd was about 65% British and Irish.

And I remember the try – Fitzpatrick dropping it, Dewi seizing it, putting me away down the right; my efforts to draw Kirwan's attention; and Kirwan finally coming in to take me, and Rory streaking away to score.

In the wild exultation immediately after the match, I tended to sit back and savour things. I looked around. Rob Andrew was in the same state I imagined him to be in when Emily, his daughter, was born. Even the quiet Peter Winterbottom, who had played so well, was showing emotion. I remember the door constantly opening and closing, people demanding to speak to individual Lions.

Dean Richards actually went back out, roused by distant roars of 'Deano, Deano.' He sang with the crowd who were besieging the dressing-rooms. The ITV cameraman poked his nose and camera in as well. In the medical room, Brian Moore was a celebration waiting to happen. He was stuck trying to fulfil the obligations of the drug test.

It was a great win, a win based on our forward play, kicking and defence. The tour was revived, and we had the momentum for the final and deciding Test. I felt that I had fulfilled all the personal goals I had set myself, had done enough in defence in Wellington and elsewhere to gain respect as an all-round player, not just an attacker. It was all a tremendous feeling.

After the midweek shambles at Waikato, a sad way for most of the midweek team to end their Lions careers, the preparation ground on. The media interest in the third Test back in Auckland was incredible. It seemed as if the whole of the British Isles and New Zealand had stopped for rugby. And our training stopped for no one.

People droned on about history in the making, our chance to become immortals, our chance to put Northern Hemisphere rugby on the top of the pile. Gavin made glorious speeches. To me, it was an important match, but still just another match. To be too carried away about history would mean less concentration on the match.

And in any case, we missed the appointment with history. The Test was lost, 30–13. We did make a great start, with a penalty by Gavin and a try by Scott Gibbs, but we were muscled out of the line-out. In the backs, we spent the whole afternoon chasing, and never had a chance to show what we could do.

The All Blacks were improved, their line-out functioned, and they scored tries through Bunce, Fitzpatrick and Jon Preston. In the final stages they forced us to ship out ball that should have been kept tight, and in the end they won with something to spare. They did not convince me at any point in the series that they were unbeatable, but they had won. It was a desperate way for the tour to end.

Our final record, with only seven wins from 13 matches, looks poor on paper, although even New Zealanders recognized that we had come close to winning the Test series. We could still look back at referee Kinsey's decision to award a try to Frank Bunce and the disputed penalty to Grant Fox in the first Test. If we had won that Test, the whole psychological balance would have shifted. New Zealand would probably have won the second Test, as a backlash, and we would probably have won the third. Even as it stood, if we had won the same amount of line-out ball in the third Test that we won in the second, we would have been home and dry anyway.

The All Blacks were a very good team, highly motivated and focused. But they were nothing frightening, and it seemed to me that we became frightened anyway, frightened of expressing the talents we had in the team. Certain teams in history have taken the game into another dimension – the Australians in 1984, the All Blacks later in the 1980s. We had the chance to do the same and we missed it. We had the ability in the party to beat the All Blacks by 15 points in every Test match, which really would have established rugby in the British Isles for the next decade.

We missed the chance by gradually moving away from the style we showed at the start of the tour, in beating North Auckland, North Harbour, Christchurch and the Maoris. The drift from attacking rugby to conservatism was difficult to spot. It happened below the surface and slowly, but it happened.

At the start, the backs were highly effective. Ieuan Evans played as well as he has ever played. He was the best finisher playing the game at the time. All four centres who started the tour played well. We had strength all round – Ben Clarke had a tremendous tour. I can't remember him taking one backward step, and to play out of position at the level he achieved is exceptional. Nick Popplewell impressed me. To see him taking tackles head on was a great sight. It was a party which had every ability and which could have played some brilliant rugby till the end.

By the end, however, we were playing by computer, with Rob Andrew kicking it down the field. It is not entirely a criticism of the coaching and management, because we allowed it to happen. With hindsight, I should have spoken out when I sensed the conservatives taking a hold, but I did not. And I am certainly not saying that I had a perfect tour while the others didn't, because I made mistakes too.

Ian McGeechan is a good coach. He could always say that the players had a licence to perform, to do what they wanted to do. He was, he said, only giving the players a basis, a platform to perform on. But when the pressure was on, there was more and more programming, less and less spontaneous rugby. The interminable session before the second Test proved that.

I admit that I am biased towards Stuart Barnes, but only because I admire him as a player. He was the best fly-half in Britain at the time and one of the three best in the world. My idea of beating the All Blacks was not to go plodding round the pitch saying that we'll do this here, and we'll do that there. It was of Barnes and the backs playing the match off the cuff, as they saw it at the time.

McGeechan and the rest of us spent an awful lot of time watching videos. In his mind, I am sure that he had a perfect, programmed game of rugby and believed that his players could get close to it. It worked well if we won the line-out, sent the ball back to Rob, and Rob kicked it; or if, one pass on from Rob, a centre went into contact, sent it back and then Rob kicked it. There are few mistakes to be made in this style, very few things that can go wrong. It was a style based around McGeechan's favourite players, Rob and Dean Richards.

It worked brilliantly in the second Test; and who was going to speak up after that victory and before the third Test? But when the line-out ball dried, it was simply not effective, it left us nowhere to go.

Perhaps the change in style was subconscious, even in McGeechan and Dick Best. Geech certainly changed the style without causing all the backs to think: 'Christ, we've just changed style.' But change we did. We changed because we started losing, started letting the opposition in with our mistakes, as we did against Otago. But if we were to beat the All Blacks, we had to go the extra mile to find the extra yard of space. Instead, we sat back.

After the 1989 tour, when I ran into Ian McGeechan, he was apologetic about having had to spend all his time sorting out our forward play, which meant he could never devote enough time to releasing the potential of our backs. I don't know what his final verdict would be on the 1993 tour – except that he was as disappointed as anyone that all his hard work didn't achieve a series victory.

Did the Lions distrust Barnes, as England have apparently distrusted him over the years? Probably. He did not always play as well as he can. He was injured at the wrong time, too, but even at the best of times he was never given the chance to show what he can really do. When he was trying to mount a challenge, the rest of the team collapsed around him.

Gavin Hastings had a good press, and was hailed for his inspirational leadership. He did play well and sometimes spoke well. But I am disputing the Gavin legend just a little. He made errors in all three Tests, and you would hardly expect a player like Gavin to concede the kind of soft tries which he did. He made elementary mistakes in the final Test, failing to appear at all when Frank Bunce scored a try and missing Jon Preston completely when Preston scored near the end. Some players would have been vilified in the press for those errors. Gavin was also essentially a conservative player, like his coach.

On some occasions he was indeed inspirational. He was very quiet to begin with, a contrast to Finlay Calder in 1989. There are times when he finds it difficult to express what he feels. Sometimes, he retreats to his own planet, his own zone.

He is also probably a little less confident than he sometimes appears. In the first Test, he came up to take a shot at goal from longish range. He ran past Will on his way to play the ball. 'I'm going to have a go, so chase it,' he said. He ran past me. 'Chase it to f–k,' he said. I looked at him as he went past. You're going to miss this, I thought. He missed.

Even so, it was all a marvellous experience. Lions tours are unbeatable. For me, it was different in tone to the 1989 trip. There, we were playing on hard and fast grounds, we were dominant, and to a player completely new to international rugby, it almost seemed like a party. But for days on end in Australia on that tour, you were aware that some of the people around you hardly knew there was a tour on, hardly knew who you were.

New Zealand may not have had the sun and the hard pitches and the excitement of the new experiences, but in a sense it was a better tour – chiefly because of the way the tour and the Lions were perceived and respected in a country that understands rugby. But it would have been more marvellous still had we not retreated into our shell, if we had taken the chances we had to beat New Zealand as we should have done.

11
All Roads Lead to Tormarton
Waiting for the million from the rugby league scout

We all know the scenarios in which a rugby league club tries to entice away a young rugby union player to a contract and a career in the north of England. Indeed, the whole mythical scene has almost become a music-hall joke in both codes of rugby.

It goes something like this. The young player is summoned to a secret meeting in a secret location, usually the dark corner of a pub. There, he meets a few suited-up northerners, and in the best imaginary stories, one of them is always Alex Murphy. For many people in the rest of the country, Alex represents the loud voice and face of rugby league.

After a little flattery from the rugby league men – how well they think the young man will do in rugby league, and so on – they always produce a briefcase bulging with a contract, with a space on the bottom for the player to sign his union career away and move away to St Helens, Leeds, Widnes or Bradford. And together with this contract, they produce a chequebook, with a cheque already made out in the player's name, and containing a decent number of noughts at the end of the amount.

It never happens that way in real life, of course. Or does it? Visitors to the Compass Inn, in Tormarton, near the M4 junction for Bath, a few years ago may have noticed a group in a deserted corner of the dining area. It had everything from the supposed traditional scenario: it had the northerners in suits, one of whom was Alex Murphy himself; it had the flattery, the briefcase, the contract, the big cheque. And there was the young rugby player with a chance to sign away his life and move lock, stock and barrel to the north. Me.

Because of something about my abilities and my image I have always been deemed fair game for an approach from rugby league and, especially for writers running short of ideas, fair game for a major story discussing the latest offer I was wrestling with – whether or not I had actually received the offer. After the second Test between Australia and the British Lions in 1989, when I scored the try which sealed the match, several papers began their report, not by praising the try, or the Lions' victory, but by estimating how much this had increased my estimated transfer value to rugby league clubs. Strange.

However, I have received a stream of offers from rugby league over the years. Those which became public caused no end of speculation. I apparently added fuel to this by my stock answer: 'I would always consider joining rugby league if the right offer came along.' This is always interpreted in several ways: that I am about to sign any day; that I am desperate to sign for league; or even that I am touting myself around for a good offer.

But there is no hidden meaning. It is a statement to be taken at face value. How can you rule out ever signing for rugby league? Someone may offer me £1m, in which case I would sign tomorrow. Half a million? Only maybe.

The first approach I ever had came before I was even established in the Bath team. One evening when Bath were in pre-season training at Bath University, I came upon a gathering of local journalists and TV crews. They came running up as soon as I arrived. We know you have been approached by Hull Kingston Rovers to sign for rugby league, they said. Are you going? And could you be faithful to your region and give us the scoop?

I told them that I hadn't been approached, and I could see that they didn't believe me. So I told them that I had yet to accomplish anything in rugby union, that I wanted to achieve my ambitions in union and had therefore decided not to accept the kind offer from rugby league which I had never had.

Soon afterwards, Hull Kingston Rovers did contact me. They asked me to go up to Hull, to look at their set-up. They gave me the flannel, about how they knew I would be a big success. I declined. I never found out if they intended to make an offer and the reporters got wind of it, or if they were just reacting to the flurry of reports and decided that, since the papers said they were interested, they had better be interested.

Over the years, offers arrived. Widnes, Wigan, Salford and some God-forsaken second division club all rang. The chairman might ring, or the secretary. Would I like to see their set-up, they knew I'd be a sensation in rugby league, they were just ringing on the off chance I'd be interested, and so on. I usually gave the same reply. Not interested at the moment, but I had no objection if they wanted to call back in a year – I was still leaving the door ajar for that £1m!

I had an approach from a third party who wanted to arrange a meeting between myself and Doug Laughton, who is now with Leeds but who at the time was manager of Widnes and had signed Jonathan Davies from Llanelli. It was hardly a lavish hard sell, because Laughton, so the intermediary said, wanted to meet in a lay-by near Bath. I was intrigued and agreed to the meet. I drove to the appointed lay-by. Laughton never arrived, so I never found out if he had the £1m standing by.

There have been two approaches from Australian rugby league. While I was playing a season in Wollongong in 1987, still only 20, I was contacted by Balmain. They had me driven down to Sydney, where Benny Elias, one of the most famous Australian players of the era, met me, took me around the club headquarters, and told me what a massive hit I would be (even though they had hardly, if ever, seen me play).

Later, after establishing myself with England and the Lions, I was called by Manly-Warringah, the famous club across the harbour from Sydney. Graham Lowe was their coach at the time. I had a call from an intermediary, then Lowe himself came on with the usual procedure and the flannel. He mentioned the lovely hard and fast grounds, which at least made me think. But again, as far as a concrete offer went, we never passed 'go'. Also while I was in Australia, this time on the 1989 Lions tour, Ellery Hanley telephoned me. He was playing in Australian rugby league at the time. He had just heard a rumour, he said, that I was joining St Helens. He said that I should not join St Helens when I could join a better club like Wigan. I thanked him for his concern, but yet again we were discussing an offer I had never had.

The two biggest and most sustained approaches of all came from

St Helens and Bradford Northern. Joe Pickavance, chairman of St Helens, telephoned, and from the tone and content of the call it was clear that they were keenly interested. Soon after, Bath were in the north to play a league match against Liverpool-St Helens. After the match I showered and changed, climbed into my car and drove to Joe Pickavance's home. Alex Murphy was there.

We sat down. The usual story emerged – about how well they thought I was suited, and how in their team, they had some good boys who would look after me. Murphy told me that he reckoned I would be in the Great Britain team after one season. There were a few awkward silences while I waited for the real offer, the sum itself. They never mentioned it. I was tempted to say: 'All right then, how much?' but I could never bring myself to ask. The conversation petered out, and I solemnly told them that I'd go away and think about it. Think about what? They hadn't told me. It was a shame that I was not more experienced. I could have had much more fun with them.

Soon afterwards, Pickavance called again, suggesting a meeting in my area, and so we all trooped up to Tormarton and to the Compass Inn. Pickavance and Murphy were joined by the club treasurer, and this time they had come to talk turkey. Alex Murphy sat on my left, Pickavance on my right and the treasurer in front of me. Murphy gave it the big sell and then produced the contract and the chequebook. They offered me £150,000 for a four-year contract. At the time I was still bricklaying. I did not have a massive salary. But even then, it was no big deal. I was not going to sign everything away for that amount.

They handed me the pen as if it was all sewn up. If they were trying to hurry me into signing, they failed. I told them that I still had an enormous amount left to achieve, still had things to do, and did not want to leave the West Country. Murphy affected to be put out that I had not signed, but they put the contract back into the case, and we all went to our cars and drove off. I can't remember if we actually ate the lunch they promised to buy me. St Helens stayed in contact. They sent me little notes when I came back from tours.

Bradford Northern have been easily the most persistent. They kept trying to entice me right up until the time of my injury in the 1993–94 season. Chris Caisley, their chairman, gave it the hard sell on the phone, and showered me with flattery. Soon afterwards I went up to the north to play a divisional match, and I went on to meet Chris in a hotel. Peter Fox, the Bradford coach with the battered features of the typical retired rugby leaguer, was also there. We sat in the coffee lounge, and they told me how devastating my sidestep and swerve would be in rugby league.

At a subsequent meeting, Bradford began to get serious. They offered me £300,000 for a four-year contract. I retorted that I needed a career, that I needed some security, because to move to Bradford I'd have to give up work.

'What sort of job are you thinking about?' asked Caisley.

'Marketing, PR, something on those lines,' I said.

They came back quickly. They had made a deal with a PR company to take me on, at £27,000 per year. They had put their money where their mouths were, and suddenly, I was freaked out. In all the history of 'negotiations' with the other clubs I have never for a second seriously contemplated signing. I always went along for the fun of it, to be nosy, to see how far they would go. I am sure that any player would play ball for a bit, just to see how golden the opportunity really was.

For the first time, I stopped in my tracks. Even then, it did not take long to decide against it. I said that I would go away and think about it. Caisley telephoned on the 1993 Lions tour, the day before one of the Tests. He apologized for bothering me before a big game, but he had important news. Would I consider signing if they added £25,000 to the signing-on fee?

I said no, and looking back, it was never even close. Not even when I was dropped by Bath in 1990 for the cup semi-final and every newspaper in the land ran a story which was effectively waving me goodbye as I disappeared up north in a huff. If I did sign it would mean uprooting myself and my family, and moving away from a city which has meant so much to me. Jayne has always said that the decision would be mine, that she would stick by me whatever I decided. But we never got as far as poring over our bank statements and saying: 'Christ, with that money we can buy this, or that.' If I did ever sign, I would sign simply for the money and not because I think that rugby league is a particularly great game. I am sure that, with hand on heart, all former union players who have gone to the north would say the same. I would sign the contract, train and play as hard as I could, then go back to my family and friends, regarding it simply as a day at the office.

In 1993, when the Bradford approach was at its height, I let it slip that I was seriously considering an offer. The media closed in, demanding to know. I had fun with them all. I even made a statement a day before I was due to announce my go-or-stay decision, solemnly thanking them for all their support and wishing them well for the future. I was teasing. I was going nowhere. But at least it focused everyone's attention on my column in the *Sunday Mirror* that Sunday. My editor was pleased.

Until recently, Wigan would always send me a videotape of the latest Challenge Cup triumph. A few days after each Wembley victory, the tape would arrive. It made very good viewing, too.

Of course, all the stakes changed in April 1995 with news that, as part of a battle over TV rights in Australian rugby league between Kerry Packer and Rupert Murdoch, a Superleague was to be set up in England, starting sometime in 1996. The Superleague plans caused no end of fuss in rugby league as teams tried to fight for their survival, campaigning not to be swallowed up in amalgamations.

Murdoch's organization put an enormous amount of money into this Superleague concept, which was badly needed because the league game in Britain was, apparently, bankrupt. So, as sure as night follows day, my name was appearing in the papers. If you believed everything you read I was receiving offers to join this Superleague, and also the new Star league in Australia, at the rate of five per day.

I was in Atlanta filming *Body Heat* when the news broke. Co-presenter Mike Smith had a computer with him that could pick up British newspapers on a kind of Internet. He came into one of our meetings, laid down the computer in front of us and said, 'The drinks are on Jeremy.' The story was that I was looking at half a million pounds. It was great to hear of yet another offer I had never had.

But obviously, it was time to be a little less flippant about rugby league because the money was coming direct from Murdoch. When I got back, Chris Caisley phoned and asked for a meeting. I was too tired to go all the way to Bradford to discuss something only in outline. He then phoned back again to say there was an offer on the table from Australia. Then he called back again and said: 'What about

£200,000 a year to play for Bradford in the Superleague.' I told him that I was simply not interested in playing rugby league in England for that money. I had to be honest and tell him that I have never really been attracted to league in England, and that I have always been more attracted to Australia. And I was certainly not going to talk about anything with anyone till after the World Cup.

My position as I returned from the World Cup was fairly clear in my mind. I had a number of possible offers away from sport to consider, and there was the promise of more money from life in the England squad. But I would have no qualms at all about accepting, say £350,000 per year for a two- or three-year contract with league, hopefully in Australia. If the terms and conditions were right I would be very tempted and nobody can really compete if someone offers to treble your salary for roughly the same amount of work. I had never really come close to signing before, but suddenly there was just a chance that serious offers might come along.

12
The Best-Dressed Millionaire?
Life under the crumbling wall of amateurism

I have always been used to winning. Not to come first was a new experience for a man who had played for the best club team in the world and also for an England team which dragged England rugby out of the doldrums, won two Grand Slams, back to back, and dominated European rugby for nearly six years.

Not to come first was hard enough. But fourth? It was a disaster. It was difficult to know how to cope, but with the support of Jayne and my family I pulled through. And in the final analysis, at least I could rest assured that I gave it my best shot. And after all, I beat six other top contenders to stand at Number 4 in the top ten. It was a tiny consolation.

I have often examined the qualities of the men who beat me, trying not to be bitter. It was George O'Dowd, formerly Boy George, who edged me out of third place. 'At the moment,' he said, 'I wear religious things, long, flowy robes, a lot of Indian stuff. Clothes are important but not as important as what goes on in your head.' What a contender.

In second place was Malcolm McLaren, former manager of the Sex Pistols. 'The idea of having a personal tailor in a world that has become so homogenized is really a very nice thing.' It sounded good, whatever he was on about.

The winner was Terence Stamp. 'I was keen to get into texture. In that sense I was a sensualist about clothes,' he said, in his acceptance speech. He sounded like a worthy winner to me.

My clothes consisted of 'Polo-neck by The Gap, jacket by Marks & Spencer, trousers from Blazer.' 'I never used to be a great one for wearing clothes,' I commented, when asked about my dress style. 'When I was a brickie I used to dive into a shop after work because I needed something for that night.'

Eventually, with the passing years, the disappointment became less. I now realize that to be named 'Britain's Best Dressed Man,' by Esquire *– or even fourth best – is an honour which comes to but a few men.*

By the end of 1989 I had become aware that for a man of my increasing profile, not to mention outstanding good looks, there was an ancillary world worth investigating. It was not a question of greed, just of taking opportunities which came your way and which sportsmen of similar profile had been enjoying in other sports for decades. It was about then that I took part in a commercial for a company associated with Brendan Foster, the former athlete. It was shown on Sky TV and, being inexperienced in the extreme in the commercial world, I was paid a pittance. I was so green in the ways of the medium and did not even realize that a couple of hundred pounds for the commercial was feeble reward.

It was only a few months after the time when I had scored my try for the British Lions in Queensland, and a member of the crowd had pronounced, in the hearing of Kevin Murphy, our physiotherapist: 'That boy will never lay another brick in his life.' He was right. I never did return to bricklaying, and I was now looking for a change of career direction. British Gas were soon to loom.

David Robson, then Bath coach, did some valuable and much-appreciated work on my behalf on the career front, and Malcolm Pearce, the businessman who has been so generous to the Bath club, helped to set up a modelling assignment which was covered in depth by BBC2 and reported widely. From that time on I have become known as Jeremy Guscott, part-time model, as if I am away on modelling assignments for three days every week. I wish.

But these things opened my eyes. I had already opened a business interiors office and showroom in Bristol. I had been paid £300. Bloody hell, I thought. It was incredible for one hour's work. The ancillary offers did not gush in, however; they trickled. But they gave me an insight and made the whole idea worth investigating.

Just before the 1991 World Cup, David Gay, the former Bath and England No. 8, introduced me to Maria Pedro. Maria was from

Real World, a company based near Bath but also in London, and which handled the affairs of luminaries such as Peter Gabriel. They were later to take on men of rather lesser musical talent such as Gareth Chilcott and Ben Clarke. I was later to meet Peter, who seemed a nice, rather shy man. He also insisted on playing us the tape of his latest album at the Real World studios. It was a difficult moment, as it was not really my kind of thing. Luckily, Jayne, who knew his music, intervened with some informed comment and we were saved.

Maria and I talked. It was very informal. I told Maria that I might be looking for someone to handle some of the extra work. She explained what she might be able to do for me. It was basically that I could hardly make all the deals and attend to all the details and still have a full-time job, a sport and a family. And that she could take all the hassle and the administration out of the whole thing. She mentioned a percentage which she would retain and I said yes. Let's go ahead.

That was the signal for an avalanche of papers to come through from Maria to David Gay, my solicitor. I have an aversion to signing things. I had heard all the horror stories before, of stars and musical people suing their manager and all that. I did not want to be stuck in a contract for years to come.

I phoned Maria from a train one day when I was returning from London. I told her about my misgivings. After some discussion she could see that I was on edge, but also that I really wanted to be taken on by her. She suggested we take it on a handshake.

'Perfect,' I said. The paper was thrown away and the deal was done. Every year an informal memo arrives, a reminder of her obligations to me and mine to her. It is then filed away and forgotten. I was in Real World.

Perhaps Maria had not quite got the full picture. She was gravely talking about taking the hassle away from all these details, as if they were coming in at the rate of a medium-sized avalanche. I think she sat around for a time waiting in vain for the phone to ring. But eventually, the phone did begin to ring.

There were no lectures from Maria about image and behaviour. However, I have always been determined to take every job seriously. If you are being false in the way you act you won't be around for very long. She did find it very, very difficult to come to terms with rugby's laws, with what we could do and what we could not do (so she was no different to most other people in that respect). 'Why can't you do this? Who makes these rules?' was her standard reaction in the early days.

An immediate difference was that, whereas before I would arrive in trains and taxis at the location, for the first six to eight months Maria always sent someone along with me, whether the job was a simple personal appearance or opening or a modelling assignment. This led to a bizarre communication problem. People would not speak to me. They would speak to the girl Maria had sent. 'Do you think Jeremy would mind doing this, or that?' My colleagues would then answer, while I stood around whistling to myself and feeling like a dummy. Chilcott was doing a fair number of appearances too. At training, we would always compare notes and experiences and funny stories.

It was an entry into the strange world of celebrity. Not every job would be undertaken for a fee; some would just be done as favours or to heighten the profile. But I appeared in the 'My Childhood' feature in *The Times*; and, more improbably, in the 'What's on My Mantelpiece' feature in the *Sunday Express*. The answer was not much. I did reveal that I kept a clock there which had been presented to me by the Bath club for the achievement in beating Wasps in one of our cup final triumphs. Helpfully, I explained that the clock was 'just something which tells the time'.

As well as the (scandalous) defeat in *Esquire*'s Best Dressed Man competition, I began to appear in the style magazines, the sports glossies. I was invited to golf tournaments, which I thoroughly enjoy. The Terry Wogan Golf Classic in Ireland was an exceptional event from every point of view, especially for the golf and Guinness. At the moment, I have an excellent deal with Rover.

Perhaps the most eye-opening assignment I have undertaken to date was part of a very good modelling contract with Littlewoods. I had to go to Miami, Florida for a total of eight days for an experience that was weird, superficial and fascinating. Perhaps Miami is somewhat divorced from the real world anyway, but add a modelling assignment into the mix and it becomes something else again.

The shoot was for clothes for one of the Littlewoods catalogues and it took place in the Art Deco area of the city where all the shoots are done; apparently, the light is perfect and remains good enough for the photographers until later in the evening. There were four professional models, two male and two female, all from America; and me, an amateur rugby union player from Larkhall, Bath. We were photographed in various kinds of sports clothing, in various different poses. Jumping up and down. Running on the spot. Making crazy faces. I was laughing all the way through.

The lads back at Bath expected that I would feel totally embarrassed. I didn't. It was work. All the others were doing exactly the same. It was all acting. When the crew called for action, you would assume the expressions and the poses. Then they would finish, you would snap out of it and become normal again. Then, the fingers would start clicking on the shutters again and you would be back in the false world.

In the time off, the models asked me about rugby. I asked them about modelling, and travelling the world. If they were jealous of this unknown entering their world they never showed it. I was probably a little stiff at first, but they were helpful. I have also been asked if I thought I actually earned the money, posing around in the sun of Miami. I thought in one sense it was easy money, because I enjoyed the experience. But again, it was work and some of it was hard work.

On the final day in Miami there was no work, just a free day prior to flying back to Britain. Walking along the beach in the course of a leisurely day, I came across a strange scruffy guy, obviously just drooling at the girls playing beach volleyball. It scared me. The whole place was weird. There was a constant parade, a promenade, going on. People parading on roller skates, people with long blonde hair and shorts and shades. There were convertible cars with cool dudes and blonde bimbos. It was a different world.

Once, when we were doing some shots in an outdoor beach gym, we came across a German model being photographed in lingerie. The girls I was modelling with said that she was probably being exploited, that she had probably been walking down the street and some guys had come up and said: 'So you want to be in modelling. Will you come and wear these for us?'

There have been times when Maria and I have had fairly sharp words because I haven't wanted to do things. I have a rigid cut-off point in that I am given a set number of days in a year by British Gas to do the ancillary things. If a job would take me beyond that number, however lucrative, then I turn it down. That period has therefore to be prime time, so that I can get the most benefit. Maria would like me to have 150 days and, indeed, I could fill 150 days on my own if that was all I wanted to do.

But I have British Gas. And I have a family. At the beginning of each session, Jayne and I talk about the forthcoming commitments and how we will approach them. We have come to terms with the absences, and Maria and I have come to terms with the fact that when the fax comes through from her offices with prospective work for the immediate future, I will put a Yes against some and a No against others. *The Word* want you; Paula wants you on the bed on *The Big Breakfast*. There is this awards function, that dinner needing a speaker. Adidas want you for a shoot. There are many different requests from many different areas.

Jayne might say: 'That will be a nice one to do.' On the other hand, there are one or two I have simply never fancied. *The Big Breakfast* from Channel 4 have asked me several times to 'go on the bed' with Paula Yates. For the uninitiated, she conducts her interviews lounging on a bed on the set. Up till now I have been able to resist the temptation to get up at half past six in the morning just to loll around with Paula! I am also leaving the delights of rugby club dinners until I am long retired.

One of the recent highlights has been my role in the TV programme *Body Heat*, as co-presenter with Mike Smith and Sally Gunnell; the programme's producer seemed to be happy with my performance. Of course, I am fully aware that I am fortunate to have the capability of this earning power from my name and fame. I fully realize that such openings would not be available to the same extent to, say, Jason Leonard or Martin Johnson, who put so much into the game without gaining the same opportunities.

But my conscience does not prickle. It is just the way of the commercial world. Graham Dawe is a great player, he drives thousands of miles to play for Bath, and he is one of the central figures of our run. But just because he is not asked to model in Miami, why should I turn down the job? It is the same in most team sports. In soccer, Collymore and Shearer and Le Tissier will get most of the attention because they are the high-profile goal-scorers. I never go out to the public and the commercial world and demand that they use me. I will also say, however, that things are improving and that, soon, many of the leading clubs will have their own pools into which a proportion of all ancillary earnings will be paid and from which all the players will be able to take a share. This seems fair, as it is the team's success which creates the high profiles. The newly established Bath Players' Initiative is a good example.

It is, of course, a matter of public record that the England team have their own company, called Playervision, for all the commercial activity which the squad conducts as a squad. At the time of writing, we are signed with the Parallel Media Company, which markets the squad and which has so far signed up major sponsorships with firms like Courage, Isostar, Scrumpy Jack cider, Cellnet and Scottish Provident. In exchange for the sponsorships we undertake to take part in the sponsors' activities, company days, golf days, product launches and the like, and to wear their distinctive logos on T-shirts and caps and the like while training or in photographic sessions or when otherwise appearing in public.

For a Five Nations season the amount earned by each individual member could be £3,000–£5,000, with about £2,500 from each tour. In fact the reality has come nowhere near some of the excited predictions in the press when we started out, and there have also been years when the expenses have been so high that the pay-out was very small indeed. But there is potential in the next five years for a leading player to look to earn between £30,000 and £40,000 per year, which is a tidy sum for duties which are not too onerous. At the moment, it is the London-based players who bear the brunt of the activities, purely because they are nearer the headquarters of the major sponsors. The Bath players have been called on to do a few duties, but most jobs are given to the Londoners.

These bare facts disguise years and years of trouble between the RFU and the players, trouble which has become extremely well publicized. I originally refused to sign along with the rest of the players, when they first decided to join up with an outside organization – in that instance, the WHJ outfit led by Bob Willis, the former England fast bowler, with which we had a short and rather controversial relationship. No one in WHJ or the team had convinced me it was a good idea, and some of the terms seemed laughable. I was not so much suspicious of it as simply not attracted to it.

My refusal to sign did not cause too much dissent, because not everyone at the time realized that I was indeed staying on the outside. However, the situation appeared to become more settled later and, partly for the sake of squad harmony, I did sign up for Playervision and with Parallel Media. If the tie-up does not prove to have a very lucrative future in this era when the profile of the sport is so high, then someone, somewhere, will deserve to be hauled over the coals.

The basis of the years of acrimony is that the Rugby Football Union has stopped us as a squad from making the same commercial deals that are common all over the rest of the world. I must admit that I have ignored the ridiculous tangle of by-laws about amateurism and about the need for deals to be 'rugby-related'. Why should I spend a long time trying to interpret the regulations if even the people who were party to framing them have consistently failed to clarify them?

I don't believe there is a commercial deal I cannot do, and I have acted on that basis. Occasionally, Maria is unable to make a deal for me because of the involvement of Playervision with a sponsor in the same field. She had a good opportunity with Lucozade for me, but to be fair to the relationship between Playervision and Isostar, we did not conclude the deal. Because Courage are a squad sponsor, breweries too are largely ruled out.

As an England squad we are at a disadvantage in comparison with our fellow international players in Australia, New Zealand, South Africa and Italy. They are not placed under so many silly rules and restrictions, and in things like the All Black Club in New Zealand and the famous fund-raising dinner extravaganza in Australia, the Unions are actively helping their players and giving some compensation for all the time and effort put in. The news in June 1995 of a massive \$505m investment by Rupert Murdoch in southern-hemisphere rugby, with much of that money to go into trust funds for players, has changed the stakes in a massive way. It is now imperative that the RFU and other European unions respond. In England, the Union are actively hindering and have been for four years or more. That was the root cause of the Carling Affair in May 1995.

In the media coverage of the running battle with the RFU, and our demand for clarification of the tangled undergrowth of the petty by-laws, it has come across that we are demanding money for playing, which is bad PR for us and completely untrue. All we are asking for is a level playing field. The way that level field had been denied us or postponed by the RFU, thus turning away companies interested in us, is disgraceful.

It is in their interests, of course, if the England squad are portrayed as a group of money-grubbers, and they are portrayed as the White Knights. Every now and again, a chink of light appears or a discussion panel is set up between RFU members and some of the players. But again, I am not convinced. It seems that panels are set up sometimes just to see what the players are up to rather than to take quick action. Rugby history proves that talking shops are the answer to nothing.

But there must come a time soon when all the restrictions and rules against commercial activity by the players, both as a squad and as individuals, are removed. We did not want to be paid wages to play, but the commercial world is showing enormous interest in rugby and in the England squad itself, and we have a right to take advantage of that interest. As I write, it seems that progress could at last be made at the autumn 1995 meeting of the IRB.

Of course, we have a certain amount of division in our own ranks, as was shown by Stuart Barnes's criticism of Brian Moore's role which appeared in his recent book. Brian and Dudley Wood have been the leaders of the two major factions, and there has been any amount of bitterness and mud-slinging as the RFU try to ease us out of another deal or accept the future with a bad grace, still rooted in their time warp.

But there is also not enough trust and information flow between Playervision and Parallel Media and the sponsors. I do feel very sorry for the people like Brian and Rob Andrew who have to spend so much time battering their heads against a brick wall. I also chuckle sometimes at the role played by Brian. He, after all, is a solicitor, who looks after our legal affairs very well, but he is hardly the most marketable player in the squad to be the front man for the marketing aspects. Still, he brings typical tenacity to the battle. Meanwhile the battle goes on, with at least a victory for us over the Carling Affair.

In an ideal world a player would be able to make enough money from commercial activities in, say, ten years at the top in rugby to give him the option of not working again. That would be wonderful. But it would take some doing.

I would not like to see rugby going fully pro and not only because only the bigger national Unions and only a very few of the bigger clubs could afford to pay players a proper rate. I would fear for some of the individuals involved. The great thing about rugby at the moment is that almost all the players are still in full-time jobs. However much people want to laugh about that, it is true and only the employers and the player really know how much work is done.

Brian Moore laughs at Ben Clarke and myself because we are given some time off – by British Gas and National Power respectively – for other things, while he, apparently, is the only one who has a real job. He can think whatever he likes! Working keeps you in touch with everything, it keeps you balanced. Besides, rugby is best left as a recreation, but I fail to see why it should not be a recreation with proper commercial possibilities for the top teams and individuals.

If you turn professional, you give up your place on the working ladder. If you then break your leg or have your playing career ended by injury, you are in a terrible position. Your working career has to start again, probably from scratch. Even if you stay injury free, unless you could make enough as a full-time pro not to work again, then all that would happen is that you would stop playing and find you have gone ten years without a career and still have to start again. There are so many sad examples in many sports, especially boxing and soccer, of great players fallen on hard times because once the sport was over and the money ran out, there was nowhere else to go.

I would love the day-to-day life of a pro player. Waking at 9; perhaps a stretch and a massage in the morning; some swimming; a hard track session in the afternoon. Nice thought, but not really practicable and not, at the moment, the wish of the majority of the leading players.

People are predicting a time when national teams are almost in perma-camp. It will not happen. There is no future in a circus which only plays against other countries. But there is definitely, however, a chance of a breakaway by senior clubs. They are the real strength of the game, and they are impatient at being dictated to by the RFU, which is still based on the old county structure.

If the clubs do not get a more direct line to all the vast incoming sponsorships and gate money currently being directed to Twickenham (all they get at the moment is some of the proceeds from the BSkyB secondary TV rights deal) – then their patience will wear ever thinner. The feed of funds, after all, is being pulled in partly by the top players and the top clubs who are the shop window of the game, week in, week out.

A battle on those lines would test the real strength of the RFU, especially if it became so bloody that third division players had to be sent out to play for England because the top clubs had pulled out of the RFU.

I can also see some kind of superleague structure coming across from football. It has been dreamt about for so long, but an event which would include the best clubs in England, Scotland, Wales, Ireland, France and Italy, with a qualifier for the rest of Europe, even for smaller national teams, would certainly have the commercial potential to float itself with no help from the Unions. We may be some time away from a superleague, but not all that far from a breakaway.

At heart, the interminable debate on amateurism bores me to tears. It is time for the whole business to be sorted out and for the game to decide how it wants to proceed towards the next millennium. At least there are now some signs that the International Rugby Board, and even the snail-like RFU, are grasping some of the nettles at last.

A final observation: if I had played to the same standard in another sport as I have in rugby, and for the same length of time, then I and players like me might now be approaching millionaire status. Something to think about! Then I might become the Best-Dressed Millionaire in Britain – a title I would hold with pleasure.

13
A Journey Below the Waist
A season lost and a career in doubt, 1994–95

It was early November, 1993, only a few weeks before England were due to meet New Zealand at Twickenham in a match which was awaited eagerly by every English rugby follower and every member of the team. I had hardly started my season. I had played only three matches for Bath – the league fixtures against Orrell and Northampton, the tour match against the South African Barbarians. That was it. The injury I was carrying in my pelvic region had caused me problems for several months, and was now agony if I so much as turned over in bed, got in or out of a car or even walked along the street.

My international caps had been won in an unbroken line since my first against Romania in 1989. I had enjoyed a career free of serious injuries. Long-term absence through injury was something which happened to many sportsmen, but not to me. But I felt a growing anxiety inside about the New Zealand game, and I was determined to push myself in training to try to prove to the England selectors and to myself that I would be ready.

An England cap is not something you give up on. For one training session, I met up with Ged Roddy, Bath's highly-rated fitness adviser, and Ben Clarke, Bath's highly-rated No. 8, at the sports grounds of Bath University. We did some striding out over distances from 100 metres to 250 metres. Ben is quick for a forward but not especially quick by the standards of backs. He set a steady pace and I was totally unable to keep up with him. It was sheer agony just trying to do so. I tried to ignore the pain, but it was too much.

Ben and Ged probably assumed that I was just being lazy. I said nothing to them about the injury. 'I'm just taking it easy,' I explained. But it had come home to me that I had no chance of being fit for the New Zealand match; there was also a growing resignation inside that I would not be back very soon at all. My inner feelings were proved right: I missed the whole of the rest of the season, missed England's tour to South Africa, and the start of the 1994–95 season, which was to end with the third World Cup in South Africa. A few newspaper scare stories eventually appeared which suggested that my career might even be over; and perhaps that subconscious suspicion rose inside me, as well. After seasons when I had become famous for my play and even famous for being famous, I was suddenly famous for being injured.

Ian McGeechan, the Lions coach, was conducting one of his monster training sessions just before the second Test of the 1993 Lions tour of New Zealand, the Test we had to win (and did) to keep the series alive. It was a closed session – i.e. with no prying cameras and pressmen – held on a muddy and heavy school field in Wellington. I slipped on the surface during the session and seemed to wrench a muscle in the groin region. I had done the same sort of thing in the past, and I thought nothing of it.

The injury was strapped as the Test was approaching. I had some treatment from Kevin Murphy and James Robson, our medical team. But often, when I had arranged a visit to the medical room which Murphy set up in every tour hotel, I didn't attend. I knew that the room would be packed by Lions and that there would be a queue. It was always the same on tour. I couldn't be bothered to wait around. I would rather be watching television in my room, playing cards with the lads and whatever else we did in the tense days before a major match. I thought it was merely a niggle, and went through the rest of the tour hardly thinking about it.

When I came back I took a holiday with Jayne and Imogen, and by mid-August I had started training for the new season. I had come back from holiday with a bad back. I assumed it came from pushing the pram and carrying Imogen while we were on holiday. This was something that, since I was away from home often on work and sporting duties, I was not used to doing.

Training began, but the niggle resurfaced around the area of the hip joint. Originally, I told myself that because of the heavy programme that was behind us and in front of us, I would delay my first game for Bath until October. But as usual, when the season approached the training sessions became more urgent and the adrenalin at the club began to flow. I was caught up in it. I thought: 'What the hell.' So I started aiming for the first match after all.

The niggle became a little stronger. I went to Julie Bardner, the Bath physiotherapist. 'I don't think it's anything serious,' she said. But she did add that the groin/pelvic areas could be extremely complicated, and she was proved dead right on that score. For the time being, she prescribed ultra-sonics and massage. I played my three games at the start of the season, dragged along by the urgency of the new season and the need to play well before the New Zealand match at the end of November.

But in my heart I knew by then that I was fooling myself, that I should not have been out there and that the little niggle was possibly something more serious. Julie continued the treatment, but she also mentioned something I had never heard of called 'Gilmore's Groin'. Apparently, there was a Harley Street medical man called Jerry Gilmore who had identified a particular problem which sometimes occurred in the groin area of sportsmen and was in fact making his living by treating that particular complaint. He boasted that he had operated on millions of pounds' worth of footballer.

For the time being, operations were out of my thoughts. But not the injury – it was around now that the pain in bed, in the car and when merely walking around became more intense. At first, I could train fairly well. The region took time to warm up at the start of the session, after which it was not too painful. But next day it would stiffen up. It would be nagging in the morning and would worsen as the day went on. And as I was training every day, it got progressively worse as the days went by.

It was time to move on from treatment by Bath's medical people; it is no slight on them, but it was clear that simple physiotherapy was not going to work. So I began a search for fitness and a journey around the field of medicine, and particularly sports medicine, that I was eventually to find extremely frustrating and confusing.

One of the first people to consult was obviously Nigel Henderson, the Rugby Football Union's honorary consultant surgeon. Nigel arranged various investigations, including an anti-inflammatory drug given under general anaesthetic; an MRI scan, which involved lying in a claustrophobic tunnel while the scanner did its scanning; and some sort of special X-ray for which I had to drink litres of water.

The diagnosis was basically a loosening around the pelvic bone, and it meant that when I ran or twisted there were shearing forces in the groin and pelvic area which aggravated the pain and the problem.

Nigel is a very nice man indeed, and he was to supervise my injury and recovery – or lack of it, through no fault of his own – for over a year. At first I pinpointed the Five Nations of 1994 as a come-back target, but well before then resignation was beginning to set in. Nigel did tell me that I could be lucky to make it, but at least it was a carrot.

I was given exercises to do by Don Gatherer, the physiotherapist attached to the Rugby Football Union, and Don also did some research into how the injury was treated in other sports. The exercises were meant to strengthen the muscle groups around the pelvic girdle. The idea was that this would make everything a little more stable and cut down the shearing forces which caused the aggravation.

There was no improvement. I officially withdrew from the New Zealand match, the first Test I had missed since beginning my England career, one week before the match itself. It was a strange feeling. But I was not distraught. I was not gutted. Everybody deals with these things in their own way and my way was to tell myself that there was nothing I could do, I was not fit to play and there was no point dwelling on it.

But I did dwell on the injury. I had to. It was always there. And with a sense of inevitability, the name of Jerry Gilmore cropped up again. Nigel Henderson decided that it was Gilmore time, so I travelled to Harley Street to see this great man of the groin. He was very welcoming, flamboyant and incredibly laid back. I wanted his diagnosis in black and white, I wanted his plan of action in black and white, and I wanted, also in black and white, his estimate of when I would be playing again.

It didn't happen like that. He gave me some background on his specialist area, then told me to take off my trousers and underpants. He began the investigation and found the problem area by inserting his fingers up through the scrotum. He had to drag me down off the ceiling to give me his findings. 'There is a bit of a problem there,' he said. And if there hadn't been before, there was one there now, I thought. 'And I believe it is my problem, don't you think?' ('How the fuck do I know?' I almost answered.) He decided that I should go away for a couple of weeks to actually aggravate the problem. If I aggravated the area, then he knew that it was indeed the problem; it was a confirmation. That was the theory.

So I went into the next stage. Henderson liaised with Gilmore and I was sent for a fortnight at Lilleshall for a residential programme of generally aggravating the injury and other treatment. Jan Molby of Liverpool was there, so at least I got the lowdown from him on the Graeme Souness saga and similar inside knowledge of the soccer world.

I also picked up the vibes that the physios there were resigned to the fact that I would have an operation with Gilmore and that was that.

The regime was boring. Treatment and exercises started at around 9 in the morning. There was tea and biscuits at 10; followed by swimming. Lunch was from 12.30 to around 2; then there were more exercises, more tea, more biscuits, more treatment and more exercises. For recreation, we had a few drinks in a small bar there and, on a couple of occasions, I went out for a few more with Steve Tallboys, the Wimbledon footballer who was also having treatment. In the outside world, the rugby season was slipping by and the England tour to South Africa, with Jack Rowell to take charge, was looming ever closer.

I went back to Jerry Gilmore. He stuck his fingers up through the scrotum again, dragged me down off the ceiling and gave me his opinion. 'Right,' he said. 'Operation!' Then he added: 'But it's up to you. No guarantees.' I know he was only trying to convey that it was not necessarily a miracle cure, but I was dismayed again by the fact that black and white had faded into all the usual greys.

In March, at around the time when the Five Nations was at its height, I went to the Princess Margaret Hospital near Harley Street and Gilmore did his stuff. By that time, I was so bombarded with advice from medical people that I had no real idea what his stuff was; nor did I care, but he did it anyway.

Next day, I left the hospital and went home. I could not stand it in there any longer. I was in total agony. I walked like an old man, almost bent double. It seemed when I tried to stand up straight that a string was tied to my testicles and was jerked tight as I straightened up. When I arrived home, Jayne looked anxious. 'What on earth is wrong with you?' she asked. Funny, that. I had been asking myself that question for months and months.

The rehabilitation period after the operation was around six weeks. After a week I could walk around properly. Just before the end of the rehab period I had to go to La Manga in Spain to film the final of *Body Heat*, the TV show on which I was co-presenter with Mike Smith and Sally Gunnell. I had done all the studio work and the location work for the programme before the operation, and I was able to complete the filming of the final with no problems.

Even better, Rex Hazledene, the RFU's fitness adviser from Loughborough University, was there as the consultant for the programme. We had a chat, we did some training together, and at that stage, having been selected for the England squad to tour South Africa, I was still, at least on the surface, hoping to be fit to make the tour.

Deeper down, I think perhaps I knew that I had no chance. For a time, I worked on a plan that I would make the tour, play the games and not train in between. Eventually, not long before Bath played Leicester in the Pilkington final at Twickenham, I rang Jack Rowell, the tour manager. I told him that I might be able to tour and take part in the matches, but that I could not train in between. I did not ask Jack to make the decision. There was no point.

I said: 'I don't think it would be the best thing to do. It will be best to miss the trip and work on getting fit for next season.' Jack agreed, Stuart Potter of Leicester came into the touring party and the withdrawal was officially announced on the morning of the cup final, which I attended as a spectator and a TV interviewee.

I had returned to Gilmore for a follow-up consultation. He told me that the scar tissue was healing well. But I politely and firmly turned down his request to make another examination in the scrotum area. There no way he was going to do that again.

I left him disillusioned, in that the problem and the pain were still there. However, one of the sensations which I had been feeling around the lower abdomen had now gone, so the operation had taken away part of the problem and probably achieved its goal to some extent. Gilmore had not promised a miracle cure.

But I was not en route for South Africa. I had missed out, therefore, on a total of seven caps and one cup final appearance. I got together with Nigel Henderson again and he decided now that the only solution was total rest. Apart from the odd game of tennis I did nothing over the summer of 1994 whatsoever; I switched off from rugby apart from the odd appearance in the ITV studio to commentate on England's progress in South Africa. I switched off from the injury too. There was no other way.

The Bath club had come up with a reward for the players for all the years of triumph. They paid a good part of the bill for the first team squad, together with wives and girlfriends, to have a break in Barbados. We spent ten days there, had a marvellous time, and everybody seemed to get on famously (which was a world first for travelling groups of Bath players).

I think it was in Barbados that my patience finally began to wear thin. Perhaps it was seeing the players training hard for the new season and realizing that I still had the nagging pain in my groin and that I would still not be available to play when the season began. It was to be a major season too, with the World Cup in 1995.

I was also sick and tired of the thousands and thousands of enquiries. When would I be back? What exactly was wrong with me? Did I think it could be that I would never play again? I realize that people are only interested, but it all started to become incredibly tiresome.

And I also began to realize that I had not chased the medical people enough, not pressed them for, if not solutions, then the ways to progress. It was not so much the lost caps – I could put up with those, because nothing could bring them back. It was just the lack of progress.

Jayne certainly seemed to pick up my new mood, as she showed in an interview in the autumn of 1994. 'For me, the injury has been by far the most difficult thing I have had to cope with with Jeremy and the rugby. He tends never to get too upset about losing games. Even after the World Cup final against Australia he only went a little quiet. It did not seem to affect him too deeply. He was not in tears or anything.

'But he became very, very frustrated when nothing seemed to be happening with the injury. After he had the operation and he still could not come back he was hell. He began to talk about not being able to come back at all. Nigel Henderson rang him just before we went to Barbados with Bath, and Jeremy told him that he couldn't even begin to think about it until we came back, which was a sign of his attitude.

'He sometimes does keep things to himself and doesn't discuss them. I tried to encourage him to be more assertive. Eventually, he went to them and said: "Look, I want a proper training programme. I want something I can work towards." '

Nigel and I got our heads back together on returning from Barbados. As part of my new approach, I told him that I wanted a course of action that I was happy with; in which we said: 'This is the problem. Let's try this. If it doesn't work, then let's try the other.' I needed a goal. I needed to be working towards some sort of conclusion.

I also asked Rex Hazledene to tap the RFU contacts around the world, particularly in Australia, to see what treatments there were and what exercise regimes could be put in place. This was intended to be Plan B, to be used if the Plan A worked out between Nigel and me had no effect. There was also a possible Plan C, an operation which would fuse the ligaments across the pelvic area so that they became rigid and everything was kept in place. I asked for enquiries to be made about the length of sporting life this usually gave to the player operated on – if it was only a year or 18 months, I would be prepared to chuck it in and tell myself that I had had some great years; if it was four or five years, I would be prepared to try it.

But towards the end of 1994, these emergency plans were still being held in reserve. Nigel was always very sympathetic and helpful. Plan A was for a few weeks of low intensity exercises to mark the end of the period of rest, which had begun at the end of the previous season. These low intensity exercises went well. Nigel and I gradually worked up to higher intensity exercises, and by the middle of October 1994, these too were going well and I was contemplating, at last, taking part in a rugby match.

Occasionally, I would still feel a twinge from the injury. But once I was warm in training I did not feel it. I no longer felt it in the bath or the car. The pain was confined to the odd little tug. I had become very cynical about the whole thing by then and I realized that it could have come back at any time but at least there was progress.

There was another boost, too. I went to the Human Analysis Laboratory in a Bristol hospital. Glen Hunter, the director, put me on a machine that can measure strengths of individual parts of the body. We found that my left adductor was weak compared to the right, and that my hip rotation was poor, so that the hip was tugging to release itself and causing some damage in the region. I was put on exercises to strengthen the relevant parts.

Near the start of the 1994–95 season many newspapers sent their writers down to Bath to see what the progress was. Mick Cleary of the *Observer* was one of them. After speaking to me, he wrote an article which attacked the Rugby Football Union for neglecting me. 'Concrete evidence of neglect' was the headline on the article.

I was quoted as saying: 'They could have done a hell of a lot more. It just shows how unprofessionally and poorly run the sport is. The welfare of players is way down the list of priorities.' There was also a quote from Dick Best, who had been relieved of his post as England coach only two months before. He referred to injuries suffered by Mike Teague and Jason Leonard and his view that the treatments organized for them had been lacking. 'Their cases were an outrage,' said Dick. 'The same is true of Guscott. It's a cock-up and someone should be hauled over the coals for it.'

The article hinted that I had been deserted. Dudley Wood sent the paper a letter of reply, and rang Cleary in angry mood. Nigel Henderson, understandably, was a little cool when we next spoke, although when I said that I would understand if he wanted me to move on to consult someone else, he would not hear of it.

In fact, although the article did reflect my impatience at the time, it was not representative because it did not give both sides. I emphasized that the RFU, through Nigel, through Don Gatherer and others, had made strenuous efforts on my behalf. I did not hold it against them, least of all against Nigel, that success had not been achieved for a long time.

And I know that the medical profession is not like a plumber, who can come and give you the quick fix. But I also felt on some occasions that the science of sports medicine can be a kind of confusing shambles. Explanations are not their strong point. At one stage, I was talking to Jayne about the possibility that I would never play again. She was encouraging. 'Even if you don't,' she said, 'look what you've achieved in the game.'

Perhaps I was also made even more impatient because of the way that the likes of Tim Horan were treated. Tim, who suffered that terrible knee injury in the final of the Super-10 tournament against Natal in Durban, was treated like the major asset he is. He and his family were moved *en bloc* from Brisbane down to Sydney so that he could be near the Australian Rugby Union's chief physiotherapist, Greg Craig. They worked out every day. He was given every single possible help in resources, technology and treatment to rehabilitate himself. He was loaned a house on the beach front by an anonymous benefactor and given time off with pay by Castlemaine, his employers. I didn't want a beach house and time off. But I was prepared to go wherever necessary – America or Australia or Siberia – to get rid of the injury. I sometimes used to ask myself if I would be hanging around at home, waiting for something to happen, if I were an injured Linford Christie or Alan Shearer.

Eventually I came back, playing for Bath at West Hartlepool, in October 1994. I was reasonably confident about the injury, but I knew it was not going to be easy, if only because of all the media interest. I also realized that a bad game would indicate to many people that I would never be the same and that I was now an inferior player. They would forget the simple fact that I might merely have had a bad game! Still, a bad game was a world better than no game at all. Soon the wasted year was a memory.

14
High Veld via Hartlepool
The domestic season 1994–95, and the third Grand Slam

The season began belatedly, especially since I decided to delay my comeback for Bath two weeks later than was really necessary, just to make sure. The West Hartlepool game was an odd affair, and because we were lucky to win, there was the huge distraction of hordes of media asking the familiar 'how do you feel?' questions. I was off the pace, and rusty, but I got through, and, in many ways, it soon felt as if I had never been away. I was surrounded by cameras and reporters at the end, gave them some of what they wanted and that was that. There seemed to be an air of celebration that I was back – from the media, my friends and my family. And all those 'will you ever be as good?' enquiries to get through.

One week later, Bath were playing Leicester in the league, which was obviously a stern early test. Jack Rowell rang me the night before the game and asked me if I would be ready to play for England two weeks later against Romania. I was not about to turn down England. I told Jack I would be ready. I wanted to play. It was an odd feeling the next day playing alongside Phil de Glanville, because I knew that if I came through the Leicester match well I would be taking DG's place in the England team. It was also annoying that we let Leicester back for a draw when we had the match won.

I put myself through it against Leicester and the injury stood up; and, to be honest, I've hardly had a single doubt about the injury, or a single twinge ever since. It faded away almost as if it had never been. Soon I was back at squad sessions, with Will and Rory telling me in less than heartfelt tones how much they had missed my biting wit and sarcasm. It was only towards the end of the season that my reflexes and reactions were fully re-tuned, but all the way through my pace had not suffered, and I was still running the same times in the fitness tests.

For many England players, the atmosphere was now different on the squad. Cooke had gone; Jack Rowell had come in and eased his way through in South Africa. For me, there were no surprises, because I had been working with Jack for ten years. I knew his ways, his man management, the way he wound people up and got the best out of them. I knew all his little foibles – and his big foibles – which most of the squad were experiencing for the first time.

For a long time in the early season, Carling was a little like a fish out of water. Towards the end of the Cooke reign, Carling had almost taken over the squad, which was fine. Now Jack was the central figure, he did not tend to let too many people in on his secrets and there was a bit of 'what's going on here?' in the whole attitude of the squad. It had all probably become too comfortable in the past, so Jack's fresh approach was what was wanted. And even if his methods were different, then the squad caught on to the general message. He began to give confidence to a team which, perhaps strangely, was lacking confidence. And as usual, he was outstanding in setting down a plan of campaign for each match.

He began the much-publicized switch to a more fluid approach, with backs and forwards in tandem, ultimately a failure. He began his work one to one, falling in with, say, Martin Johnson as they walked off the training field for a sharp aside, and telling people that what they did with their clubs was not good enough for England, even players like Dean Richards (ironic, because he also used to tell us at Bath that what was good enough for England was not good enough for Bath!).

The players certainly took to him once the transitional period was over, and we struck out for what turned out to be my third Grand Slam in the England team. It was perhaps a measure of our horizons then that as soon as the whistle blew to signal our Grand Slam, after the victory over Scotland in March 1995 at Twickenham, I could only think of the forthcoming World Cup. I felt nothing like the same sense of elation that I felt after the earlier Slams, simply because this time, the job was only half done. It was a season in which we established ourselves as one of the favourites for the World Cup and in which, at last, the England forwards produced the goods consistently. They tuned in to the fact that the whole game depends on them. Frequently they were awesome and, for me, it was a pleasure to see players like Ubogu, Clarke and Rodber running and handling.

We met for the Romania game on Wednesday, 9 November, the official start of my return to the squad. We used to start training at 7 p.m. on the Wednesdays but that has been brought forward to 2.30, lengthening the weekend. Victor Ubogu had to accept the new timing even though he always had problems meeting at 7, owing to his work commitments.

Strangely, although we had four squad sessions at Marlow prior to this match, when we trained there still seemed to be some confusion as to what we were doing and what style we would play against Romania. During the session, Will often appeared bemused by Jack's ad hoc approach. Whereas Cooke's sessions were always well structured, with heavy input from Will, Jack was doing his level best to confuse everyone by telling the forwards to run moves they had not even practised. It brought back echoes of some of the old Bath sessions.

In the evening, Les Cusworth, the backs coach, outlined his role to the players, gave his version of how he saw England playing. Jack weighed in with a plan which he called the players' plan but was, in fact, his. There was plenty to think about as we watched *Beverly Hills Cop 2* in the evening. It seemed apparent, as I have said, that Will no longer pulled so many strings. Jack was stamping his authority. One thing had not changed in my absence. Dewi Morris, as ever, seemed on the verge of a nervous breakdown.

On the Thursday, I had a long session with Kevin Murphy, concentrating on a good stretch and mobilization of the groin. We had a team meeting at 9.30, in which Jack showed a video of the England–New Zealand match from the previous season, and after a lightish run-out, concentrating on backs and forwards linking, we looked at line-outs and quick tap penalties. There was a major session of three-card brag in the team room that afternoon, and in the evening the whole squad minus the management went to Bellinis, in Richmond, for an Italian meal. Ben Clarke favoured us all with his impression of an Italian waiter, which sounded exactly like a Northern coal-miner. He had the piss ripped out of him as a consequence. Dewi and Jason Leonard sat near me, and we reminisced about the Lions tour of New Zealand.

Will came to the fore a little more next day. Jack had to miss the session to attend a business meeting for Dalgety. In front of a massive media presence, we trained at the Stoop Memorial Ground. The session seemed to go well, but Will was not happy. He said at the team meeting that evening that he would be asking individuals what they were going to contribute to England being successful on Saturday. I had to think of something just in case he asked me. He didn't.

At the dinner following the team meeting, Dean Richards rose to make a presentation to Will on behalf of the team, to mark his 50th cap for England. He handed over a picture to Will, declaring that it showed Will and his friends. It was a picture of Will and 20 other players, all of whom were Jeff Probyn. Later that evening, after watching *Frankenstein* at the pictures, Dean and I found Mike Catt, Kieran Bracken and Graham Dawe playing three-card brag. We joined in, and 45 minutes later I went to bed richer by £30. Thanks, boys.

Rob Andrew and I decided to wear Adidas boots for the match, and decided not to bother to blacken out the stripes and logos as we were supposed to. The trouble was that everyone was expecting us to beat Romania by 50. That meant that we had to keep concentrating and not assume too much. We did beat them easily, 54–3, and tried with varying success to play our 15-man game. We probably gave ourselves six out of ten at the end. This was still the crossover period from the old set-piece dominated game. I had two tries disallowed and was still waiting to resume scoring exploits following the injury. Sympathy from the rest of the squad was sorely lacking . . .

Obviously, the whole game is moving away from the old days, where the forwards battled for possession then tried to send the backs away. It is more of a war of attrition, the game is moving towards the bigger and stronger players, and the question being who is the biggest and strongest and who can maintain it for the longest. You do not get those flashes of individual brilliance too much any more, you get a busy field clogged up with backs and forwards.

People ask me if I am upset that there are few chances for the searing outside break and the bursts of individual skills, that the game has drifted away from my type of player. The answer is yes. I have come to terms with it, and other people should come to terms with it too. I can be involved as much as I want, I can go and chase the ball – provided I get back to make the tackles. I enjoyed the old days when there was space to run, but they are gone. The laws should be changed to try to bring them back.

The key man at the moment is the scrum-half. He now has so many decisions to make, things that are easier to see from the centre. He has to decide whether he should throw the long ball out, throw the short pass to the runner on the fringes, or run himself. Ironically, what the world lacks at the moment is an outstanding half-back combination. The last great combination at 9 and 10 were Nick Farr-Jones and Michael Lynagh, but all countries are struggling to get anywhere near the standard of that pair.

A squad day was scheduled in late November, the week before the match against Canada at Twickenham. Jack made himself unpopular with the squad by calling a training session for Twickenham that afternoon, which meant we would not be able to watch the Wales–South Africa match live on television. Wives and girlfriends were included for the weekend, at the request of Will Carling. A shopping trip to Harrods was arranged for them, and in the evening there was a boat trip on the Thames. The training went well, but still there was a bemusement factor as we tried to catch up with the new thought patterns of Rowell and Knobhead, or Les Cusworth, as he was also known.

There was bad news after the session for Dewi Morris and Steve Ojomoh. They were the two left out when the team to play Canada was announced. Steve told me on the way home that he knew he would be left out because Carling could not look him in the eye at training. Dewi was so upset that he dropped out of the boat trip and went off to drown his sorrows.

At further training for the Canadian game at the start of December, Carling handed out questionnaires. The form asked for players' views on how we approached training and how we could improve. He expressed concern about our attitudes to the World Cup, which did not go down a bundle. Jason Leonard was eventually singled out for some unfriendly rebukes because he had taken the piss out of the form and filled it in using schoolboy language.

Jack Rowell returned from the team managers' conference in South Africa with a warning. The vibes he had picked up suggested that all the teams were going to give it a real blast in the World Cup tournament. Jack declared that we had to be better prepared than everyone else if we were going to win the tournament. At about this time, Austin Swain, a sports psychologist, was introduced to the squad. Previously we had only really dabbled in that field, and some of the forwards used to ridicule the mental rehearsal tapes Geoff Cooke prepared.

Another part of our build-up for Canada was to watch a video including a study of John Monie, the rugby league coach, preparing a team mentally for a game. We had a Thursday session in atrocious weather, but it was easily the best session I had been involved with since returning to the squad. We were very definitely gathering strength.

In the afternoon, I went to the *Daily Express*/Yardley Gold sports awards, where I was presented with the Yardley English Blazer Award for the best-dressed sportsman. The major awards, for the sportsman and sportswoman of the year, were won by Linford Christie and Sally Gunnell respectively.

I was back for a team dinner in the restaurant. Our media liaison man, Colin Herridge, is usually extremely mild-mannered. Yet, that evening, he lost his rag totally after being made to wait and wait and wait for his food. He attracted the attention of a poor little waitress by bellowing: 'Oiiiii! Is anyone serving dinner tonight?' The waitress panicked. Sadly for Herridge, all the squad heard his outburst and he never heard the last of it. It was totally out of character, but that did not save him.

On the morning of the Canadian match, after my usual back rub from Kevin Murphy, I went to a backs' meeting. I was still awaiting my first try since returning, and Carling tried to crack a laborious funny at the meeting at my expense, saying how hard everyone had to work to get Jeremy a try, which didn't really come off – either that or my sense of humour failed me. But I felt better later. I didn't score, but we thrashed Canada with an excellent performance in which our new style seemed to work well. We won

60–19, with Mike Catt beginning to show some of the running from full-back which gave us an extra dimension.

Indeed, it worked far too well for Gareth Rees, the Canadian captain, who spent most of the match whinging to the referee about various things. To reach 50 against Canada is no mean feat; there were some great tries and great rugby. Canada bitterly disappointed me. After their World Cup performance in 1991 I expected something much better.

That night, we celebrated in champagne. I stuck to champagne all night, switched to vodka at midnight, and paid for it with a tremendous hangover next day. At least I was able to stay in bed, because I was staying in London for the *Sportsview* Personality of the Year Award ceremony, which was in London on the Sunday night. They gave it to Damon Hill, for coming second. Only in Britain.

Over the New Year 1994–95 period, we returned to the familiar surroundings of Club La Santa in Lanzarote. We had a big squad of 34, all hoping that they would be in for the Five Nations. I was by now, of course, a veteran of these trips, and the memories came flooding back when we reached the barren volcanic desert. Two years before, Jeff Probyn had been telling all the young props how to conduct themselves, how to give the right impression to the management. He really lived up to his own advice. We had all gone for a meal at a local restaurant to break up the monotony of lounging around La Santa all day. When it came to leaving the restaurant, there was no sign of Probyn. After intensive searching, some of the lads checked out the toilets. After they knocked on the cubicle and called out Jeff's name, there was a low moaning and groaning. Jeff could not open the door from inside so the lads charged it. It almost flew off the hinges and when the boys investigated further, they found Probyn inside, clinging to the toilet pan with vomit all around. He did not have a clue what was going on. In typically Probyn fashion, he flatly denied next day that he had been drunk.

I suppose that if the 1995 Grand Slam seemed comfortable in hindsight, then at least some of the games loomed as major problems beforehand. It is said so often, but the intensity of the Five Nations is so great that you can't look beyond the next game. To play in

Dublin is always a potential problem. But when we arrived, despite an horrendously bumpy flight, we were extremely relaxed. We played well, especially in the first half, and there were tries by Will, Tony Underwood and Ben Clarke. The forwards played brilliantly and completely got the better of the Irish front row, who had drawn all the publicity before the match. Dean, Ben and Tim Rodber were playing really well in the back row. Considering the fact that we had won in Dublin, it was a night of only average-sized celebrations. But leg one was in the bag, by 20–8, which away from home is a hammering in anyone's language.

We met on the Wednesday before the French match, grimly determined to keep our grip on the French, even though they had a superb series win in New Zealand in the previous summer – an extremely rare home defeat for the All Blacks. On the Wednesday, I had an early start from Bath because I had to open a sports hall at Westerbrook High School, and also had to meet up with Bob McKenzie, the rugby writer from the *Daily Express*, with whom I have a column. I signed a three-year contract with the *Express* just before the World Cup to continue the column until 1998. The squad had all been to a Cellnet lunch before we all met. It was a long sesson on a heavy ground, but Rex Hazledine provided some light relief by devising some *It's-a-Knock-Out*-style games. It was so taxing on the heavy pitch that I spent a relaxing evening playing chess on my lap-top computer.

The preparation dragged on. On the Thursday, Will decided on a squad dinner out of the hotel and we went to The Naked Turtle, which, despite its name, turned out not to be too bad. Even these squad weekends cannot be divorced totally from real life. On the Thursday afternoon I had held meetings with the makers of the *Body Heat* TV programme, to sort out the details of my role as co-presenter.

At this stage of the season, the actual training runs were getting shorter and sharper. Even Brian Moore's attempt to goad the French through the media was more half-hearted than normal. I was confident of victory, especially because our forwards were now playing so well. The French had Sella and Lacroix in the centre, two players we had to respect, but our forwards had been so superior against the French pack for so long that we hoped to shut France out completely.

On the day before the game, after a training run that amounted to little more than a showpiece for the media, I set off for the Institute of Directors in Trafalgar Square, where I was guest of honour at their lunch. The team meeting that night was short; we were ready. I took a considerable amount of stick during the day over an article written by Stuart Barnes which had revealed my former career as a bus driver, with Badgerline. I went to bed early.

We hammered the French. The score was 31–10, but it could have been more. People say they played badly, but they played as well as they were allowed. We dominated them in the forwards and we allowed them to break out just once, when they scored a great try, launched from their own line and touched down by Viars, one of those tries even the opposition have to admire. But they escaped only once. I managed to end all the jibes about lack of try-scoring by scoring our first, in the 33rd minute. Until then, I had been followed around the squad sessions by the lads humming the theme tune to *Mission Impossible* because of the supposed impossibility of my ever scoring again. Tony Underwood scored two, including a brilliant try from a scrum set up by a run by Mike Catt, and Rob Andrew kicked his goals. It was a dominating performance.

With a large Bath contingent in the squad and the team manager a resident of Batheaston, the venue for the gathering of the squad before the Welsh game at Cardiff was the Bath Spa Hotel. It is a very nice hotel, but when we met it seemed that I had taken up permanent residence there. We met on the Wednesday of the Welsh match, but already that week I had had a business lunch there with a sales team, and done a fashion shoot for the *Sun*, which was a great laugh. Training was held at Bath University in foul conditions, a low-key affair, and even though it was supposed to be a closed session, there were lots of students there. Who knows, they could easily have been Welsh spies in disguise.

At the meeting that evening we concentrated on Welsh strengths and weakness. We went through a flip chart prepared by Jack, who gave us various things to remember, and as usual, Jack had a go at Ben Clarke, asking if he was really fit after his ankle injury. Even though we were staying in Bath, I loyally decided to remain with the squad, rather than disappear back home to the family. Cynics would claim that as our house was in the middle of refurbishment, and as Imogen might easily have woken around 7.30 and come to wake me up too, I made this decision for reasons other than squad loyalty. That is a disgraceful slur.

It didn't do much good. We had a very good session on the Thursday; everyone seemed clued in and to be thinking ahead – except me. I dropped far too many balls and made too many unforced errors. I also discovered the reason why the previous day's session had been a light one. Apparently, Rob had been working on a project at his work. He had been on it for eight days, working from 7 a.m. to midnight most days. So he needed a rest, the poor love.

On the Thursday after training we moved down to Cardiff, where another tear-jerking tragedy occurred. Will Carling lost about £70 at three-card brag, as did Dean Richards. It was a big school, including such sharps as Catt, Callard, Morris and myself. I finished the evening playing a golf game on my lap-top.

There was a 10 a.m. team meeting on the Friday. As usual, the coverage of the match in the papers was enormous, and as usual, there was savage ribbing for anyone shown in an unfortunate light. The *Daily Express* featured Victor Ubogu in the money section, explaining how he spends money like it is going out of fashion on clothing, and his favourite designers are Versace and Ralph Lauren. Why spend £60 on a shirt when you can afford £600? The team run, when we all stopped laughing, was short and sharp. I contemplated going out shopping in the afternoon in Cardiff but I decided against it. I can take stick from the locals but I thought there might be a bit too much of it for one day. My nerves grew steadily. I was dreading the next day, match day. Wales didn't worry me, but I was anxious about the reception my feature in the *Sun* would get from the lads. Luckily, it was not too extreme.

Wales were not much to worry about. I could see in their eyes that they did not expect to win. They kept it going to around 30 minutes, then they slackened off considerably and we came through to win 23–9. I was angry to be called back after being on my way to score, but on the replay afterwards you could clearly see an offence, with Martin Johnson scooping the ball back from a ruck on the floor. John Davies, the Welsh prop, was sent off for stamping, and Victor Ubogu opened the try scoring.

When we got back into the dressing-room Victor was shouting, ranting and raving about buying the whole squad champagne. He had instructed a friend to put £100 on him to score the first try of the match at odds of 18–1, so was in the money in a big way. At least, he would have been. But his friend, by now his ex-friend, hadn't managed to get the money on. The squad, of course, were heartbroken on Victor's behalf.

Victor was out of pocket, we were one step from the Grand Slam. Meanwhile Scotland, after a dreadful start to the season when they were thrashed by South Africa, had somehow staggered through and won in Paris and were also going for the Grand Slam. That fact, and the memories of 1990, were all the motivation we needed.

On the Wednesday before the Grand Slam match, we met up at the Bank of England ground, Roehampton. There was a lunch thrown by Courage, one of the team sponsors, amid much press hype and with speculation and demands for interviews at an all-time high. The session after the lunch was the worst I had experienced since Jack took charge, and it was all his fault. He completely disorganized the session by continually changing tack, and after messing around with the back row, he started messing around with the backs as well and no one knew what on earth was going on. A strange way to start the build-up!

The evening, I shared a few glasses of wine with Dean, Dewi and Graham Dawe. Dawe, who had sat patiently on the bench all season, had to drop off the bench because of injury.

Jack rescued the build-up a little with a better session at the Bank of England on the Thursday and we continued monitoring the papers for embarrassment. Rory was the target that day. In the *Daily Mail*, a piece on him had appeared with the heading: 'I don't believe I'm sexy.' That accurate revelation earned him any amount of stick from the players. There was a meeting with Adidas later that day, a photo call with Cellnet, one of the squad sponsors, and still the build-up raged on, with the media anxious for one of the camps to insult the other so that they could build up the old war between the two countries.

They succeeded on Friday, when Craig Chalmers made some silly comments about us in the papers and the article was pointedly read out in the 10 a.m. team meeting. The sheer volume of press was now becoming so intrusive that, for the Friday session, we decided to arrive and take the field as one, depart as one, and leave all the interviews until later in the day. We decided that we were in danger of losing focus because of all the attention surrounding the game, and if we had let Scotland through to the Grand Slam we would all have felt like retiring. That afternoon Tony Underwood and I ventured into Richmond, and in the evening I took a full part in a piss-take video, which sent up Will Carling's famous Quorn commercial a treat.

The match was probably something of a disappointment, considering all the fuss beforehand. We won 24–12, Rob kicking all our points. He dominated the possession, but the Scots came to spoil and they succeeded. After the match, Brian Moore attacked them on television, saying they had come to kill the game. The Scots were angered, but I agree completely with what he said. I had no sympathy with their complaints at all. The Scots had won in Paris just before the England match because they went out there to win. They were positive. By the time they got to Twickenham, they no longer had that attitude. They didn't really believe they could win – and they didn't win – but they spoiled the game for all the followers. I regret that fact that we didn't really pour it on them. They were not a great side at all. I never saw players like Eric Peters and Iain Morrison in the whole game, whereas in the old days you would always see the likes of Finlay Calder and John Jeffrey.

I did get through the defence once. Gavin Hastings came across to tackle me. I knew that Gavin is always a person you can cut inside, wrong-footing him as he comes across. As I got to him I cut inside but he stayed where he was, stuck his arm out and caught me. At the dinner in the evening, I asked him what the hell he was doing standing his ground like that. 'You normally let people run inside you,' I said. 'Yes,' he said. 'I knew you were going to try it.'

As I say, the final whistle brought no feelings of great joy, or not for me. Some of the players who were relatively new and had not won a Grand Slam before – Mike Catt, Kieran Bracken, even Phil de Glanville on the bench – were excited. But there were other hurdles to conquer.

For the moment, I was back in the team, had a third Grand Slam under my belt (plus a case of white and a case of red from the RFU to mark the occasion); I felt that I was approaching top form.

As the World Cup approached it was a little difficult to keep focused, with a new baby, with a new house needing plenty of work, and, I suppose, with life after the World Cup to contemplate. But as we went through more sessions at Marlow, as the team began to build up mentally for the biggest challenge of all, and as everyone, rugby fans or not, began to talk about the World Cup, I felt that I was completely restored after the season away and was ready for anything. Perhaps our vision of an expansive game had faded, but perhaps they would rise again in South Africa.

15 Ambushed by All Blacks

Talking a Good Game in the World Cup, 1995

I never thought I would see anything to compare with the outstanding drop goal with which Stuart Barnes won the Cup for Bath in injury time in the 1992 Cup Final, a kick which I watched first hand from a range of about five feet. I never thought I would ever again feel the same emotions on a rugby field. So I never realized that there could be a kick, and a moment, that would leave that 1992 kick for dead – blow it away.

We were level at 22–22 with Australia in the quarter-final of the World Cup 1995 at Newlands, Cape Town. It was already the most emotional game I had ever played in; not just because of the emotion in the stands or the incredible interest of the people at home which had been reported back to us, but because of the emotion on the pitch, the ebb and flow of two teams desperate to win, to keep their World Cup hopes alive. And with the match approaching injury time, I think that both teams had accepted that extra time would have to be played.

But Mike Catt kicked a lovely long touch from a penalty award to give us a foothold in the Australian half. Martin Bayfield won the ball in the line-out, and our forwards drove it on about 15 yards, to a point where we were just about in range for a drop goal. Rob Andrew had already told me he was going to go for the drop goal, just as Barnes had told me in advance in the Cup Final. It still seemed a long way out.

Dewi Morris fed Rob and Rob let fly. The strange thing was that I knew it was there two feet after it left his boot, while Rob kept looking and looking, watching intently over his shoulder as he ran back, as if he couldn't quite believe it. I was already celebrating, ages before it actually went over the crossbar. It was a brilliant kick. The ball just went on and on, and over. It was my happiest moment in an England jersey. It was to be followed by some of my worst moments in an England jersey, but I was not to know that at the time. The whole team was in a state of euphoria as the final whistle blew and we were in the semi-finals. Mission Trophy, our own name for our World Cup build-up and campaign, was on course.

The 1995 World Cup was a tremendous commercial for the game in so many ways. It was very exciting, often very entertaining. Because it was in the European time frame, it was shown on peak-time network TV and must have done wonders for the growth of the game in Britain, especially since ITV's audience figures were very good. There was some excellent rugby played and an emotional final when South Africa upset the odds and beat New Zealand, who had earlier played easily the best rugby in the whole competition.

The crying shame was that ultimately so little of the memorable rugby in the competition was played by England, because we had indeed set off with high hopes, and I believed firmly as the tournament began that we could win it. We did play a match against Australia which, as Jack Rowell said afterwards, would remain in memory, but that was about it and even that match was hardly a rugby classic, just a great contest.

We had begun the season, back in the autumn against Romania, with high talk of a faster and more expansive game, a 15-man game. We talked about it before and after every game in the whole long season (we played 12 test matches); we talked about it in our team meetings and, through the management, in the media. The truth is that we never played it. In the end, and for various reasons, talk was all it ever was. We did well to get through to the semi-finals but the prevailing mood at the end of the tournament was that, when set against our high hopes, the World Cup campaign had been a failure.

We left home in mid-May, already with months of preparation behind us. Jon Callard and John Mallett, the two Bath players, joined me for the drive to London and to our traditional headquarters, the Petersham Hotel. There was a lunch thrown by Scrumpy Jack, not another of Jack Rowell's businesses but the cider makers who sponsor Playervision. Brian Moore was the speaker. We could hardly say that we had not heard enough from Brian over the years, but there he was, on his feet. In his speech he referred to my supposed vanity: 'Jerry is so vain,' he said, 'that when he climaxes he shouts out his own name.' Many people wanted to know how Moore knew that.

There was another farewell dinner that evening when the Sporting Club of England threw a function at the Café Royal. This time we had to listen to another man whose tones were hardly unfamiliar, Jack Rowell. He waffled on for around 45 minutes, combining wisdom and wit. He related the following conversation he claimed to have had with Victor Ubogu.

Victor: 'Jack, why do people take an instant dislike to me?'

Jack: 'Quite simple, Victor. It saves time.'

Jack rambled on for a little too long, and we did not reach the Petersham until midnight. Thanks, Jack. We left for the great adventure next day, numbering off on the coach so that we could guarantee that we had left no-one behind as we motored over to Heathrow. And we hadn't left anyone behind. Except Graham Dawe.

We travelled to Durban, where we were to play all three of our Pool games and where we were based on the seafront in the Holiday Inn Garden Court. There, we showed our unity of purpose by considering whether we should take advantage of the commercial opportunities which were there for us during the World Cup, and deciding against it. We all felt extremely virtuous as the rand went out of the window.

The hotel itself was something of a sore point, as was the attendant organization of the whole tournament, whatever the likes of Louis Luyt tried to claim otherwise. The Holiday Inn was not a terrible hotel, but nothing like as good as the hotel in a resort up the coast that we had picked out on our tour of South Africa the year before. This was where the World Cup was badly run. The organizers insisted we all stayed in the Holiday Inn chain for the Pool matches. It meant that we were in establishments which were full of supporters and media, and all kinds of other distractions. We loved our supporters dearly, but even they would understand that proper preparation is difficult with distractions. At the Petersham before Twickenham internationals, basically, only the squad and a few others are in residence.

When we qualified, we and the other teams still in the event in the knock-out stages had to go through an appalling pantomime. We had to base ourselves in the Johannesburg area all week, then fly down to the weekend match venue late in the week, sometimes as late as Saturday, and return to Johannesburg after the match – sometimes on the evening of the match. This was meant to ensure that no-one had an unfair advantage in being more acclimatized to the altitude on the high veld. It was all garbage.

What the organisers should have done was to stop treating every team like a bunch of schoolboys and allow them to make their own arrangements. Both our quarter-final and our semi-final were in Cape Town. We had been told by our medical people that if we got through, and provided we travelled up to Johannesburg less than 48 hours before kick-off for the Final, we would be unaffected by the altitude. We could have based ourselves in the Cape and not bothered with the stupid rigmarole of flying back and forth. It is not an excuse to say that it was ridiculous that teams were not allowed to prepare properly for rugby's biggest tournament.

The early culinary experiences were nothing dazzling, either. One day we were served some boring soup and boring sandwiches. By chance, Rex Hazledene, the RFU fitness adviser and the man who had contacted the hotels to order all the food in advance, was to arrive in Durban the day after. We prepared to give him some.

One of the aspects of the trip that we had all been looking forward to with fervency bordering on delirium was the Welcome Lunch in Cape Town, to which all the teams were summoned, no matter where in the country they were based. Just what the lads needed was the 6.15 am wake-up call, the snatched breakfast, the tiny airport waiting room shared with the Argentinian team (our first opposition), and the delayed flight, which had hopped around half the country picking up other teams. At the function, held in a giant tent at the Groot Constantia Wine Estate, were all 416 players, plus their management teams, all in a competition to see who could look the most pissed off.

The Australians were deemed to be the winners – in addition to the other reasons for looking pissed off, they were kitted out in green-and-yellow striped blazers which would have looked perfect at Henley Regatta. The South African team looked notably relaxed and the Ivory Coast team were – uniquely – glad to be there. They were collecting autographs and posing for photographs alongside some of the better-known players. We reached our base back at Durban late at night, having wasted a day so badly that only a few of the lads had enough energy to contemplate a quiet, winding-down beer. Leonard, Clarke, Morris, Hopley, Johnson, Mallett and I sat down together to bemoan a joke of a day which everyone bar the Ivory Coast lads hated.

However, I did have time in the tent for a chat to Tim Horan, whom I looked upon by now as an old friend. I had rung him when the Australian party had first been announced to congratulate him on his remarkable achievement on returning to the squad less than a year after his horrendous knee injury. He seemed to have put on some weight, and said that at least he might be chosen for a test or two during the campaign – even that sounded a little optimistic. We spoke about our respective families, about how rugby union was changing.

I bumped into Michael Lynagh and David Campese as the reception was breaking up. I also remember spotting a vaguely familiar figure rolling around several of the tables, slightly rotund and with a glass of red permanently in his hand. After some time trying to remember where on earth I had seen him before, I realized that it was Stuart Barnes, by now a journalist, trying to set up some exclusive one-to-one interviews in his new life.

On the journey back from training at King's Park on the Monday, six days after we had left London and still five days before we opened against Argentina, we discovered two things. First, the team to play Argentina. Dean Richards was unfit, and Steve Ojomoh came in. Dewi Morris took over as scrum-half from Kieran Bracken. Otherwise, the team was the same as that which ended the Five Nations. We also learned about Victor Ubogu's name problems. Ubogu was idly musing on the coach that his name was sometimes misheard, and that people would call him Vincent, so that Victor, annoyed, would have to correct them. It was, of course, the death knell for his real name. From that day on, he was known as Vincent. Later, at training, Dean Richards stood up in the middle of an exercise, rapped Victor's lips with the fingers of his hand. 'Vic, I've always wanted to do that to you,' said Dean.

It was a relief when the whole thing began, with the South

Africa–Australia match at Cape Town. We settled round the television and saw an epic battle. The South Africa half-backs, Joost van der Westhuizen and Joel Stransky, played well, as did the foraging back row of Pienaar, Kruger and Straueli. The front five did the sort of donkey work which now appears to be beneath the front fives of some other teams. South Africa were superb when they attacked, and, on the day, the Springboks were more hungry than the Wallabies.

It gave us the appetite for our first burst of action – all that remained was to commiserate with Tim Rodber. He had taken a phone call in his room from a girl called Tammy. This surprised him because he didn't know anyone called Tammy. She recalled the events of the night before, talking as if Tim should know exactly what had happened because he had been there, and said she had dropped him off later at the hotel. Rodber asked the girl to describe him. She said he was tall, played in the back row, and had dark hair. Tim revealed that he was tall, played in the back row, and had blond hair, and that some unknown person had taken his name in vain.

When the tournament finally went live for us we fulfilled to the letter the final pronouncement of Jack Rowell that England 'must hit the ground running'. We were true to his words, but unfortunately we hit the ground running backwards. We had trouble in the scrums, we did not play well at all, and we won only by 24–18. If Argentina had had anyone who could kick goals, they would have won. We discovered what could have been partly to blame. We had been taking salt replacement tablets to combat the heat and humidity of Durban and, eventually, we were told that they reacted badly with the Isostar isotonic drink we were taking, causing some kind of chemical reaction which, allegedly, made us feel lethargic. But it was still something of a shock, even ignoring the chemical reactions, that after all the training and all the talk in team meetings, we played as if rusty and ill-prepared. The talking-shop inquest resumed at full throttle afterwards.

On the day after the match, Jayne, Imogen and Holly arrived in a group of wives and girlfriends. It was great to spend an evening with them and I decided that I would stay the night in their hotel so that I would be able to give Imogen and Holly a hug when they woke up.

Back at home, readers of the *Sun* were regaled by what was portrayed as the real reason why England had not performed – the nervousness and unrelaxed vibrations given off by Jack Rowell. 'Jittery Jack' was the paper's headline, above a major article. Jack was sufficiently riled by the story to point out at the next team meeting that he was relaxed, that he had never enjoyed himself more in his life and that anyone who felt he was acting in a strange way should speak up.

I later discovered how the story had reached the Docklands, where the *Sun* is printed. On the morning of the game against Argentina, Ben Clarke was sitting with Stuart Barnes, John Mallett and Chris Hewitt, the rugby writer of the *Bristol Evening Post*. Will Carling spotted them and wandered over. Amongst some general light-hearted chit-chat, Barnes asked Carling how Rowell was bearing up – Barnes, of course, knew Rowell of old. Will replied light-heartedly that Jack was nervy and that by the time of the quarter-finals he expected Rowell to be in a right state. There were a few laughs and the subject was forgotten. That night, however, Hewitt happened to mention the jocular remarks to Steven Howard of the *Sun*. Without checking with Will, Howard ran the story next day and half the country got the impression that the England manager was cracking up under the strain. Jack, apparently, did have a nasty turn on the golf course. He was explaining to his caddie after a few holes that he didn't play golf too often. 'You don't have to tell me that, sir,' said the caddie.

Our play did not rise much above the standard of Jack's golf when we played Italy. We were talking a big game as usual before the match, but we didn't produce one. I still felt the training was going well, but I also felt that something was missing. Certainly, even though we were still talking about our much-hyped 15-man game, there was no sign of it on the match days, just as it seemed to peter out in the home season after a reasonable start against Romania and Canada. We beat Italy by 27–20, scored two tries against two by them, but to be ahead only by one score at the end was not the form to worry Australia and New Zealand.

We still had to beat Western Samoa to ensure top place in the Pool after Samoa had beaten both Argentina and Italy, and although they never looked as dangerous as they had in the 1991 World

Cup, we still respected them. We also knew that, whereas Italy and Argentina had simply tried to kill the ball, the Samoans would be looking to dig out a quick ball for themselves – that would help our game to flow. We gave a run to everyone in the party who had yet to play, except Damien Hopley and John Mallett, neither of whom had been capped, and who were waiting impatiently.

It seemed to be that the buzz began to grow in the camp as that match approached. Mike Catt was at 10, with Phil de Glanville alongside in the centre and Will as his co-centre. For me, it was a match off. The only check on the growing good feeling was provided by Dean Richards. Out in Durban Bay are shark nets, placed to protect the swimmers and the surfers near the beach. Dean organized a boat trip to see the nets lifted, and to see the sharks. The drawback was that the boat left at 5.30 am, but eight forwards and Dewi Morris, who has forward blood in his veins, rose at the unearthly hour, were joined by an ITV camera crew, and off they went. They saw the nets lifted, looked on expectantly and found that there was not one single shark in sight. One of the boatmen was even heard to say that they hadn't seen a shark for ages. Dean Richards romped home with the Dick of the Day award, the others shambled back to bed.

Two days later came the lift against Western Samoa. It was a far better performance. England won 44–23, scoring four tries. There was more pace and urgency about the whole thing. Les Cusworth, the backs coach, seemed to have more input because although Will was in the team, he did not train until the last session before the match. There also seemed to be less chatting, fewer discussion groups.

I was interested to watch Catt and de Glanville in the mid-field. I have explained before in this book that Rob Andrew is not the easiest fly-half to play with from the point of view of an inside centre, not being a running fly-half. Catt played like the all-round talent that he is, and Catt and DG seemed to be comfortable with each other after a year of playing together at club level. DG was hungry and eager, and soon rumours were surfacing that my own place might be in danger.

Jack Rowell declared afterwards that it was a great England performance. It may have been good in some phases, and it did improve the atmosphere in the camp, releasing a little of the tension that the poor displays had built up. But the subject of my selection seemed to be raised around the camp again. I was prepared to admit that things had not gone brilliantly for me in the tournament to date but I was annoyed at some of the suggestions from the media that I may be left out.

I made no comment whatsoever, said nothing to the media or to Jack. But if I had been dropped, I would certainly have asked what I had done wrong – did they all feel I had been given any opportunities, what had I done to deserve to be dropped? Alan Shearer is picked so that when balls are crossed to his feet in a certain position, he is expected to score. Ryan Giggs is expected to take players on, then whip over the crosses to Andy Cole and the United strikers. I had been picked to play in a certain role, to exploit gaps and create chances for the full-back and the wings. In the tournament to date, and indeed, in much of the previous season, I had merely run up and down the field chasing kicks. I would have taken on Jack at his own mindgame, and blamed him if I had been dropped. He'd picked me, but he hadn't played the system that would bring me into the game. We were still talking about our new style rather than playing with it.

You could tell how intense the build-up for the Australian match was going to be. At a team meeting early in the week, after we had travelled up to Johannesburg (for no apparent reason bar the pig-headedness of the organizers – the game was to take place in Cape Town, where both sides could and should have gone), Will stood and made a sensational suggestion – a complete ban on alcohol until after the match.

The move, I understand, was partly motivated by rumours that one or two of the lads were taking more than they should have. The two props, Jason Leonard and Vincent (formerly Victor) Ubogu, raised their voices in protest but they were overruled. It was reported in all the papers that we had gone teetotal, although many of us still took the odd glass of wine when Will was looking the other way.

After one of the first high-altitude sessions of the tour, Jack issued me with the summons to his room for a chat. 'Nothing heavy,' he said, as ever defusing the situation. We spoke about life, the universe, the tour to date, and how my game was progressing. The conversation covered the way that Rob, Will and the rest of the backs were trying to play and I also picked up the fact that Jack wanted to assess my mood, whether I was interested or committed enough to really get involved. I was, and felt better for the opportunity to get some things off my chest.

The chat hinted that I would be in the team to play Australia, and that he wanted me in because of what I was capable of delivering. I left the Rowell chamber in happier mood. After the press conference to announce the team, the assembled hacks asked how it felt to have made the side. Was I pleased, how did I feel? You know, all the really tough and searching questions. The match approached, the pace of training began to pick up. It was fluid, controlled and sharp, and, thankfully, there were fewer interruptions for pow-wows and talking-shops. The tension, even for a player as laid back as myself, grew and grew.

It was also important to let off some of the steam by relaxing. We had an afternoon of war games, in which you stalk and shoot each other in a mock war terrain, using paint balls instead of bullets. It was forwards against backs, and when the big guys emerged from hiding to claim victory, they had all decided to hold up two fingers, in Churchillian style, to celebrate and rub it in. They must have had their own Churchill in Nigeria who gave his own Nigerian salute, because Victor came out holding up three fingers. He romped home in the choice for Dick of the Day when it came to light that, while in hiding at the paint-balling session, he was making calls on his mobile phone. There was also a round of golf, as Phil de Glanville, Tony Underwood, Jon Callard and myself had what amounted rather more to a nice walk in the country, and rather less a threat to Nick Faldo.

There was even time for a dinner with four members of the media, and Tony, Ben Clarke and myself had a good dinner in Sandton, one of the safer suburbs of Johannesburg, with Jack, Jack, Jack and Jack. It must be very confusing for the press lads, because they all share the same nickname. As for Johannesburg, we did see a little of the City en route to training. It was probably all we wanted to see, too. It is not a nice city in any shape or form.

We moved to Cape Town on Friday, and even that was a concession from Rugby World Cup, who wanted us to travel down the day before the game. Jayne and the girls were still in the country, and on the Saturday I went to the hotel to pick them up for lunch down at Cape Town's Waterfront complex, the centre of the city's nightlife. My father had also travelled out to catch the final stages of the World Cup, and it was great to see him.

That evening, Jack Rowell went through the final stages of the game plan to take on Australia, the match that would decide whether the World Cup was a disaster or not. Austin Swain, our psychologist, gave us a mental exercise to complete. He gave us a sheet of paper with the numbers 1–21 printed down the side, representing the team and replacements. He asked us to write something positive about every member of the team and bench. When we had finished, we had to cut up the paper and put each comment in the correct envelope. Later that night, he slipped our envelopes under the door of our rooms, each containing 21 positive comments about us. It was a good exercise. So much so that I kept all the positive comments about me, and took them home at the end. In the circle of the England team, with all the traditional flak flying, you need all the positive comments you can get.

We got even more positive comments on the night before the match. They played us video and audio tapes with messages of support from various people at home, including Bill Beaumont, Damon Hill and Gary Lineker. It gave us some indication of how much support at home had mushroomed and how big the whole thing had got.

Will's final words were pointed. He said that he had dedicated himself to the World Cup for two years, it was all he had thought of, that if we lost to Australia it was the end of our dreams. He said that he wanted it so badly, and knew that we all felt the same.

It was a fantastic occasion. It was incredibly hard and hectic and, in its way, the best of the four quarter-finals. One moment it seemed to be flowing our way, the next minute Australia seemed to be on top. We probably even surpassed ourselves when we led 13–3 just before half time and 13–6 when the whistle sounded for the break. We had been very concerned about the way they were attacking. Michael Lynagh was passing to Tim Horan and using him as a pivot. When Lynagh got the ball back from Horan he had hordes of dummy runners and was able to fire off long, short or medium-length passes. We really had to concentrate. We were working in channels, and, for one move, Jason Little was in my channel. Lynagh started to come round into the channel in possession, then Lynagh and Little fumbled between them.

Rob seized the ball, gave it to me and for an instant I thought that there was something on for me. However, inside a few strides the space closed down dramatically so I handed on to Will. The pass may or may not have been forward but we kept on running. Will passed on to Tony Underwood and Tony went blasting down his wing. The run seemed to go on and on, outside Damian Smith, his opposite number. Smith made a last desperate dive to try to catch Tony around the shoulders, but Tony was past him and scored. I was particularly thrilled for Tony, because he has sometimes got away on runs of 40 and 50 metres in his career without quite managing to finish. To lead by 13–6 at half time was a tremendous position.

The intensity grew. Our back-room analysts always said that we tended to concede more tries on our right hand side, and that also we seemed to be most vulnerable just before or just after half time – and in the early stages on the second half, we duly conceded a try down our right. Lynagh put up a perfect kick, Tony Underwood and Mike Catt seemed momentarily to hesitate, Smith made a brilliant jump and catch, and he fell over the line to score. Lynagh kicked the goal and it was level at 13–13.

It was still level at 22–22 as time ran out, with each side having put over three more kicks. I asked Will in a break in play what would happen if we finished level: was there a count back on tries or on number of players dismissd, or what? He had read his rules, and confirmed that there was injury time. The final stages of the match went by in a desperate blur, but we were all almost conditioned for extra time, even at the line-out, when Rob told me that he was going to go for the fateful drop goal. As I have said, it was the kick of a lifetime, the greatest moment. Jack said afterwards that the match would be remembered for a long time, and as a contest, no doubt it will be.

The Australians were gracious in defeat, despite their intense disappointment. However, Bob Dwyer was still hammering away at our approach, saying in the post-match press conference that he would not have been happy being involved with a style like ours. It was all nonsense. Australia had hardly tried to set the world alight in the match – it was not that sort of game. And which would he rather? Being through to the semi-finals, or being dumped and ready to fly home? I was tempted to wave him goodbye, and tell him to do his whingeing somewhere else. We had avenged in some way our defeat in the 1991 Final, we had reached the last four in the World and we certainly fancied our chances of beating South Africa, if we and they reached the Final. It was a great feeling.

On Monday morning, extremely hung over, I said goodbye to the family, who had to leave for England. We had planned two days at Sun City as rest and recuperation, although it was a sign of the times when Dean Richards and Tim Rodber suggested to Jack Rowell that we should do a spot of training up in Sun City. Jack thought for a while, then decreed that the Sun City trip was the Sun City trip, no training. Jack is extremely devoted and likes nothing more than long training sessions and team discussions. But he is also a social animal, and, like the rest of us, felt like a few days without the pressures and all the fuss of the World Cup. In any case, when we got back and had a major Wednesday training session, Jack made up for the days off with a severe verbal lashing and then a physical pasting out on the field. Thanks again, Jack.

So to the All Blacks. One thing had changed over the years. They no longer had an aura about them, which used to mean that we were beaten before we started. They were just another team, a team we had beaten as England and as the Lions. But if they were just another team, then they were an outstanding team. It wasn't so much aura we had to worry about as ability. The familiar intensity was still there, but there was also the pace and skill of their new wide game, a game which sometimes in South Africa had bordered on Barbarians-style, very courageous and fast.

I had first seen Jonah Lomu a few months before the World Cup in the Hong Kong Sevens, when he was player of the tournament. I did not find his pace as remarkable at that time as his strength. He blasted through tackles in Hong Kong with sheer power. In the final, he ran through again until only Waisale Serevi, the Fijian captain, was left to tackle him. He never even bothered to try to run outside Serevi. He just ran straight through him. Serevi tried to jump on Lomu but after yards and yards, he simply fell off.

In South Africa, Lomu showed even more. He started going around players who I knew were really quick, so he obviously had a tremendous turn of pace. He showed that he could run straight but also could go left or right, could swerve or sidestep. If everything else failed, which it usually didn't, he also had the old-fashioned fend-off. And if he looks big on television, then I can tell you that he looks even bigger close up. We spent ages trying to lay plans for him, but, ultimately, you can do little more than try to get in on him quickly, and to make first-time tackles. He has the ability to be the greatest player rugby has ever seen, whether or not he decides to take the money and depart at some stage for rugby league. He will be a great in that code too, if he does make the switch. But it was good to hear that the New Zealand RU were making strenuous efforts to keep Lomu, because union needs players of that explosive quality and entertainment value.

The first few minutes of the semi-final provided the shock of our rugby careers. We conceded two tries inside the first four minutes, which blew apart our game plan. The first time Lomu had the ball in earnest we were on the back foot, and he simply battered his way through three tackles to score. It was a devastating blow. Only minutes later, the All Blacks attacked from deep and I missed Walter Little. I looked up from the ground and saw the black jerseys attacking in strength, and Josh Kronfeld eventually came up in support to score. I was gutted, and we were 12 points down inside five minutes.

I don't know why I missed Little. Perhaps I did not hit him hard enough, or didn't hold on tight enough. As the move came straight from our kick-off after the Lomu try, with Rob not yet up in the line, perhaps our defensive alignment was wrong, although through no fault of Rob's. In fact, Little had an outstanding World Cup.

If to begin with we did not realize that it was not our day, then all remaining doubts were lost after about 18 minutes. Zinzan Brooke, the No. 8, picked up the ball and dropped a goal from 45 metres. That was rubbing it in. Early in the second half, we were actually down by 35–3, staring perhaps a 50-point margin of defeat in the face. It was unbelievable.

To be fair to Will, he did his best to keep us going. Behind the posts he would keep insisting that we were as good as them, that we could strike back, that the shock of the early passages, when the All Blacks were dynamic, had passed. But we were simply never in the game long enough to get back.

There was a rally in the last quarter, when both Will and Rory Underwood scored two tries each. Will scored one from a solo run and chip, showing what he could do when he really tried to extend his horizons. In the end, with a final score of 45–29, the final margin was only 16 points. It was a reasonable effort, considering we had been thrashed in the first hour of the match, but it was still a heavy defeat and the end of all our aspirations. It really smacked us in the face.

The dressing room was eerily quiet, of course. I find many of the gestures a little empty. When I arrive at Twickenham and walk from the team bus to the dressing rooms, I feel I have to put on the face which says: 'I am an England international, I must look serious.' In the dressing room at Newlands, I joined everyone else in holding my head in my hands and staring at the floor. From time to time, I peeped to see if everyone else was maintaining the same grieving posture. I realize that some people really did feel devastated, but after a decent interval had elapsed, I stood up and began to get changed. I didn't fancy the inquest, it changed nothing, it was not in my nature to brood about it and feel suicidal.

The truth is that although we thought we were prepared for the onslaught of the All Blacks, with their incredible intensity and pace, when it came to it we were still taken by surprise. To try to lift us, Jack Rowell blamed 'a couple of aberrations out there'. I could not agree. It was not some sort of fluke. We had been heavily defeated by a superior side, a side which spoke of its wide game and then played it, and team which had incredible strength and tenacity. That night, the drinks ban was torn up with a vengeance and I had a major night with Messrs Leonard, Hopley, Ubogu, Ojomoh, Andrew, Bayfield and Morris.

At least, it was a major night after something of a false start. We first had to return to Johannesburg, and to share the plane with the All Blacks. When we boarded we found that not only were they already in their seats but that they were in business class and we were in the back. I wondered if we would have been in the front if the result had been reversed. As we walked down the corridor, the atmosphere was cordial enough, even friendly. But Eric Rush, the All Black wing, told me later that as soon as we had all disappeared, there was a spontaneous outburst of piss-taking and hand-signals from the Blacks. 'But you would have done exactly the same if the roles had been reversed,' said Eric. He was right.

The next day, I found that the world had not ended. I spent some time in a recovery session at the Health and Racket club in Pretoria, I slept all afternoon and in the evening, I went to the cinema to watch *Dumb and Dumber*, which was brilliant. But instead of travelling in triumph to Johannesburg and preparing to meet South Africa, a team we knew we could have beaten, we had to face the losers' final, the third-place play-off in Pretoria against France, who had been beaten by South Africa in a monsoon-lashed Durban in the other semi-final on the previous Saturday.

In a way it was a nothing match to prepare for, but in another way it was highly significant. The winner did not have to pre-qualify for the 1991 World Cup in Wales, and there was still the chance to show that we were a better and more exciting team than our critics would admit. We spent a long time talking about the challenge and we managed to convince ourselves that we were up for it. We also told ourselves that we would not allow the French to beat us and end our wonderful run against them. We had won all the previous eight matches between the teams, a remarkable achievement. The incentive seemed to be there.

The major training session before the game was fraught. Tim Rodber contemplated filling me in for what he considered a cheap shot when I tackled him. Then Jack, trying to avoid confrontation, decided to tell Dean Richards he was dropped from the team to play France without actually telling him. He tried to persuade Dean that his shoulder was too bad to play. Dean kept politely insisting that all was well and that he was ready. Jack also suggested to Tony Underwood that it might be helpful if he had a rest after the battering he had taken from Lomu. In the end, Jack and Will had to come clean and they had to tell Dean and Tony that they weren't playing. Steve Ojomoh and Ian Hunter came in for our final game in South Africa 1995.

The final build-up day began on the wrong foot when a relative of Tony Underwood, with whom I was sharing a room, was kind enough to wake us up at dawn with a phone call. In the evening, we watched a video prepared by Hale and Pace, who had laid down a cod soundtrack over pictures of us being interviewed or off duty on the tour. It was extremely funny, though not quite as delightful as the realization that we had trained our last for the tournament, and that, give or take a few final words before kick off, we had had the last of our interminable sessions where we tried to talk ourselves to glory in team meetings.

But there was to be no big-send off. France won 19–9, scoring tries near the end by Emile N'Tamack and Olivier Roumat. Far from us showing something in the backs, there were even shouts of 'boring, boring' from the crowd. This time, I would not blame Rob Andrew for the lack of a running game. The forwards did not play well and they did not support us well, either. Throughout the tournament, we had worked on the principle of backs supporting backs, because we had no flyer in our big back row to help us out in a hurry and, therefore, we had to look after ourselves until the forwards arrived. In Pretoria against the French, backs supported backs, but very little happened after that. There was nothing happening anywhere, in fact. There was a lack of heart. If Australia had been the high point of my England career, then the demise of the team in a poor match in Pretoria was probably the low point.

The only thing left was to watch the final between the two southern hemisphere teams, and to see that New Zealand, for whatever reason, never came closer to repeating their brilliant performance against us. It seemed to me that they took too long to get into their game chiefly because Sean Fitzpatrick seemed completely unable to hit his jumpers with the throwing-in for the first 20 minutes. Like most of the Rugby World Cup 1995, it was an exciting match, but there was a shortage of real attacking rugby.

Will Carling's demeanour changed as soon as we lost against New Zealand. You could almost see Will shrinking as the disappointment and the end of all our dreams hit home. He lost the aloofness of captaincy and just became one of the team, no longer locked in discussion with the likes of Geoff Cooke or Jack Rowell about what went right or wrong, now simply one of the boys talking about life and Lomu. In a sense, it was the end of the road for him and for all of us.

He had changed his style of leadership for the World Cup; indeed, he had gradually changed throughout the preceding Five Nations. 'This is what I want you to do, and this is how I want you to do it,' became his theme, which suited me because it meant more authority and less talking. He would ask for a show of hands from the players if he had decided that a communal team dinner on a certain evening would be a good idea. If only four or five hands were raised, he would simply carry on as if he had been given a unanimous vote. 'I'm glad you all feel like that, because that is what we are all going to go,' was the gist of his response to a less-than-ecstatic vote. To have held out against his wishes would only have caused tension and friction.

I had an indication of how much the England captaincy meant to him when I rang him in the middle of the Carling Affair, when he called the RFU committee '57 old farts'. History now shows that he was quickly reinstated after a vivid demonstration of player power, but while he was still sacked it was obvious that he was extremely shaken and bewildered. I detected a huge low when I spoke to him, as if he could not believe that his world had collapsed. The captaincy was obviously a major part of his life, and an integral part of his business career.

His honesty in South Africa impressed me. He said in one team talk that he realized that the captain is rarely popular. I thought that he was coming to terms with captaincy in that statement. Will, like many captains, is not popular, and that is simply one of the responsibilities of the office. That is why I would never consider holding such an office. When all the players rallied around in support when Will was sacked by the RFU committee, it was not a personal crusade made on his behalf. The team realized what was best for the squad itself, not for Will or any other individual. As we returned home, Will announced that, contrary to expectation, he did wish to carry on as England captain.

I was delighted to be home after the tournament and relieved not to find an endless stream of people asking me what had happened against New Zealand. One person did ask the question, but I made a joke of the response. He had seen the match and he knew as well as I did what had happened.

Personally, I was disappointed when I got back home to Bath. I had trained hard for the World Cup and, probably, I was fitter and as quick as I have ever been. As one of the top players I have to accept the criticism that I did not make the impact on the tournament that I had hoped. I also feel that we stand condemned of merely talking a big game.

English rugby, generally, is in a healthy state and we have a team that is capable of beating anyone in the world on our day. But while New Zealand made an impact with their running style and I would have loved to have played in that style, the truth is that we never achieved it. All rugby nations have their own particular style. England's style is set-piece orientated and because we are so good at set-piece rugby we can be extremely effective, even if not everyone finds the style enjoyable to play. Critics should bear in mind that South Africa won the World Cup with a set-piece approach.

To claim that a lack of entertaining rugby is an English disease is inaccurate, because in many ways the lack of spectacle in South Africa is an indication of the way rugby is going, and there is no point in pretending otherwise. There are more people thinking about the game, more videos, more people trying to cancel out the opposition. Teams know each other inside out. And with the field crowded and with forwards carrying the ball up, it is getting more and more like rugby league. Surely, the administrators can't allow it to get that far; surely, they must realize that many international players these days are not enjoying the game. But it is now almost totally a game of power and strength, in which we in England probably have to become ever fitter and stronger to compete. The field is now crowded almost to the point of suffocation.

It is no use demanding that the forwards stick to their normal habitat and leave space outside for the backs. Some of the forwards don't want to go back. They like it in the open spaces. The only way to give backs more space to work is to drag forwards all back by reversing the turnover law, giving possession at the scrum after both rucks and mauls to the team that was going forward. Then you might drag the forwards back where they belong.

This is not just a whingeing back complaining. It must be obvious to anyone that the game has changed and that players like David Campese and Jason Little, who hardly had a chance in the whole tournament, are being phased out. No wonder that Tim Horan was quoted in the press as saying he didn't enjoy the game any more, and that Bob Dwyer announced that he was abandoning the traditional flat alignment of the Wallaby backs just to give them more space to operate in.

I have to admit that 1989 was probably my most enjoyable year in the game. I have never enjoyed it as much since then. After 1989, there have been the Grand Slams and the World Cups and the tremendous experience of playing for your country. There have been big rewards. But that old joy in the actual playing of the game has declined quite sharply. I am as streetwise as any other player and I am not one to shirk the dirty jobs on the field. But to me, my role should be more than running up and down the field chasing kicks, making and missing tackles. It should be about running with the ball in your hands and if a centre, any centre, is not doing that any more, then something must have gone wrong.

But it would also be too easy for us to pretend that it was a global problem and excuse the fact that we never developed our 15-man game. In fact, in the last eight or so internationals of the season, we hardly saw it at all. Perhaps we lacked the ambition, perhaps the English are too conservative by nature. I spoke to Walter Little at the final dinner. Little's view was that England had the best three-quarter line in the world but we hardly ever used it. But if we are going to be serious about changing style then we have to change personnel and individual attitudes. New Zealand have managed to make a similar change and they were not only entertaining to watch but highly effective. People may carp that New Zealand did not win the tournament, but to many people they were the best team in it – and who would bet against them winning it next time, and being the team to beat for the next four years?

Since Stuart Barnes left the game, we simply have not have had enough half-backs throughout English rugby to switch on that style. Rob Andrew has tremendous value to the England side in many departments, and if he was left out of the side we would miss his superb kicking dearly, especially since Mike Catt at full-back is not yet in the same class as a goalkicker. But just as Barnes had his weaknesses, Rob is difficult for centres to play with, not being naturally quick off the mark. He does not have the ideal style for launching back play at pace. There do not seem to be many fly-halves around who would be a natural for the expanded game which we in England must develop if we are to compete, and to entertain.

We also have to cut down the amount of talking we do, especially in the national set-up. Someone, hopefully Jack Rowell, who would be the man for the job, has to start talking big about the game we are going to play, but then stick by his words, rather than offer the whole squad a say. I tend towards the dictatorship in a rugby team rather than the democracy. If Jack Rowell has a vision of the game, he then chooses the players he thinks will fulfil that vision. He, or any team manager, should then declare: 'This is the way we are going to play.' The alternative is endless discussion in which your jaw gets more tired than your legs.

But in terms of the famous expanded game to which we were all supposed to be aspiring, it is time for English rugby to put up or shut up. We do have the potential to beat any other team. There is a strong belief in the squad that we are a far better team than we showed in the 1995 World Cup, even though we beat Australia. But we felt short of that potential in South Africa.

Certainly, when I returned home to enjoy the summer I felt in need of some reassurance, perhaps even a chat with Jack, still one of the best coaches I have come across in the game, to establish how he sees my role and the role of the backs in any future England set-up. I made up my mind on returning from the tournament to carry on playing for Bath, where it all began. I hope I can also remain as part of the England team, but it would help my decision greatly if I thought that we in the backs were going to carry the ball upfield, rather than merely chase it.

Epilogue: A Question of Balance

It can be difficult when the sporting media, and even your own friends, ask you to summarize instantly your innermost feelings about your career. To the outsider, I may have made considerable strikes on and off the sporting field after coming from a modest background, a troubled early life. But there can be little time to sit back and assess on a frequent basis while you are still riding the rollercoaster.

At the end of every season, people like to put you into retrospective mode. What did you think of this? Did you enjoy that? What do you regret? I don't think that way. If it is past it is history. Perhaps I might take part in analysing an England performance to see what we can learn about it for next time. But that is as far as the contemplation of regrets about the past ever goes with me.

But I always think I am lucky to be where I am, doing what I do. After some effort, I have found a balance between playing, working and family life. There is no doubt at all, as I have said, that the biggest change I have had in my life came with the arrival of Imogen and then Holly. Everything is now geared around them, and it is difficult to think of any major alterations I would make to improve the balance.

Everyone is entitled to dream, of course; and perhaps in dreams I could think of things I would like to improve. But it would have to be some sort of miracle. Perhaps a miracle cure of an injured groin would have come in handy during my year away from the rugby field. But that is merely a detail. Jayne and I discuss what we want, what we don't want, and how we can go about achieving things.

She is aware of how much the arrival of Imogen changed things for me. 'I noticed a major change in Jeremy after we had Imogen,' she said last year. 'He dislikes being away from home more than ever. When he comes in from work he wants to be with her straight away. He walks straight over to her.'

There have been sacrifices because of sport, as well as the good things that sport has brought us. When I was 20, Jayne and I were renting a flat in St James's Square, Bath. As I mentioned earlier, we planned to buy a flat which was available at about £25,000 and which would have put us on the housing ladder at an incredibly advantageous time. But I had been invited to go to Wollongong for six months to play rugby for a local club. I decided to go. We lost out on the flat. But so what? I enjoyed Wollongong, it was an experience, and it gave me an admiration of the Australian style of rugby. I couldn't say I would change that, or, as I say, that I would change anything.

I have anxieties, like anyone. The night before I make a speech I might get anxious. How are they going to receive it? Will anyone laugh? It is a horrible feeling. You try to wish it away. Sometimes, you feel almost nauseous. There is anxiety too about British Gas, who provide the bread and butter. There is a massive reorganization going on in the company and it is impossible to look far ahead. There may not even be a job for me at the end of it all.

But I have enjoyed the balance and the security of my involvement with a big company such as British Gas. They have been good and sympathetic employers and they have granted me enough time off for other activities. I have committed myself more to British Gas recently in terms of time and input. I want to be as competitive in business as I am in sport, and I want to be the best at what I do.

Perhaps my ultimate working goals will not be achievable with British Gas. It could mean branching out on my own, into some area of that vast field which comes under the heading of 'media', in broadcasting and journalism. I want a role where I am a communicator.

When I retire from playing there will obviously be scope for a major hit with Maria Pedro and my commercial activity. There may be a chance to go beyond the two years of fame that a retiring sportsman tends to have before he is superseded by the next retiring sportsman. But I simply do not see it as a major challenge. Maria and I have yet to discuss the scope and extent of the work we will do together.

The priority will be to become as integral a part of my family as I can possibly be, and the best time will be the time I can spend with Jayne, Imogen and Holly. I have spent a large part of my life away on short trips, and the occasional long trip. But there is also the possibility that, as a means to an end, by taking on some more work and opportunities through Maria, I can make things a bit more comfortable for us in the medium and longer term. That could even mean that I am away even more in the early years of retirement than I was before. Difficult choices. I know there will be a time when Maria says: 'These are the possibilities. We can move it further forward and start planning.' If we really went for the big hits, it could be that I would not be able to stay with British Gas. It all depends on fitting together the jigsaw, from the pieces we have at our disposal when the time comes to throw the boots into the River Avon.

And if it sounds that it is all meticulously planned out, and needing only the final decisions, then it is not. My plans change by the day and so do my perceptions of the future. Some of my Bath friends have their lives mapped out moment to moment in their diaries. I am sure that they have this kind of entry:

9.00pm Bed
7.00am Awake
7.30 Teeth
9.00 Office

They set out their goals, mark down their retirement dates, stick to it. Then they follow through their other plans. I would never plan. It is partly because, if I have no future rigidly planned, then I can't be disappointed if it fails to map out. That is why I cannot, ultimately, be disappointed with my injury and other defeats. I lost some rugby, but it was not rugby that I had pinned up on a giant wallchart of sporting ambitions. I could say that I will aim for the 1996 Lions tour. But it wouldn't be true. I would prefer to see how things go first, and discuss my future role with Jack Rowell.

When I retire it will not be a retirement like Les Cusworth's. Les announced his retirement a season in advance, and it all became a kind of public wake. I will either become too old and decrepit to play, and fade out; or, perhaps, I will find that other parts of my life begin to eat into my rugby time and make it impossible to devote enough time to maintain my standards of performance.

Whatever the reason, and unless I receive a massive league offer and change careers, I will leave quietly. I will tell the coach at Bath that I am leaving, that they should begin to plan ahead. When training starts for the next season, I just won't be there. It will be done privately and the news will pass only by word of mouth – till the papers get hold of it.

I realize that many sportsmen have found the transition from player to non-player an awful experience. But at least what you cannot lose for a couple of years is your tag as an international player and celebrity. You will always get reminders – I have had some early experience because of my year out of the game. 'If only you were playing . . .' I have heard it so many times, even when I knew I would have made no difference.

My wish would be that when I have stopped playing, the break is clean, and the feelings are not hard. Thank you very much. Goodbye. But life is not always like that, of course. I will probably get impatient at all those people who go on laying bad England performances at my door! 'Jerry. What's going on . . .?' There are also some people who take the technical view, and say: 'You shouldn't have missed that tackle.' You try to be polite, but unless you are talking to someone who has been out there and done it himself, it can be hard to keep an even temper. I admit that I have sometimes found it difficult to take silly comments on the chin, the people who call across crass comments at golfing pro-ams, the players from small clubs with their jibes in the night clubs of Bath. I admit that when I lost my temper with them I tended to go in a big way; that I can still be cold with people who are bothering me. But I would say that these days I usually manage to drift away at the first opportunity but without cutting people dead.

Some of the leading players on tour have taken to carrying red cards to stop the harassment. There might come a time when someone is bothering you too aggressively or for far too long. The red card is flourished, which means: 'Sorry, I am not at home to you.' Richard Webster, who was on the 1993 Lions tour and who has since signed for rugby league, has a different approach. 'Hey,' he says to the real bores. 'Fuck off!' That was Webby taking dismissiveness to extremes!

But Jayne believes that I am still the arch villain in the Bath winding-up process. 'Jeremy has changed through maturity,' she said not long ago. 'He can sometimes put on a cruel exterior, and I sometimes think it would be nice if more people knew what he was like underneath. Unfortunately, he still loves to wind people up. He still does it to this day. It normally happens after a few beers. He doesn't know when to stop; or at least, he knows when to stop but he doesn't want to. There have been a couple of times when he has picked on someone and I tell him to stop but he says: "... Oh no. It's all right..." They all do it at Bath. Any outsider would wonder what the hell is going on.'

In the final analysis, it does not bother me if people go through life thinking that my myth is true and that I am arrogant. I don't mind them saying it if they hardly know me, because people who do know me would not agree with the assessment. And I do have a bit of fun with the rugby writers as we try to lead each other a dance. But I don't think it is taking advantage too badly. There is never any malice in it from me. I hope that enough people I have come across have been left with the impression that I was one of the good guys.

As I say, I have no ambitions mapped out in diaries of the future. If I have any picture of the future on Saturdays then it is probably of playing golf in the morning, then going down to the Rec to watch Bath play, having a couple of pints afterwards; perhaps even starting every conversation with the players with: 'In my day...' and then being shown the red card!

I cannot imagine myself as chairman of Bath, or sitting listening to debates on the Rugby Football Union committee. I am not a born rugby official in any shape or form. I don't have any desperate wish to stay in the game on a formal basis. I cannot imagine myself in a formal coaching capacity. One of the problems is that when things you do on the field are instinctive it is impossible to teach them to someone else. I would have to go through the chore of attending coaching courses to learn how to teach rugby, how to pass things on. If there is one thing that my past life tells me, it is that classroom situations are not my favourite environment.

I believe I could coach. I like working with children because of their incredible enthusiasm. They want to learn, which is why the atmosphere is so good. The other area which might interest me is the opposite end of the scale – the challenge of helping really good players take that extra step. I would like to help players rising through the ranks at Bath on an individual basis.

But a long-term commitment? Taking up the reins of a club? I admire Richard Hill and Gareth Chilcott for stepping straight off the playing field into the coaching arena. But when you retire the commitment of training and playing suddenly lifts off and I think I will enjoy that new freedom, when it comes, too much to give it up again almost immediately.

I will have a few minor regrets as far as the playing side of my life is concerned. I could have helped Bath players more as a senior player, although I have spent time recently talking to some players. I would like to have been a bit more forceful about how I feel the game should be played, and piped up at team meetings like Brian Moore. I have always tried, possibly a bit too hard, not to come over as a bad guy in the dressing-room, but I have probably gone too far the other way and left unsaid the things I should have said. I would have liked to encourage a more expansive game, an open game.

That might sound like a selfish back talking, and I was glad enough to accept England's Grand Slams and ignore the 'boring England' jibes. But in most recent seasons I did not get involved in rugby as much as I wanted to. The style of the game and the laws dictated that. You have to play for the team at the expense of shining as an individual, and you tend to be carried along by changes in the game, even if they mean it has become less entertaining to play and watch.

But I enjoy the Australian attitudes towards the game. If I had been born Australian I would probably have spoken up more. To have expanded on my thoughts in this era and with the kind of players I played with would have not have been so appropriate. It is a chicken way out, but I would like to have laid down the law more while avoiding the adverse reaction. In any case, I cannot be bothered to spend ages explaining in painstaking detail my philosophy of rugby. You either understand it or you don't. And I am not saying that it has not been a fantastic experience.

Many great players have shared it with me. I did not notice all of them. I have never been a student of the game. I can remember the names of very few players I came up against in the early days. Nigel Redman can remember every moment of every game he played in; who scored, who came on as replacement. I could not match him. Take a team like Northampton, one of the better known teams around at the moment, even if their days as a contender at the top of Division 1 seem to be over. I might be able to name about five of their players, on a good day.

I have few heroes. Pele in soccer, but few in rugby. Certainly, I spent very little time as a boy hanging pictures of England rugby players on my wall. David Duckham used to stand out because of his blond hair. No one else did. I did watch Wales. It was a bit like watching Liverpool. You knew that even if they were trailing in the last 15 minutes, they would always win in the end. Even the glories of French rugby used to pass me by. I can remember Lescarboura, but only because he used to drop some incredible goals.

From the current era, I have already picked out the great Jon Hall of Bath earlier in this book. For a different sort of player in a different position, I believe that, until his appalling injury in the Super-10 final last year, Tim Horan was the best player in modern-day rugby. Horan seems to be in every phase of the game. He is only 5′ 7″ but he is very quick, and he has great hands. Speed is essential – speed of thought as well as speed over the ground, and Horan has both. He understands centre play; that you are a provider, a little like a midfielder in soccer. Sometimes you might score yourself, but usually you are trying to lay on a score for someone else.

I have only seen him miss one tackle. He missed me when England played Queensland in 1991. I looped around, Horan came covering across, I got my hand in his way and fended him off and scored in the corner. But generally his defence is brilliant, his commitment incredible.

He and Jason Little have proved themselves an outstanding

partnership. We used to regard Little as the weak link. He had the speed over the ground but not the speed of thought. He used to come up in a dog leg so that there was space around him. But they worked it out, improved and became more solid. Perhaps Horan's greatest game was in 1992, when he played for Australia in a one-off Test against South Africa at Newlands, Cape Town. He took the ball out of defence in an attack in the second half, kicked up and chased, won the ball back and passed underneath the full-back to make a try for Campese. It was Campese's 50th in Tests.

Horan's complicated knee injury was so bad that even two months after the operation to repair the damage he could hardly walk. I rang him in Sydney last year, while he was staying in the beach house loaned by an anonymous benefactor. He is a good guy, well-balanced and well-adjusted. Australia were already exposed for the 1995 World Cup, owing to the retirement of Nick Farr-Jones. It was great news that Horan had fought his way back into the squad for the World Cup 1995 in South Africa.

Philippe Sella, of course, is a tremendous player, although his greatest years were probably before I arrived on the scene. Ieuan Evans, also badly injured in 1994, never ceases to amaze me. He has the ability to fade outside and to lose his man, slipping tackles. Sometimes, even though seeing is supposed to be believing, you still can hardly believe that he has done it. He and Rory have an incredible ability to finish off tries that no one else around would score. They both have the ability to go running down the touch-line, to be tackled while in the air, to transfer the ball from one hand to the other and to reach out and score in the tackle just before they hit the flag. Rory has thought out all these processes. There is no greater finisher.

On a more homely note, Richard Mogg of Gloucester used to give us a certain amount of trouble. He used to play like a Gloucester boy, he used to come bustling up, he used to get in the way. And you knew that if you were caught by Mogg at Gloucester you were in for some pie. But it was the roar and intimidatory crowd which caused the problems, as well as Mogg himself.

In the forwards, I would single out another Australian, John Eales, and a former Bath Scotsman, David Sole. Eales is very tall but without much obvious physical presence. When he and Dooley first met, Dooley used to outgun him in the line-out. Dooley was once standing at the very back to take the long ball and Eales had not gone back to mark him. 'Hey, you dull student. I'm back here. Come and mark me,' shouted Wade. But Eales's work away from the lines-out amazes me. The Australian team in the 1991 World Cup final were like a Brazilian soccer team in that they could all play, their skills were interchangeable. At one stage of the final, I thought that Rob Andrew was streaking away, but these long arms of Eales snaked out and reeled Rob in. Sole was also a forward who could perform some of the handling and running skills like a back. He came up to Bath from Exeter University in the 1980s, and the work he did around the field was amazing, both then and later in his career. The hard-core front-row men like Gareth Chilcott and Jeff Probyn would say that he couldn't scrummage. People say the same thing about Victor Ubogu, and you wonder how much of it is valid and how much is sour grapes. Even after Sole was apparently being stuffed in the scrum you would always see him flying around the field. He was refreshing. He was what spectators wanted to see.

Apart from the brilliant Jonah Lomu, I would include no All Blacks in the list of the individual players who have really impressed me. Basically, that is because they are a great team: with them, teamwork is everything and individuals are not given the framework to shine. I have a respect for what they have achieved because, in its simplest form, rugby is New Zealand-style. But for someone like myself or Serge Blanco to be allowed to thrive out there is unthinkable. The only player I saw who appeared to have some striking individual talent was Steve Pokere, the Maori centre. And he did not always seem to fit in too well.

There is no getting away from the fact that if the England team had their stern mentality, we would be world-beaters, a great side. But here, there are things that are more important than rugby. In England, kids want to be Shearer; in Scotland, McCoist. In New Zealand, they want to be Sean Fitzpatrick or Frank Bunce.

But whoever I have played with and whoever I have played against, rugby has been a rich experience. I hope that there are brilliant rugby experiences to come. But I would always settle for those I had already had. It may have surprised people to learn that I was not the slavish follower of all the training regimes that I may have been portrayed as, that I always had an affinity, socially, with the forwards; I have always roomed with Rory Underwood but found the company of Leonard, Richards and Teague especially congenial. They would always stay around and have a few more beers. I couldn't name the pub itself, because the landlord might get into trouble, but there have been some memorable nights in a Richmond pub after England business has been concluded.

And if I appear aloof out on the field and if I have been accused of not being a team man, then I would say that I do like the closeness of a rugby team, especially of the Bath team. You see so much of each other through training and playing, and I am sure that the people who have left have missed it, that 12 months down the line they realize how close it all was. You cannot beat team friendships and what goes on inside club teams – especially at Bath with the savage jokes, the friction, the things that boil up, only to be quickly forgotten. Some of the England teams I have played in to date have got close as well, others not so close.

People also ask me, because of my air of arrogance on the field, whether I feel superior to the other guy, to my opponent. If you are the best you should be like a chief executive walking into a room – everyone sits up and takes notice. Whether or not I secretly feel superior, I would like to be able to get across a feeling of superiority to the other guy; but unless you are in the forwards and you can be intimidating and fierce, it is difficult to get that across without becoming unpopular and looking arrogant and forced. I would love to be a headbanging tackler and get stuck in and frighten them, and establish superiority that way.

The most difficult thing of all is explaining rugby talents. Mine is natural. People have told me ever since I started playing that I was good at rugby; there would be comments that this lad Guscott will play one day for Bath, or Somerset, or England. All my coaches, from mini-rugby and Walcot Old Boys upwards, have told me that I have a talent for the game. I never took any notice. I did not want to be buoyed up with it all, simply to fall down.

But something in me in the early days always wanted to come out and say: 'I'm brilliant.' It used to come out wrong, and put people's backs up. That was just immaturity. You don't have to say it, just do it.

I also admitted in an interview in 1990 that I never sat down before games and worked out what I was going to do; that it all came naturally once the match started. Obviously, that changed a little as time went on, because when players in the opposition had worked me out I had to put some thought in.

But not much. Other players study the opposition with a magnifying glass. I might show some interest if they say that Tim Horan is better tackling on the right than the left, but again, not much. I don't bother assessing all my opponents from top to toe.

I never bothered with all the books and papers that Geoff Cooke used to produce in his time as England manager. I even used to get mildly annoyed with it all. Cooke might say: 'Look at Tuigamala. He steps off his left foot, steps off his right, then he comes straight at you. When someone runs at you like that, it should be easy, you just tackle him.' I used to look at Cooke and think that unless you had actually done it yourself then it was difficult to know what you were talking about.

I rarely take part in the games to improve one's mental build-up either. Cooke used to try to get us to imagine we were tackling someone, or going past your man, or scoring a try. I would lie down and try some of these visualization techniques in my hotel room. Then I would get bored and turn on the television or go for a chat with one of the other lads.

And all you can really hope for is that when you retire, perhaps going on into charity events and the after-dinner circuit, enough people still look at you as one of the good guys, that you came across as well as possible, that you were liked by as many people as possible and that you played a great game like rugby pretty well.

Some years ago when the top English and Welsh clubs still used to put out strong sides against each other, Bath went to St Helens to play Swansea. Both sides had most of their good players on the pitch. Of the game, I can't remember much at all. I think that Bath won. But I scored two tries, and I can remember them vividly, almost as if I can replay them in slow motion in my mind.

For the first, the ball came to me in the centre and all I did at first was to stop, dead. I stood still in my tracks. Then I came back on a line towards the forwards. It was like running through a tunnel

I was creating myself. Like a mole coming up against roots, I was sensing when to move out of the straight. As I was going through the tunnel it was as if I had sensors on all around me. If I sensed anyone coming from the left side I would veer out and away. The same from the right. I carved a path through the whole mêlée, and came out of the other end into the open. The Swansea full-back came across. I changed direction and he was stuffed. The line was there. I ran under the posts.

The second try was a mirror image of the first. The same tunnel, the same sensors, the same exhilarating burst into the open. This time, the last defender managed to brush a hand across my stomach as I went past, but he was in no position to tackle me.

I'll never play in that kind of game again. I enjoy the pressure games of modern rugby, but that was a game with most of the pressure off. The tries brought me total satisfaction. Not just because of the points. It was a fantastic feeling. It was so easy. It was running free.

Index

In the index, J.G. refers to Jeremy Guscott

Ackford, Paul 51, 101, 103, 105, 108, 116, 119
  and the British Lions tour of Australia (1989) 73–4
Adams, Gareth 54
Aland, Jayne *see* Guscott, Jayne
Aldred, Dave 135
All Blacks 94, 115, 133, 158, 237
  and the Lions tour of New Zealand (1993) 156, 157, 158, 159, 162, 163–4, 165
  and the 1995 World Cup 220, 221–3
Allen, Bull 159
Allen family 13, 16
Andrew Rob 41, 77, 90, 95, 108, 198, 227, 228
  and the 1991 World Cup 106, 110, 115, 237
  and the 1995 World Cup 208, 224
  and the British Lions tour of Australia (1989) 73, 77, 78, 79, 80, 83, 84
  and the Five Nations matches
    (1991) 101, 106–7, 108
    (1993) 128, 129–30, 131–2
    (1995) 203, 204, 206
  J.G.'s relations with 136–7
  and the Lions tour of New Zealand (1993) 152, 154, 155, 156, 161, 162, 164, 165
  and the RFU 182
  and Stuart Barnes 134–7
  and Will Carling 141
Armstrong, Gary 46
Ashton Brian 52, 54
Australia
  1991 tour of 109, 110, 111
  and the 1991 World Cup 114–16, 237
  and the 1995 World Cup 208, 209, 216–20, 236
  British Lions tour of (1989) 57, 67, 70–85, 168, 169
  rugby union players 181
    treatment of injuries 194
  trip to Wollongong (1987) 20–1, 169, 240
Australians, England 'B' match at Sale (1988) 60–1

Back, Neil 68, 133
Bailey, Mark 60, 95
Barbados, trip to (1994) 55, 191
Bardner, Julie 187
Barnes, Stuart 39, 41–2, 44, 49, 51, 65, 72, 81, 86, 101, 118, 203, 227, 228
  and the 1992 Cup Final 29, 30, 208
  and the 1993 Five Nations 122, 123, 128, 130–1, 132–3, 145
  and Brian Moore 182
  as Bath captain 50, 56
  and the John Player Cup (1984) 32
  leaves Bristol to join Bath 37
  and the Lions tour 146, 148, 149, 152–3, 155, 156, 159, 160, 164, 165, 203
  retirement 52, 134
  and Rob Andrew 130–8
  and Simon Halliday 46, 47, 48, 58
Bates, Steve 69
Bath
  city of 24–5
  Larkhall 8, 22, 25
Bath Colts 13, 31–2, 80
Bath Players Initiative 54, 180
Bath Rugby Club 38–55
  and the Barbados trip (1994) 55, 191
  and the England team 126
  Lambridge Training Ground 15–16, 30, 33, 55

match against Swansea at St Helens 239–40
Recreation Ground 15–16, 17, 33, 41, 233
Bath Technical College, J.G. at 11
Bayfield, Martin 116, 118, 119, 125, 162, 208
BBC (British Broadcasting Corporation) 94, 104, 105
Beaumont, Billy 141
Berot, Philippe 63
Berry, Mr (deputy headmaster) 11
Best, George 135
Best, Richard 43, 93, 116, 117–18, 125, 126, 134
and the Lions tour of New Zealand (1993) 150, 152, 157, 165
on the RFU and injuries to players 193
Big Breakfast, The 179
Bishop, Dave 113
Bishop, David 57
Blackett, Peter 13, 17, 19, 22, 31, 35, 37, 58, 65, 71
and J.G.'s wedding 22
Blanco, Serge 94, 95, 107, 112, 113, 237
Body Heat 24, 172, 179, 190, 202
Bracken, Kieran 133, 198, 206
Bradford Northern, approaches to J.G. from 170–3
British Gas
and J.G.'s commercial activities 179–1
J.G.'s employment with 26–7, 175, 183, 230, 231
as sponsors 104
British Lions
tour of Australia (1989) 56, 67, 70–85, 165, 166, 169
tour of New Zealand (1993) 83, 124, 143–66, 171
Bucharest, 1989 trip to 66, 67–9
Buckton, John 60
Bunce, Frank 154, 156, 158, 163, 165, 237
Burnell, Paul 147, 148

Calder, Finlay 71, 73, 74, 80, 81, 82, 83, 85, 113, 118, 166, 206
Callard, Jon 40, 53, 54, 133, 204, 209, 217
Campbell, Bill 80
Campese, David 61, 80, 82, 83–4, 114, 212, 227, 236
and the turnover law 124
Canada, 201
1992 match at Wembley 123, 127, 139
1994 match at Twickenham 199–201
Carlin, Simon 8
Carling, Bill 139
Carling, Will 51, 53, 56, 57, 59, 62, 64, 66, 71, 74, 89, 91, 93, 94, 95, 96, 97, 100, 127, 128, 181, 182, 196, 197, 198, 199, 200, 204, 206, 221–2, 224–5
and the 1991 World Cup 108, 111, 112, 113, 114
and Barnes 131
character 139
and the Five Nations matches
(1991) 102–3
(1992) 118, 120
(1995) 202
J.G.'s relations with 92–3, 138–42
and the Lions tour of New Zealand (1993) 154, 156, 159, 160, 161, 166
marriage to Julia 139
withdrawal from Lions captaincy 146–7
Catt, Mike 52, 135, 198, 201, 203, 204, 206, 208, 213, 219, 227
Caisley, Chris 170–2
Chalmers, Craig 76, 78, 205
Charlton, Jack 115
Charvet, Denis 94, 95
Chilcott, Gareth ('Cooch') 17, 30, 33, 37, 39, 40, 42, 43, 44, 48–9, 52, 54, 57, 103
and the British Lions tour of Australia (1989) 71–2, 78
and coaching 234
commercial activities 176, 177
and David Sole 237
and the England–Scotland international (1988) 62
J.G.'s first experience of 89
Christie, Linford 200
Clarke, Ben 54, 125, 133, 176, 183, 185, 197, 198, 202, 203
and the Lions tour of New Zealand (1993) 146, 151, 154, 164
Clarke, Eroni 162
Cleary, Mick 193
Clement, Tony, and the Lions tour of New Zealand (1993) 147, 153, 161
Cooke, Geoff 51, 59, 60, 62, 99, 91, 93, 95, 96, 98, 117, 127, 196, 200, 224, 239
and the 1989 Bucharest trip 68
and the 1991 tour of Australia 110
and the 1991 World Cup 111, 114
and England's defeat at Murrayfield (1990) 98
and the Five Nations matches
(1991) 100, 102, 103, 104, 105
(1992) 117, 119–20
and the Lions tour of New Zealand (1993) 145, 150, 152, 155, 159
and Rob Andrew 131–2
and Stuart Barnes 131, 138
and team meetings 125–6
and Will Carling 127, 140
Cooper, Trevor 26
Courage Leagues 50, 59–60
Craig, Greg 194
Cronin, Damien 153, 154
Cusworth, Les 134, 138, 197, 199, 215, 232
Cutler, Steve 80, 81, 82

Daly, Tony 116
Davies, Alan 60
Davies, Jonathan 169
David, Mervyn 144
Davies, Phil 103
Davies, Steve 17
Dawe, Graham 40, 49, 53, 103, 108, 126, 179, 198, 205
Day, John 26
de Glanville, Phil 41, 42, 48, 51, 53, 64, 132, 196, 206, 215, 217
Dean, Paul 73
Devereux, John 75, 77
Dixon, Carlton 17
Dooley, Wade 74, 78, 79, 103, 105, 115, 119, 120, 125, 129, 156, 236–7
Downey, Peter 54
Dubroca, Daniel 113
Duckham, David 235
Dwyer, Bob 82, 219

Eales, John 115, 215–16
Edwards, Bill 26
Edwards, Gareth 144
Edwards, Neil ('Eddie') 118
Egerton, David 43
Elias, Benny 169
Evans, Ieuan 77, 84, 130, 215
  and the Lions tour of New Zealand (1993) 154, 156, 157, 158, 160, 164

Fallon, Jim 140
Farr-Jones, Nick 81, 82, 199, 236
Fiji
  1991 tour 109–10
  match against at Twickenham (1989) 89–90
Fitzpatrick, Sean 143, 162, 163, 237
Five Nations matches
  (1990) 93–8
  (1991) 100–8
  (1992) 118–21
  (1993) 123, 129–33, 145–6
  (1994) 133, 188
  (1995) 202–6
  earnings from 180
Foster, Brendan 175
Foster, Christine 27
Fox, Grant 136, 158, 163
Fox, Peter 171
France
  England 'B' match with (1988/9) 63–4
  Five Nations matches
    (1990) 94–5
    (1991) 106–8
    (1992) 119
    (1993) 129
    (1994) 133
    (1995) 202–3
  South African tour of (1992) 128
  1995 World Cup 223
Frankcom, Gary 13, 31

Gabbitas, Charles 34
Gabriel, Peter 176
Galwey, Mick, and the Lions tour of New Zealand (1993) 147, 148, 155
Gatherer, Don 188, 193
Gay, David 175, 176
Geoghegan, Simon 133
Gibbs, Scott, and the Lions tour of New Zealand (1993) 148, 154, 159, 163
Gilmore, Jerry 187, 188, 189, 190, 191
Grand Slams
  1990 86, 88, 96–8, 141
  1992 116, 120–1
  1995 196–7, 202–7
Gray, Philip 9
Greenstock, Nick 53
Gregory, Andy 84
Griffiths, Mike 75
Gunnell, Sally 179, 190, 200
Guscott, Gary (J.G.'s brother) 4, 7, 11, 12, 67, 69, 89
Guscott, Henry ('Slim', J.G.'s father) 22, 30, 67, 69, 89, 218
  background 4, 12
  and the British Lions tour of Australia (1989) 70–1, 81
  J.G.'s relations with 12–14, 27–8, 85
  and J.G.'s schooldays 8, 10–11
Guscott, Holly (J.G.'s daughter), 24, 213, 217, 229
Guscott, Imogen (J.G.'s daughter) 23–4, 204, 213, 217, 229, 230
Guscott, Jayne (J.G.'s wife) 19, 21, 66, 104, 139, 146, 176, 179, 213, 217
  and the 1989 Bucharest trip 67, 68, 69
  birth of Imogen 23–4
  and the British Lions tour of Australia (1989) 81
  and England's defeat at Murrayfield (1990) 98
  on J.G.'s character 212
  and J.G.'s commercial activities 179
  and J.G.'s father 27–8
  and J.G.'s groin injury 186, 190, 191–2, 194
  J.G.'s meeting with 17–18
  and J.G.'s mother 27–8
  and J.G.'s offers from rugby league 171
  J.G.'s relationship with 17–19, 21–3, 87, 230
  marriage to J.G. 22–3, 99
Guscott, Jeremy
  and Bath 24–5
  birth 4
  childhood 7–11
  and coaching 233–4
  commercial activities 176–86, 230–31

and daughter Holly 24, 229
and daughter Imogen 23–4, 204, 229, 230
Daily Express column 202
employment
bricklaying 1, 19, 21, 175
with British Gas 26–7, 104, 175, 179, 183, 230, 231
as bus driver 19, 203
as shelf-stacker 17
as tree-feller 16–17
and *Esquire*'s Best Dressed Man contest 174–5, 177
first drugs experience 21
groin injury 124, 185–95, 195–6
and judo 9
marriage to Jayne 22–3, 99
meeting with Jayne 17–18
modelling career 64, 175, 177–8, 179–80, 203, 204
newspaper articles 177
offers from rugby league 167–73
and racism 12
relations with father 12–14, 27–8
relations with mother 12, 13–14
relationship with Jayne 17–19, 21–3, 55, 87, 209
retirement (speculations on) 230–32, 233–4, 239
rugby heroes 214–16
schooldays 3–4, 8–9, 10–11
and soccer 9
social life 25–6
Sunday Mirror column 172
television work 24, 94, 172, 179, 190, 202
views on turning professional 183
views on future of rugby 183–4, 226–8
and Yardley English Blazer Award, 200
Guscott, Susan (J.G.'s mother) 3–4, 7–8, 10, 26, 67, 69, 81
background 4
J.G.'s relations with 12, 13–4
meets J.G.'s father 4
and Reginald Teague-Jones 5–7

Hakin, Ronnie 46
Hall, Jon 8, 37, 39, 45–6, 53, 54, 65, 117, 126, 133, 235
Hall, Mike 76, 77, 78, 82
Halliday, Simon 22, 34, 36, 37, 46–8, 57, 58, 59, 64, 72, 89, 92–3, 101, 118
and the 1989 Bucharest trip 68, 69
and the 1991 World Cup 112
and the 1992 Five Nations 119, 120
and the England-Scotland international (1988/9) 62
and J.G.'s wedding 22
and Will Carling 91, 139, 140
Hampson, Steve 84
Hanley, Ellery, 169
Hare, Dusty 65, 90
Harlequins, and the 1992 Cup Final 29–30, 51
Hastings, Gavin 79, 80, 122, 206
and the 1991 World Cup 113
and the Lions tour 146, 147, 149, 154, 156, 157, 158, 161–2, 163, 165–6
Hastings, Scott 75, 77, 78, 79, 80, 97, 98, 122, 132
and the Lions tour of New Zealand (1993) 152, 154
Hayter, Miss (headmistress) 3–4, 11
Hazledene, Rex 190, 192, 202, 211
Henderson, Nigel 187–8, 191, 192, 193, 195
Herridge, Colin 25, 200
Hilditch, Steve 119
Hill, Damon 201
Hill, Richard 1, 17, 39, 40, 49, 52, 54, 65, 86, 95, 97
and the 1991 World Cup 108, 111, 115, 116
and the 1992 Cup Final 29
and coaching 234
and the Five Nations matches (1991) 100, 101, 103, 104, 106, 107
J.G.'s disagreements with 41
Hill, Roger 19
Hirini, Steve 154
Hodgkinson, Simon 69, 95, 100, 101, 103, 105, 106, 107, 118
Holmes, Jon 141
Hopkirk, Peter 7
Hopley, Damien 215
Horan, Tim 194, 212, 218, 235–6, 239
Horton, John 34, 36, 37, 39
Hudson, Tom 39
Huish, Chris 58
Hull Kingston Rovers 59, 168–9
Hunter, Glen 193
Hunter, Ian 127, 129, 223
and the Lions tour of New Zealand (1993) 153
Hynes, Neil 120

International Rugby Board 182, 184
turnover laws 124–5
Ireland
Five Nations matches
(1990) 93–4
(1991) 106
(1993) 145
(1994) 133
(1995) 202
Ireland, Ernest 19
Irwin, David 94

Jackson, Peter 99
Jeffrey, John 74, 75, 113, 118, 206
Jenkins, Neil 105, 130
John, Barry 144

John Player Cup (1984) 32, (1985) 35
Johnson, Gary 8
Johnson, Martin 129, 179, 196, 204
Johnston, John 9
Johnston, Warren 153
Jones, Michael 112
Jones, Robert 73, 76, 79, 80, 81, 82, 83, 100
  and the Lions tour of New Zealand (1993) 148, 150, 155, 156
Jones, Simon 7
Joseph, Jamie 133
'Journey, The' 15–16, 33

Kinsey, Brian 158, 163
Kirwan, John 143, 162
Knibbs, Ralph 37
Knight, Steve 13

Lacroix 202
Lafond, Jean-Baptiste 107, 129
Lanzarote, training camp at 90–1, 93, 101, 117, 128, 201
Lascubé, Grégoire 119
Laughton, Doug 87, 169
Lee, Richard 59
Lenihan, Donal 83
Leonard, Jason 198, 200, 216
  injuries suffered by 193
  and the Lions tour of New Zealand (1993) 128, 153, 155
Lewis, Emyr 130
Linnett, Mark 92
Lions *see* British Lions
Little, Jason 115, 116, 219, 227, 235–6
Little, Walter 156, 221, 227
Littlewoods, J.G.'s modelling contract with 177–8
Lloyd, Bas 9
Lomu, Jonah 220, 221, 223, 237
Lowe, Cyril 94
Lowe, Graham 169
Lumsden, Audley 47, 58, 65, 72, 101
Lye, Robbie 32, 33, 34
Lynagh, Michael 83, 84, 136, 199, 212, 218, 219

McBride, Willie-John 145
McDonald, Carmen 63
McGeechan, Ian 72–3, 74, 75, 76, 81, 83, 85, 105, 136, 186
  and the Lions tour of New Zealand (1993) 148, 149, 150, 151, 152, 157, 160, 161, 164–5
McKenzie, Bob 202
McLaren, Malcolm 175
Mains, Laurie 133
Mallett, Jon 209, 215
Martin, Chris 35
Martin, Greg 84
Martland, Tom 31
Mason, John 103
Mendez, Federico 101
Mesnel, Franck 107
Miami, J.G.'s modelling assignments in 177–8
Michael, Andy 31
Mogg, Richard 236
Molby, Jan 189
Morrie, John 200
Moore, Brian 74, 97, 99, 100, 102–3, 106, 108, 126, 141, 202, 206, 209–10, 234
  and the Grand Slam match at Murrayfield 141
  and the Lions tour of New Zealand (1993) 148, 159, 162
  and the RFU 183
  and Rob Andrew 137
Morris, Dewi 60–1, 116, 119, 122, 128, 129, 132, 141, 197, 198, 199, 204, 205, 208, 212, 215
  and the 1991 World Cup 113
  and the Lions tour of New Zealand (1993) 143, 148, 151, 158, 161, 162
Morrison, Iain 206
Morrison, John 20, 31, 43, 56, 66–7
Moscato, Vincent 119
Mullin, Brendan 75, 76, 77, 78
Mullins, Andy 61, 62
Murdoch, Rupert 172
Murphy, Alex 95, 167, 170
Murphy, Kevin 68, 76, 161, 175, 186, 197, 200

Nadruku, Noa 90
New Zealand
  and the 1991 World Cup 112, 114
  and the 1995 World Cup 209, 224, 227
  defeated by England (1993/4) 132–3
  defeated by France (1994) 202
  J.G. misses match with (1993) 185–6, 187, 188
  Lions tour of (1993) 124, 143–66, 186
  rugby union players 181
newspapers
  and the 1994–95 season 193
  and the Five Nations matches (1991) 103, 104
  J.G.'s celebrity articles in 177
  on Pontypool match (1988) 57–8
Norman, George 16
Norster, Robert 79, 83
N'Tamack, Emile 224

O'Dowd, George (Boy George) 174
Ofahengaue, Willie 111
Ojomoh, Steve 125, 133, 199, 212, 223
Olver, John 93, 95, 100, 120
O'Reilly, Tony 144
Oti, Chris 69, 77–8, 91

Ottey, Merlene 93
Oxley, David 87

Palmer, John 33–4, 35, 36, 37, 38, 39, 49, 57, 65
Parallel Media Company 54, 180, 181, 182
Paris *see* France
Parr, Barney 10
Payton, Walter 91
Pearce, Gary 64
Pearce, Malcolm 54, 176
Pears, David 112
Pedro, Maria 175, 176–7, 179, 181, 230–231
Peters, Eric 206
Phillips, Kevin 105
Pickavance, Joe 59, 170
Pillinger, Geoff 31
Playervision 54, 137, 180, 181, 182, 209
Pokere, Steve 237
Popplewell, Nick, and the Lions tour of New Zealand (1993) 147, 148, 150, 151, 153, 155, 164
Porter, Mike 79
Potter, Stuart 190
press *see* newspapers
Preston, Jon 163, 165
Prince, Allan 154
Probyn, Jeff 85, 101, 109, 119, 125, 140, 147, 179, 198, 201
  and David Sole 237

Ralph Allen Comprehensive School 3–4, 8–9, 9–10
Real World 176
Redman, Nigel 30, 40, 51, 54, 126, 133, 235
Reed Andy 44, 46, 105, 126
Rees, Gareth 201
Rendall, Paul 85
RFU (Rugby Football Union) 108, 127, 207
  and J.G.'s groin injury 188, 190, 192
  press criticisms of 193
  sponsorship and commercial deals 105, 180, 181–2, 184
Richards, Dean 73, 83, 92, 98, 105, 106, 119, 127, 133, 141, 196, 198, 202, 204, 205, 212, 215, 220, 223, 238
  and the Lions tour of New Zealand (1993) 149, 154, 155, 158, 159, 161, 162, 165
Ring, Mark 57
Roberts, Vic 62
Robinson, Andy 20, 43, 58, 126
  and the British Lions tour of Australia (1989) 71, 72, 73
Robinson, Dave 60–1
Robson, David 26, 175
Robson, Dr James 161, 186
Roche, Tony 104
Rodber, Tim 46, 119, 126, 133, 197, 202, 213, 220, 223
Roddy, Ged 186
Romania
  1989 trip to Bucharest 66, 67–9
  England match against (1994) 195, 197–8, 209
Roumat, Olivier 224
Rowell, Jack 30, 32, 34, 38, 39, 41–2, 43–5, 52, 54, 55, 59, 66, 86, 87, 126, 195, 196, 198, 199, 200, 203, 205, 209, 210, 213, 214, 215, 216, 217, 220, 222, 223, 224, 228
  and J.G.'s groin injury 190
  replaces Best 117–18, 134
  and Rob Andrew 138
  shake-up of England team (1994–95) 134, 196
  and Will Carling 140, 197
Rowlands, Clive 56, 66, 73, 79, 81, 84
Rudland, Keith 8, 12
Rugby Football Union *see* RFU
rugby league, contracts offered to J.G. 167–73
Rush, Eric 223
Rush, Mr (teacher) 9, 11
Rutherford, Don 66, 111
Rutland, Richard 53
Ryan, Dean 53, 61

St Helens, approaches to J.G. from 95, 169, 170
Saint-André, Philippe 63, 107, 129
Saunders, Eddie 37
Schmidt, Uli 108
Scotland
  and the 1991 World Cup 113–14
  England-Scotland international (1988/9) 62–3
  Five Nations matches
    (1990) 86, 88–9, 96–8, 109
    (1991) 105
    (1992) 118–19
    (1993) 131–3
    (1994) 133
    (1995) 205–6
Sella, Philippe 94, 107, 202, 236
Serevi, Waisale 220
Sharp, Alan 64
Simpson, John 69
Simpson, Paul 41, 66,
Sinclair, Ronald *see* Teague-Jones, Reginald
Skinner, Mick 64, 105, 110, 117, 119, 120
Slemen, Mike 145
Smith, Mike 172, 179, 190
Sole, David 72, 82, 97, 236–7
South Africa 85
  and the 1995 World Cup 109, 208–28
  England team in (1994) 134, 186, 191
  rugby union players 181

tour of France and England (1992) 123, 128
Spartans 16, 31–3, 34
Spurrell, Roger 41, 57, 66
as Bath captain 33, 39
and the John Player Cup final 32, 35
Stamp, Terence 175
Stanger, Tony 97, 122, 132
Starmer-Smith, Nigel 35–6
Stevens, John 50
Swain, Austin 200, 218
Swift, Tony 40, 41, 47, 53, 54, 58

Tallboys, Steve 189
Taylor, John 30
Teague, Mike 85, 97, 98, 103, 106, 107, 117, 125, 238
and the 1991 tour of Fiji 110
and the 1991 World Cup 111, 116
injuries suffered by 193
and the Lions tour of Australia (1989) 73, 74, 83
and the Lions tour of New Zealand (1993) 155, 157
Teague-Jones, Reginald 5–7
Thatcher, Peter 9
Thorne, Willie 64
Tordo, Jeff 119
Townsend, Gregor 133
Trevaskis, Barry 35, 58
Trick, David 15–16, 17, 20, 33, 58
Tuigamala, Inga 156–7, 239
Twickenham, 1992 Cup Final 29–30
J.G.'s first match at (1989) 89–90

Ubogu, Victor 197, 204, 205, 210, 212, 216, 217, 237
Underwood, Anne 132
Underwood, Rory 72, 77, 91, 92, 94, 95, 96, 137, 196, 198, 222, 236, 238
and the 1991 tour of Fiji 110
and the 1991 World Cup 113, 115, 116
and the 1993–94 season 133
and the Five Nations matches
(1991) 106
(1992) 118
(1993) 122–3, 128, 130, 132
(1995) 205
and the Lions tour of New Zealand (1993) 143, 144, 150, 153, 154, 161, 162
Underwood, Tony 64, 127, 128, 198, 202, 203, 206, 217, 219, 223, 224
and the Lions tour of New Zealand (1993) 154, 155
Uttley, Roger 69, 93, 98, 108, 116
and the 1991 World Cup 111
and the British Lions tour of Australia (1989) 74, 75–6, 77–8, 81

Vonolagi, Tevita 90

Walcot Old Boys 11, 29–30, 238
Waldron, Ron 104
Wales
Five Nations matches
(1990) 95–6
(1991) 100, 102–5
(1992) 120–1
(1993) 129–30
(1994) 133
match at Pontypool (1988) 57–8
Wardle, Tony ('Chalkie') 13, 25, 31, 35, 65, 71
and J.G.'s wedding 22
Watkins, Alun 34
Webb, Jon 41, 51, 65, 109, 115, 118, 119, 120, 129, 130, 147
Webster, Richard, and the Lions tour of New Zealand (1993) 148, 151, 153, 154, 233
Wessels, Ronnie 20
West, Peter 37
Western Samoa
and the 1995 World Cup 214, 215
White, Derek 76, 113
Williams, Ian 84
Williams, Peter 20
Williams, Sharon 17
Willis, Bob 105, 180
Winterbottom, Peter 33, 69, 105, 113, 120, 126, 127
and the Lions tour of New Zealand (1993) 149, 151, 162
Wood, Dudley 105, 182, 193
World Cup
(1991) 100, 107, 109–16, 223, 237
(1995) 197, 200, 207, 208–28, 236
Wright, Peter 147, 148, 154

Yates, Kevin 54
Young, David 81, 82